RESILIENT WIDOWERS

Alinde Moore is chair and associate professor in the Department of Psychology at Ashland University, where she has taught since 1985. She has chaired the department since 1989. She earned her M.S. at Butler University in Indianapolis, Indiana, and her Ph.D. in educational psychology from the University of Illinois, Urbana-Champaign. Her doctoral dissertation involved a 5-year qualitative study of the coping skills of poor elderly women trying to live as independently as possible in their own homes. In Ashland, Ohio, she helped found the local hospice, served on the local hospice board for eight years, and served on the state hospice board for three years. She continues to help train hospice volunteers.

Dorothy Stratton is chair of the Department of Social Work at Ashland University, where she has taught since 1984. She has administered the social work program since 1986. She earned her MSW at the University of Arkansas at Little Rock. She is a member of the Academy of Certified Social Workers (ACSW) and a Licensed Independent Social Worker (LISW) in the state of Ohio. Her interest in men's issues developed as a result of teaching male inmates in the Ohio correctional system. She developed interdisciplinary courses in Men's Issues and in Family Violence; both courses have been taught in the correctional system and on the main campus. She is past president of the Ohio College Association of Social Work Educators.

This study of resilience of older widowers is the first collaborative effort of Dr. Moore and Professor Stratton. Their research has been supported by Ashland University and the Miami Valley (OH) Gerontology Council. They have made numerous presentations at state, regional, national, and international conferences. They have also conducted continuing education workshops. They have begun to interview widowers in Great Britain for a comparative study.

RESILIENT WIDOWERS

Older Men Adjusting to a New Life

ALINDE J. MOORE

DOROTHY C. STRATTON

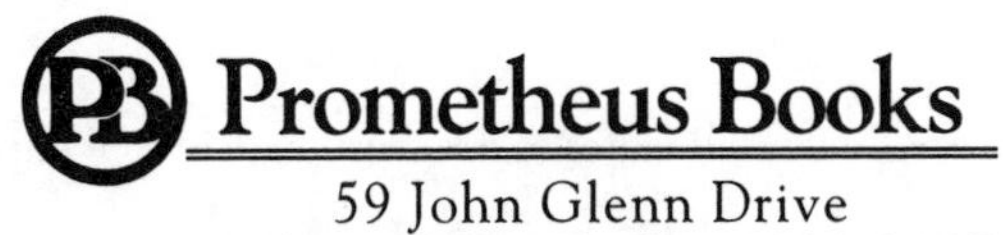

59 John Glenn Drive
Amherst, New York 14228-2197

Published 2003 by Prometheus Books

Inquiries should be addressed to
Prometheus Books
59 John Glenn Drive
Amherst, New York 14228–2197
VOICE: 716–691–0133, ext. 207
FAX: 716–564–2711
WWW.PROMETHEUSBOOKS.COM

07 06 05 04 03 5 4 3 2 1

Library of Congress Cataloging-in-Publication Data

Moore, Alinde J.
Resilient widowers : older men adjusting to a new life / by Alinde J. Moore and Dorothy Stratton.
p. cm.
Originally published: Resilient widowers : older men speak for themselves. New York : Springer Pub. Co., ©2002.
Includes bibliographical references and index.
ISBN 1–59102–082–4 (pbk.)
I. Widowers—United States—Psychology. 2. Widowers—United States—Attitudes. 3. Loss (Psychology) in old age—United States. 4. Resilience (Personality trait)—United States. 5. Adjustment (Psychology) in old age—United States.
[DNLM: 1. Men—psychology. 2. Widowhood—psychology. 3. Adaptation, Psychological.] I. Stratton, Dorothy C. II. Title.

HQ1058.5.U5M68 2003
306.88—dc21

2003008286

Printed in the United States of America on acid-free paper

This book is dedicated to the men
who participated in our study.

—A.J.M

This book is dedicated to the memory of my father,
Richard J. Jarsensky, and to the memory
of my mentor, Dr. John J. Lennon.

—D.C.S.

Contents

Preface

From the earliest moments of conceiving this research project, it has been our intent to hear the stories of real people and to convey what we learned to others in a form that would maintain that genuine "real person" quality. We were drawn to researchers such as Kaufman (*The Ageless Self: Sources of Meaning in Late Life,* 1986) and Rubenstein (*Singular Paths: Old Men Living Alone,* 1986) who listened to the stories of the persons they interviewed and then drew out themes and patterns to illuminate the thinking, feeling, and acting of those people.

Themes and patterns that developed out of our interviews appear throughout this book. Yet our findings also confirm the individuality of the widowhood experience. We went into the interviews without categories into which we would place our respondents. We listened to what the men had to tell us. Then, when we looked at the content of their stories and tried to put elements of those stories into categories, we found that the information resisted being categorized. "Were you with your wife when she died?" The answer to that question should be easy to categorize: yes or no. But it wasn't. Ben was with his wife, but stepped away for a minute to call in the children, and in that minute she passed away. Yes or no? Robert was asleep as he kept vigil and was not aware of the moment of death. Yes or no? Maybe the "yes" or "no" was not so important; what mattered was the feeling that each man attached to his part, his place, in the death event. So we discovered that it was not our ultimate aim to force placement in categories, but to let the experiences maintain their uniqueness and see how they could be placed on a continuum of similar experiences derived from all 51 interviews. When we write that "many," "most," or "a few" of the men could be categorized in some way, we are admitting that their responses could not be put in neat little boxes to be counted. We are also affirming our belief that getting a tally was not our goal. If the reader comes away from this book with a sense of knowing more about older widowed men and their life circumstances, then our purpose has been fulfilled.

We have described the situations of older widowed men, setting the widowhood experience within the context of life experience, for these purposes: (a) to contribute to the knowledge base about widowhood and about older men, (b) to inform professionals who work with older men and their families so there can be greater understanding in working with individual widowed men, and so services can be designed or modified to better serve the needs of older widowed men, and (c) to encourage researchers of many disciplines—both qualitative and quantitative—to explore more thoroughly aspects of the lives of widowed men.

This population needs more research attention because widowhood studies tend to focus on older women, people in general believe that widowed men "fix" their situation quickly by remarrying, and service providers do not know how to appeal to older men to take advantage of services.

The 51 men in this study generously shared with us their lives and their widowhood experience. We have tried to maintain the integrity of their personal stories while drawing out commonalities and exploring differences. We saw it as a indication of our success in doing that when a student helper reading over the manuscript said, "I kept seeing places where I thought, This is my grandpa!"

REFERENCES

Kaufman, S. (1986). *The ageless self: Sources of meaning in late life.* New York: New American Library.

Rubenstein, R. L. (1986). *Singular paths: Old men living alone.* Guildford, NY: Columbia University Press.

Acknowledgments

No authors ever stand alone in their accomplishment of a finished book. In 6 years of work, we have accumulated quite a crowd of supporters, and wish now to acknowledge all of them—and some in particular: (a) the many students who helped us through independent study or work study, naming those who worked long and took a special interest in the project: Tony Capra, Barb Sloan, Nicole Slaughter, and Heidi Holmer, (b) our department secretary, Cyndi Dininger, for her computer skills and her willingness to help us out whenever deadlines loomed, (c) Jordan Kosberg, the men's series editor at Springer Publishing Company, who believed in the potential of our material as soon as he learned about it, (d) our editors, first Bill Tucker and then Sheri Sussman, for their good ideas for organizing the book and for their cordiality in working with us, (e) Ashland University and the Miami (OH) Valley Gerontology Council for their financial support of our research, (f) our husbands, Scott Moore and John Stratton, who endured disrupted lives in good humor, helped us whenever they could figure out how, and otherwise stayed out of our way, and (g) friends, family and colleagues who encouraged us, gave us assistance, and did not complain when we were preoccupied with the book.

We thank all of the people who helped us get in contact with men eligible for our study. We thank the men and their families for their willingness to share stories with us. Nothing shows the basic goodness of people more than a complex enterprise that demands much of many people, yet assures them only that they are helping someone else by doing what they are doing.

ALINDE MOORE
DOROTHY STRATTON

1

Studying Resilience in Widowers

Louis' daughter recalled his saying that he was going to socialize just as he and his wife had done. He would invite people over for hors d'oeuvres and cocktails, then would take them to dinner in a restaurant. He also cooked a few favorite dishes; he made some dishes that his daughter particularly liked when she visited him, but he said that he did not cook well enough to prepare food for a dinner party. She remembered his entertaining with great fondness, as it demonstrated to her his resilient spirit. (Follow-up phone conversation after his death.)

But to speak of resilience in widowers—their ability to return to a life that has meaning and satisfaction after the loss of a spouse—may be putting the proverbial cart before the horse. First, the common beliefs about older widowed men must be confronted: (a) the man almost always dies first, so there can't be many widowed men, (b) they resolve their grief by getting married again right away and enjoying life with a new—and probably younger—wife, and (c) they get depressed because they can't take care of themselves, and some of them commit suicide. These stereotypes have some factual support, but they are not accurate as broad generalizations about older men, nor do they explain any given man's situation.

Looking for Literature

In the mid 1990s, when we became interested in older men whose wives had died, we discovered little research on that population. The extensive literature of widowhood was about women, with a few notable exceptions. Berardo's article, "Survivorship and Social Isolation: The Case of the Aged Widower" (1970) examined the cumulative losses of occupational role and of spouse, concluding that older widowed men were likely to be socially isolated and therefore at high risk for mental disorders, suicide, and natural forms of death. Vinick (1983) looked at living arrangements, health status and attitudes toward dating and remarriage of elder widowers three years after the death of their spouses, but she excluded remarried men from her analysis. Clark, Siviski, and Weiner (1986) examined the coping strategies of widowers in their first year following the loss. Gass (1989) found that widowers coped better if they faced an anticipated death rather than a sudden death. Tudiver, Hilditch, Permaul, and McKendree (1992) found that bereaved men made progress in coping with their loss whether or not they attended a support group.

Two books featured personal accounts of men's widowhood. *The Widower* (Kohn & Kohn, 1978) combined personal account with interview findings; it gave more consideration to the issues of younger men and finally is a treatise on remarriage. *Forever Is a Loving Word: A Story of a Life Together* (Schneider, 1991) is a poignant account of recent widowhood by an older man; it is presented without analysis.

Singular Paths: Old Men Living Alone (Rubenstein, 1986) dealt with widowed, never- married, and divorced men. *Widower: When Men Are Left Alone* (1996), originally published in 1987 by Campbell and Silverman, examined the grieving process using case studies of men of varying ages and lengths of time since the wife's death. Kaye (1997) wrote about men as caregivers, but not as widowers.

Several works considered widowhood in both men and women (Lund, 1989; McCrae & Costa, 1993; Moss & Moss, 1984; Stroebe & Stroebe, 1983; Thompson, Breckenridge, Gallagher & Peterson, 1984; Umberson, Wortman & Kessler, 1992). Fitzpatrick (1998) surveyed research on men's bereavement and recommended a methodology that would seek comprehensive knowledge about aging men, their health, and their bereavement within the environment in which they live.

During the 1990s many books were published about men and masculinity. The men's movement books are notably about men in their prime, many seeking something they feel has been missing from their masculine development (Bly, 1990; Keen, 1991). While some authors mention giving honor to the older man (Lee, 1991), most do not deal with the issues facing elderly men. "Love lost" is about broken relationships, not about widowhood.

COUNTING WIDOWED MEN

Some of our associates have suggested that research interest in widowers is low because widowers are rare compared with widows. We acknowledge that widowed older women are far more numerous than widowed older men. There were approximately 13 million men over age 65 in the United States in 1992, as compared with a little more than 19 million women in that age category (U. S. Bureau of the Census, 1993). As age increases within the 65+ age group, at each level more men die, so that in the oldest age groups the sex ratio in favor of women is much more than the aggregate 65+ statistics indicate (U. S. Bureau of the Census, 1993). Men over age 85 are the fastest growing segment of the aging population, but they still represent a small proportion of the older population. However, older widowers are not rare.

The Census Bureau counts 10.2% of men age 65–74 as widowed, and 23.7% of those age 75 and over (U. S. Bureau of the Census, 1993). However, the experience of widowhood is underreported in these figures because census questionnaires ask only for current marital status. If the person has remarried (as many men are quick to do), "now married" is the status that will be noted on the census form. Thus, many men who have dealt with the stressful widowhood experience are not counted as widowers.

Thompson opens his edited book, *Older Men's Lives* (1994), with a chapter entitled "Older Men as Invisible Men in Contemporary Society." Among the reasons he gives for older men's invisibility, in addition to their being less numerous, are that researchers tend to study disadvantaged groups, and older women have had a more difficult time than men in terms of resources and advantages in society. Also, he writes that "the medical-industrial complex has profited handsomely by medicalizing" old men, focusing attention on treatment of their health problems and, in the process, trivializing any non-medical problems they might have (p. 8). Non-medical services for the elderly are aimed primarily at a numerically larger female clientele.

Thompson (1994) notes the societal tendency to "homogenize" elders—as in having a common image for "the elderly"—is carried another step further when agedness is seen as synonymous with being female (p. 14). However, he writes, even the researchers studying masculinity have given unduly short attention to older men. Some scholars conclude that men and women become more androgynous—less differentiated by gender—as they age (Gutmann, 1987; O'Rand, 1987; Pleck, 1981). Even the possibility that strongly masculine qualities diminish with age may be a subtle influence drawing men's studies researchers away from confronting their own futures. If such mental and emotional factors underlie assumptions and theories within the scholarship of men's studies, it should not be surprising that the literature of widowhood—with its own mental and emotional undertones—would shortchange older men also.

Older widowed men are invisible primarily for two additional reasons. First, their identity as widowers is often masked by remarriage. As explained previously, the U.S. Census count hides more widowers than widows. Also, a widowed man who remarries rejoins couples society with his new wife, and after a short period of time the fact that he was widowed may be forgotten by his acquaintances. We found that to be true as some of our contacts admitted they had forgotten or had redefined widowed men, thereby not thinking of them as eligible for our study. Second, widowers do not socialize with same-sex friends in the visible way that widowed women often do. Among people in their early 70s, there are 76 men for every 100 women (U. S. Bureau of the Census, 1996), so when one of our respondents told of attending an activity where he found only two other men among approximately 100 women, we had to wonder: Where were the men? Several of our respondents commented on the overabundance of women at senior center activities, many implying and a few stating outright that they did not find this society of women very appealing. Another man told us that he was waiting for a call from people who had said they would call him about going out for lunch. Others told us they would like to go out to dinner but did not want a woman to get ideas about getting romantically involved. So where is the widowed older man? He may well be sitting at home watching TV, invisible to his neighbors, local service providers, national policy makers, and social science researchers.

But they do exist—the older widowers—and their situations cannot be subsumed in widowhood studies in which 75+% of the respondents are female. Gender socialization is different throughout the life span; there is no reason to assume that men and women will experience widowhood in the same way. Wortman, Silver, and Kessler (1993) suggest that "widowhood is not the same event for the two sexes" (p. 360). Actually, the experience of widowhood is a highly individualized process of grieving, adjustment, and self-definition. Gender is one factor in that process. We expected—and found—among older men a variety of responses to the loss of a spouse. Even if researchers conclude that men and women exhibit similar patterns when losing a spouse, men must be more thoroughly studied and the richness of their stories added to the extensive literature about widowed women. Thompson (1994), even as he wrote about the invisibility of older men, fell into that trap of overgeneralizing which invariably leaves some members of a population—in this case the widowed—invisible. He wrote:

> Aging does not oblige many older men to recast their lives and go it alone after the death of a spouse. . . . The point is not men's earlier

> deaths. . . . Men are not obliged to bury their spouses and live alone as often as women. . . . Older men rely on their spouses and report greater satisfaction with marriage than do older women (Antonucci & Akiyama, 1987). . . . For older men, assets—and not just their income and pension—are greater, allowing them greater autonomy. Personal care tasks are maintained by two adults, not just one. Life is experienced in the company of another (pp. 10–11).

Thompson is careful to include qualifiers such as "many," "not as often as," and "vast majority" in his writing, so the reader will not mistake his broad statements for generalizations about all older men. He goes on to explain that a much smaller proportion of African American men enjoy the "community of a spouse" (p. 11). However, by failing to note that life can be very difficult for the nonnormative men who have lost their spouses' emotional support and tangible help, he perpetuates the invisibility of older widowed men. Surely something that is so beneficial in its presence—a supportive marriage in older age—is very keenly felt with its loss.

Focusing the Study

Kaufman's (1986) focus on the life themes of her respondents was very helpful to our conceptualizing. Still, it is difficult to contain a study in which people are considered holistically. Themes and topics interweave. While we found little written about older widowed men, there has been quite a lot written about widowhood, bereavement, the process of recovery, and effects of stress on health. Life stages, life review, religious beliefs, systems of social support, relations with family, retirement, housing, health care, and finances have been studied in the older age categories. Findings about women help to inform about men, in considering either similarities or differences. We continually had to ask how far we should range in our attempts to survey the lives of older men and the issues that fill their widowhood.

The problem of focus has challenged us throughout our study of older widowers. It was easy to have far-ranging interviews with our respondents, first letting them decide the subject matter of the conversation, then filling in later with questions we would ask of all the men. The difficulty came in the organizing and analysis phases, for it was then that we learned just how broadly and deeply we had delved into the lives of these men. As we would begin to follow a theme, we invariably would embark on another search of another strand of the scholarly literature, and that might take us on to other considerations. At some point, we knew we would have to say simply, "These are the outer boundaries of our study." For the connections that we have not made in this book and pathways that we did not follow, we must allow that those are topics for further research.

Research Questions

Our most basic research question has been: What is the experience of widowhood for older men? That question leads directly to others. Since older men are not all the same, what various adaptations to widowhood do we find among them? How did the values, beliefs, and attitudes developed earlier in life shape their coping ability and their coping strategies? How did their own lifetimes of experiences help or hinder them in their adjustment? What can we learn from widowers who have been able to return to a reasonably satisfying life that would be of help to other men? To answer these questions we talked in depth to a variety of men. Interview topics are listed in Appendix B. We were also curious about how men's experiences of widowhood differ from women's experiences (which have been much studied and documented), yet we knew that we wanted to focus more on the men's experiences rather than on comparisons, at least in our initial study. Finally, we wondered how much of what we learned about older men today would pertain to older men in the future. In other words, as we looked at a cohort sample representing two generations in the twentieth century, we asked how much had they been shaped by the experiences of their lifetimes that will not be duplicated for future generations—the timings of wars, depressions, technological advances, and sexual and other revolutions? How much of what they experienced in widowhood will still be common to men born in the second half of the twentieth century?

Representativeness of Our Sample

Our research, like all research, is shaped and, therefore, compromised by the assumptions that must be made in order to formulate a research design and proceed with a sample selection. The basic assault on representativeness comes with decisions as to who should or should not be included—usually for very practical reasons—in the study. So when, for example, Johnson and Barer (1997) decided to study persons 85 years of age or older, some choices were made as to the types of oldest old who should be interviewed. Their findings and conclusions about that age group reflect a sample that is white, English speaking, in the local voting records or known to someone who was, not institutionalized, and without prominent dementia.

Likewise, our sample is biased. While it illuminates the lives of older widowed men and discovers some patterns among those lives, it cannot be said to be representative of all older men who have lost their spouses. We also ruled out dementia, because we felt we needed clear and meaningful conversations in order to get analyzable information. Our sample selection was biased because of our decision to do all of the interviews ourselves. Since English is the only language we speak fluently, we did not conduct interviews with non-English-speaking widowers. We interviewed two men who spoke another first language, but they were both fluent in English.

Interviewing all of the men ourselves is, we believe, a strength of our study. We were able to observe much about individual men that allowed us to see emerging patterns and distinct differences. Our presence, our format, and our style could be held as a constant as we analyzed themes across the many interviews.

Arrangement of This Book

Again, the holistic nature of our interest in the men's lives provided a challenge in organizing and presenting the material. In this opening chapter we have provided the rationale for the study, a brief introduction to the population of elder widowers, and a reference to our methodology, which is explained in Appendix A. In the next chapter, we pull together several models of resilience and introduce their relevance to our findings. The following chapters move through an introduction to the wives and the marriages, and on to the illnesses and deaths that made our respondents widowers. We consider the husbands' immediate transition from married men to widowers, and then the grieving and adjustment phases that followed. Life skills, health and disabilities, and finances of the men are considered in the chapter on living alone. Remarriage, a popular option for widowed men, is explored in the next chapter. Then we step back to look at the basic values that have guided our respondents through life and have affected their adjustment to widowhood. Adult children provide the most social support to widowed fathers; that chapter includes others who support widowed men as well. In the final chapter, we describe cohort effects on our respondents; they were the men who experienced the Great Depression and a world war (or two) in their young lifetimes. In light of cohort considerations, we consider to what extent our findings can inform researchers and practitioners about the lives of men who will lose their wives in the coming years. We also make suggestions for those who will provide services to older men in this new century. We have found this population to be notable for its diversity, its genuineness, and its directness. Older men are not simple creatures, nor are their lives simple. We hope researchers will give additional attention to this interesting and little studied population.

REFERENCES

Berardo, F. M. (1970). Survivorship and social isolation. The case of the aged widower. *The Family Coordinator, 19,* 11–25.

Bly, R. (1990). *Iron John: A book about men.* Reading, MA: Addison-Wesley.

Campbell, S. & Silverman, P. R. (1996). *Widower: When men are left alone.* Amityville, NY: Baywood.

Clark, P. G., Siviski, R. W., & Weiner, R. (1986). Coping strategies of widowers in the first year. *Family Relations, 35,* 425–430.

Fitzpatrick, T. R. (1998). Bereavement events among elderly men: The effects of stress and health. *Journal of Applied Gerontology, 17*(2), 204–228.

Gass, K. A. (1989). Health of older widowers: Role of appraisal, coping, resources, and types of spouses's death. In D. A. Lund (Ed.), *Older bereaved spouses: Research with practical applications* (pp. 95–110). New York: Hemisphere Publishing.

Gutmann, D. (1987). *Reclaimed powers: Toward a new psychology of men and women in later life.* New York: Basic Books.

Johnson, C. L. & Barer, B. M. (1997). *Life beyond 85 years: The aura of survivorship.* New York: Springer Publishing.

Kaufman, S. (1986). *The ageless self: Sources of meaning in late life.* New York: New American Library.

Kaye, L. W. (1997). Informal caregiving by older men. In J. I. Kosberg & L. W. Kaye (Eds.), *Elderly men: Special problems and professional challenges* (pp. 231–249). New York: Springer Publishing.

Keen, S. (1991). *Fire in the belly: On being a man.* New York: Bantam Books.

Kohn, J. B. & Kohn, W. K. (1978). *The widower.* Boston: Beacon Hill.

Lee, J. H. (1991). *At my father's wedding: Reclaiming our true masculinity.* New York: Bantam Books.

Lund, D. A.(Ed.). (1989). *Older bereaved spouses: Research with practical applications.* New York: Hemisphere Publishing.

McCrae, R. R. & Costa, P. T., Jr. (1993). Psychological resilience among widowed men and women: A 10-year follow-up of a national sample. In M. S. Stroebe, W. Stroebe, & R. O. Hansson (Eds.), *Handbook of bereavement* (pp. 196–207). New York: Cambridge University Press.

Moss, M. S. & Moss, S. Z. (1984). Some aspects of elderly widow(er)'s persistent tie with the deceased spouse. *Omega: Journal of Death and Dying, 15*(3), 195–206.

O'Rand, A. M. (1987). Gender. In G. L. Maddox (Ed.), *The encyclopedia of aging.* New York: Springer Publishing.

Pleck, J. H. (1981). *The myth of masculinity.* Cambridge, MA: MIT Press.

Rubenstein, R. L. (1986). *Singular paths: Old men living alone.* Guildford, NY: Columbia University Press.

Schneider, R. (1991). *Forever is a loving word: A story of a life together.* Westminster, MD: Wakefield Editions.

Stroebe, M. S. & Stroebe, W. (1983). Who suffers more? Sex differences in health risks of the widowed. *Psychological Bulletin, 93,* 279–301.

Thompson, E. H., Jr. (1994). *Older men's lives.* Thousand Oaks, CA: Sage Publications.

Thompson, L. W., Breckenridge, J. N., Gallagher, D., & Peterson, J. (1984). Effects of bereavement on self-perceptions of physical health in elderly widows and widowers. *Journal of Gerontology, 39,* 309–314.

Tudiver, E., Hilditch, J., Permaul, J. A. & McKendree, D. J. (1992). Does mutual help facilitate newly bereaved widowers? *Evaluation & The Health Professions, 15,* 147–162.

Umberson, D., Wortman, C. B. & Kessler, R. C. (1992). Widowhood and depression: Explaining long-term gender differences in vulnerability. *Journal of Health and Social Behavior, (33),* 10–24.

U.S. Bureau of the Census. (1993). *Statistical abstracts of the United States, 1992.* Washington, DC: Government Printing Office.

U.S. Bureau of the Census. (1996). *65+ in the United States.* Current Population Reports, Special Studies, (Publication No. P23-190). Washington, D.C.: U.S. Government Printing Office.

Vinick, B. H. (1983). Three years after bereavement: Life styles of elderly widowers. *Interdisciplinary Topics in Gerontology, 17,* 50–57.

Wortman, C. B., Silver, R. C. & Kessler, R. C. (1993). The meaning of loss and adjustment to bereavement. In M. S. Stroebe, W. Stroebe, & R. O. Hansson (Eds.), *Handbook of bereavement* (pp. 349–366). New York: Cambridge University Press.

2

Models of Resilience

Other researchers have developed models of resilience that have helped us assess the resilience of the men whom we studied. In some cases, we have modified or enlarged a model to accommodate information provided by our respondents. This chapter introduces the elements of resilience that make up the various models; it also serves as an introduction to many of our respondents. Appendix C provides basic information about each of the men.

Reorganization After Widowhood

Rubenstein (1986) identified several themes as indicating successful reorganization in older widowers. Among them were themes relating to belief that life is good, that the individual feels he has good health, sufficient income, and at least one close friend, and that he is in control of something important or in some way fits in. Religion is important, as are ties to the past. The successfully reorganized widower has a definite opinion of his own social needs and feels that he has "passed through the storm." Based on our findings, we have adapted Rubenstein's themes to include: (a) a sense of returning to a state of well-being, (b) perception of having relatively good health and sufficient income, (c) positive and forward thinking, (d) involvement formally or informally in religion, (e) realistic opinion of own social needs, (f) being productive in some way, (g) having a close friend, and (h) living in the present while keeping connections to the past.

Our additions were the themes of "forward thinking," living in the present, and being productive, as we saw these themes in many of our men who had adapted well to widowhood.

Interpreting Adversity to Find Benefit

Janoff-Bulman (1992) describes a positive worldview reflecting what she says are most people's assumptions that the world is beneficent and meaningful and the self is worthy. People who have suffered trauma transform it into something that fits their pretrauma view of the world. Our men made meaning of their loss.

McMillen (1999) writes that beneficial changes can be realized out of seriously adverse events. Categories of possible benefits are: (a) purposeful changes in life structure, (b) changes in views of others and the world that result from the experience of vulnerability, (c) the receipt of needed support, and (d) the search for meaning in adversity. We were able to identify many of our respondents as illustrations of McMillen's categories. An explanation of each category and some examples from our study follow.

Purposeful Changes in Life Structure

Included in this category would be seeing the need to take care of oneself after losing the wife who had tended to his care. A widowed man might learn to cook good meals, develop an exercise program, or find ways to get out and be with people. In our study, John and Stuart were both purposeful in getting out to socialize. Jacob and Daniel arrived at widowhood with different levels of competence in cooking, but both were trying to eat healthy, as well as observing Kashrut.

Changes in Views of Others and the World That Result From the Experience of Vulnerability

A widowed man might decide how good and helpful people are in response to seeing how much help he was given with caregiving and how much support he received after his wife's death. Frank had much praise for his son-in-law who stepped in and handled all funeral arrangements while Frank and his daughters were stunned by the sudden death of his wife and their mother. Most men viewed their children as helpful anyway, but that feeling was enhanced by the support that the husband received around his wife's death. For Russell, it worked the opposite way; he felt his daughter had taken advantage of him in his vulnerability. Craig and Stuart were very appreciative of their neighbors for the help and the friendship they had provided.

The Receipt of Needed Support

People would become aware of the man's needs; he was able to admit needing assistance, in other words, there would be a positive breakdown of the "going it alone" mentality. Ned's family and Art's family saw their fathers needed assistance with caregiving, which they provided. Then they continued to care for them when the fathers needed assistance in living alone. Curly protested that he did not need help caring for his wife, but his son and daughter-in-law insisted that she go to a nursing home. He was then able to admit that he had not been managing well.

The Search for Meaning in Adversity

A widowed man might see himself as more capable for having survived the stress of his loss, reaffirming his optimism and sense of competence for having survived this stress. He might be able to consider the loss philosophically and thereby find deeper meaning in life, including deeper consideration of religious faith. He could develop a desire to help others in similar situations or to help others avoid similar experiences. George wanted to help other heart patients. Robert was volunteering for hospice. Richard's losses greatly enhanced his search for meaning in life. Earl's faith was deepened with the death of his young daughter. Surviving life-threatening accidents convinced Eldon that his continuing life was a God-given miracle.

The work of Scheier and Carver (1985) is presented in the Grief and Adjustment chapter. They find that optimistic people do tend to experience more positive outcomes and suggest that optimistic people may work harder for the positive outcomes they expect, or they may tackle problems sooner so they can achieve the positive outcomes they expect. It is possible that the optimist could feel crushed by a devastating reality that shakes one's belief in good outcomes. However, among our respondents, we found a basically optimistic outlook can return out of the depths of despair. That was indeed the case for Richard, whose story of bedridden depression and his recovery has been referred to many times in this book. Janoff-Bulman (1992) describes ways in which people cognitively restructure traumatic events so they can keep a positive outlook, and Richard was a remarkable example of that.

Making Up for Losses

Ferraro, Mutran, and Barresi (1984) support the use of a compensation model when considering the responses of the elderly to losses. Rather than seeing a cumulative negative effect as more and more losses are experienced, these researchers report that older people find alternative means of getting support and experiencing intimacy. The losses increase in number, but the effect is not one of cumulative "loss overload" because of the tendency to compensate with new relationships and new arrangements. They report that persons widowed between one and four years increase their involvement in friendship networks, settling into the satisfying ones by the end of that four-year period. For example, Yussef had purposefully moved to an apartment complex so he would have other people around him.

Adapting by Adjusting Role Priorities

Hammel and Walens (1999) explain how older people who experience disability make adjustments in their role priorities so that they are able to continue taking care of themselves. This Adaptive-Process Model for Self-Care Manager Role illustrates the layers of roles as concentric circles with the identity core roles at the center (spiritual/human/ethical qualities). Basic survival roles surround that center circle. For the older person experiencing disability, those roles include sick role, assistive technology user, home manager, and self-care manager. These are the roles which take priority as the older person tries to remain independent. These survival roles take precedence over roles that were very important to the person: father, grandfather, volunteer/mentor, musician/artist. These latter roles now become part of the outer circle of roles, the elective roles. An older person may express a wish to give more attention to these roles, as in the old days, but the effort to care for self takes so much time and energy that it is not possible to do all that one used to do in the family and the community. To assess the personal effort going into the self-care roles, an interviewer would try to ascertain how much time is given to performing these roles. Energy spent on a role is less easily pinned down; it includes not only the physical effort of self-care, but the time spent thinking about it. A person ostensibly at rest can be worrying about how he will get his checks written and mailed the next day.

What appears to be self-centeredness, self-absorption, perhaps even selfishness may be a concentration of time and energy into the roles that will allow the person to remain independent longer. Conceptualized in this way, the reprioritizing of roles is positive. In our study, the two men who were most self-absorbed were Alvin, with his anxieties and his desperate need for a new wife or companion, and Leroy, with his regrets about life in general and his boredom. Alvin was driven by his needs to continue his search for a new woman in his life, so perhaps that was adaptive. Leroy was not moving toward any changes that he could identify as positive, so his choices seemed not to be adaptive.

Within this model, there are still individual differences in the ways that people handle the need for greater attention to self-care. Examining more closely that center circle of identity core roles may shed some light on those differences. If a person holds certain beliefs that lead to an "other focus," then self-care efforts may go hand in hand with continuing interest in others. Richard was not evasive when asked about his episode with the broken hip, but after a few comments, he redirected the conversation by saying, "Well, tell me what is going on at the university. What's new?" This congenial redirecting was not an incidental occurrence, as it happened four or five times during an hour-long visit and seemed to indicate a genuine interest in the world that had become much less accessible to him because of his disability.

Al's behavior was quite adaptive. He was giving money to his grandchildren as they needed it, thereby creating reciprocal relationships that would help him manage his increasing health problems. He had given his granddaughter money for an addition to her family's home. In return, she called him every day and took him shopping and to appointments. We found many of the older men conserving energy for their self-care routines by doing less than they used to do. Charles commented on that during a follow-up visit. He had relinquished some leadership roles in his retirement community since the initial interview.

Patterns of Resilience in Older Widowers

We found the above models helpful in assessing the resilience of our respondents. Among the men we found many ways of returning to a balance and a reasonable satisfaction with life. No one model will fit every man. On the other hand, there are commonalities that encourage us to begin thinking of our own model.

Being resilient does not mean being pain free. The men who had made an adjustment that most outside observers would term "good," had these things in common: (a) an initial very painful awareness of their loss, (b) a continuing hole in their lives (sadness), in spite of many meaningful activities, (c) an integrated belief and value system that helps them come to grips with tremendous loss, (d) a personality that was basically positive and optimistic throughout life, and (e) the ability to get social support. However, as pointed out by Wortman and Silver (1986), there is significant variability in the ways people respond to loss. Instead of looking for an individual's expected journey through particular emotions identified with grieving, researchers and helping professionals would be wise to examine the internal consistency of an individual's belief system and personal style with the outcome of his own personal adjustment to loss.

Taking into account that each man will adjust in his own way, we can categorize the adjustment choices made by the men in our study: (a) finding a new wife or companion, (b) altering their self to help adjustment, or (c) altering their environment to help adjustment.

Seventeen of our 51 respondents had remarried in older age—the youngest at age 54, the oldest at age 81. Not all married immediately after being widowed, but many did marry within a time frame that would have been associated with active bereavement. Others had found companionship with another woman. Their strategy might be termed "replacement," a way of having continuity in lifestyle.

Art's comment that he had to "recreate myself" in his debilitated old age is an example of altering the self to adjust to the new reality. Each man who learned skills formerly handled by his wife was recreating himself in order to be self-sufficient. Daniel said that he was "good company for myself." Conner—keeping the house, his daily routine, and even his diet just the same as when his wife was alive—had recreated himself to be whole in the very same environment and lifestyle in which he had been just half.

Al and Yussef altered their environments to help them adjust to life on their own. Al was solidifying his support system through cordial and undemanding interaction, and by helping family members with finances. Yussef had moved to a living situation where he could be by himself when he wanted to be and could interact with others when he wanted to do that. Extending oneself socially could be identified as altering the self in the case of an introverted man who pushed himself to socialize more, or it could be altering the environment in the case of a man like Al, friendly and talkative, who worked at ways to draw others to him.

An Example of Resilience

Throughout this book we describe the many ways in which our 51 respondents were handling the loss of a spouse. Their adaptations, in more cases than not, could be identified as resilient in their own particular situations. Here we have selected one of our respondents, Clarence, whom we met additionally outside of the interview situation and found the characteristics of his style of resilience to be even more evident in a social situation than they had been in the formal interview. Clarence was 93 years old and lived alone. His two daughters lived out of state. We highlight our observations here.

Genuinely Interested in Other People

Clarence asked questions in a give-and-take conversation. He was direct in his style, and obviously assumed that people are trustworthy and likeable. He was willing to talk about himself. His sharing about himself was just the right amount of detail for a pleasant conversation. He would tell a story completely and would keep it focused. Then he would bring up a new topic in the form of a question to another person. He responded positively to new information.

Interested in Events Happening in His Environment

He knew about and was interested in events, not only in the ways that such events impacted upon him, but more generally. In other words, he was still a citizen of the world.

Not Self-Absorbed

He spoke very little of health problems. He was matter-of-fact about his circumstances, wanted to be as self-sufficient as possible, but did not lament, excuse, or deny the need for assistance in some ways.

Pride in Being a Survivor

He was proud of being very old, especially in that he was taking care of himself and feeling comfortable with the daily routine that he had fashioned.

Comfortable with Idea of Death

He could talk lightly and contentedly about the time he had remaining in this life, acknowledging that it might not be long.

Made Overtures for Continued Contact

He encouraged further contact, thus showing the social skills for gaining social support. While letting us know he would like further contact, he was not at all pushy about it, leaving it wide open and definitely up to us to contact him.

Considered Himself Worthy

In an unassuming way, he seemed to consider himself worthy of the time we were spending with him; at the same time he seemed pleased that the other persons wanted to spend time with him.

Optimistic

In spite of devastating losses, he had been able to adjust emotionally. He looked forward to each day as it came and to special events such as a visit by one of his daughters.

Not Judgmental of Others

When disagreement arose in the conversation, he smiled and nodded, then moved on to another topic.

In summary, Clarence provided us a good example of how resilience is demonstrated in living life. He embodied the themes described by Rubenstein and our further adaptations. The well- adjusted, self-assured men such as Clarence encouraged us to look more deeply at men's perceptions of locus of control and optimism or pessimism.

Resilience and Type of Death

A resilient man did not necessarily know how to cook, clean, do laundry, and arrange social engagements while he and his wife were together as a healthy couple. But he was flexible enough to learn how when he needed to, optimistic enough to feel that he could learn well, and secure enough not to feel his masculinity was threatened by carrying out housekeeping activity.

Giving care to an ill wife seemed to enhance resilience by giving the man a chance to develop competence. It may have been tiring and emotionally draining, but it was also a training period for household competence.

Does a sudden death of the wife, therefore, rob a husband of the chance to become resilient? The shock of a sudden death seemed to leave a man at least temporarily immobilized. He had not had time to prepare spiritually, emotionally, or philosophically for the loss. He had probably not practiced housework and self-care skills enough to be good at them. The way a man dealt with a sudden death was to large measure a reflection of the way he had been living his life previous to the loss—with the addition of the loss exacerbating any difficulties he may have had. Adaptations observed in our study included being a loner, having to have a new relationship immediately, being tearful and too cautious to enter another relationship, being able to be rescued by another woman, feeling sad but reconnecting with a woman from the past, and filling one's life with service to others. These outcomes were not surprising in light of what the men had described of their lives before the tragic loss. Adaptations were in some cases quite positive, but in all cases there seemed to be an underlying traumatic residue.

Resilience and Resources

None of our respondents was in serious financial need. Some did have more money to spend than others; that gave them more options, as we see in the section on disabled men in the Living Alone chapter. Family, friends, and relatives are valuable resources for an older person living alone. In some cases they can bring disappointment and cause irritation, but in more cases they provide resources, companionship, and a sense of belonging.

Accessibility and appropriateness of bereavement support groups for men should be of major concern for professionals hoping to serve older men; if our findings are an accurate indication, the existing groups are not attracting and holding male participants who could find the group support very helpful.

REFERENCES

Ferraro, K. F., Mutran, E., & Barresi, C. M. (1984). Widowhood, health, and friendship support in later life. *Journal of Health and Social Behavior, 25,* 245–259.

Hammel, J. & Walens, D. (1999, December). Testing a model for examining how older adults develop a self-care manager role following acute and long-term disability experiences. Paper presented at The International Meeting of the Rehabilitation Engineering Research Center on Aging, National Learning Center of the American Society on Aging and the Rehabilitation Engineering and Assistive Technology Society of America, Arlington, VA.

Janoff-Bulman, R. (1992). *Shattered assumptions: Towards a new psychology of trauma.* New York: Free Press.

McMillen, J. C. (1999). Better for it: How people benefit from adversity. *Social Work, 44*(5), 455–468.

Rubenstein, R. L. (1986). *Singular paths: Old men living alone.* Guildford, NY: Columbia University Press.

Scheier, M. F. & Carver, C. S. (1985). Optimism, coping, and health: Assessment and implications of generalized outcome expectancies. *Health Psychology, 4*(3), 219–247.

Wortman, C. B. & Silver, R. C. (1989). The myths of coping with loss. *Journal of Consulting and Clinical Psychology, 57*(3), 349–357.

3

What Was Lost: Wives and Marriages

To begin to understand the widowhood experience of older men and their adjustment, we must set a context that shows what the men had lost. In this chapter we offer the men's descriptions of wives and marriages. These descriptions come from each man's perception and recollection alone, and are valuable for that reason; they establish the perspective and context for all that he had to say about his loss and his adjustment thereafter.

DESCRIBING A WIFE

We asked each respondent to describe his deceased wife. Some adjectives such as "nice" and "good" and "wonderful" were commonly offered, in which case the interviewer would probe for a more specific description. Describing the wife was difficult for many of the men. Possible reasons include a lack of expressive vocabulary, little experience in thinking about how to describe someone, and perhaps knowledge and experience so broad that expressing it in a few words seemed impossible. Bill, who was in general very articulate, said, "I guess I'm not very good at describing her," and later, "I wish I could do a better description of [my wife] but I can't." He followed these statements with some information about her work history and her helpfulness to other people.

Words That Describe

The adjectives that the men used to describe their wives were almost all positive, and they all praised their wives, although to varying degrees. The word "good" was associated with personal qualities: good-hearted, good sense of humor, good Christian. It was associated with role performance: good mother, good grandmother, good cook, good housekeeper. It was also associated with nondomestic talents and skills: good voice, good speaker, good manners, good driver, good dancer.

Some men used positive descriptors that were vague in terms of painting a picture for the interviewer, but obviously very meaningful for the man. Art said, "She was the sweetest, most wonderful thing that ever walked on earth." Carlo referred to his wife as an angel, and Joe said his wife was a doll. Jerry and Curly referred to their wives as sweethearts.

Many of the descriptions included the wife's physical attractiveness. Seven described their wives as pretty, five as beautiful. Conner described how he was in his office one morning and "this gorgeous creature walked in the door." Jacob described his wife as "winsome." Arch showed a photograph of his wife as a young beauty queen with her court. Bill said, "She was a nice-looking, good lady. She was round, a little. I like women with rounded corners." None of the men said his wife was unattractive or plain. A few men commented that their wives had gotten heavy, but none gave any indication of feeling that made her unattractive. It was common for the men to show photographs of their wives in old age and to comment on their good looks at that time.

Many of the men used terms such as "outgoing," "social," "friendly," and "well-liked" to describe their wives. Some of them said that their wives were the social directors of the couple, keeping them actively involved with other people and keeping them in touch with families. They typically described their wives as very giving and caring towards all, and especially attentive to them (the husbands). Conner said that his wife was the social one of the two, "a great reacher-outer, a friend to everyone and a helper to anyone." Jim said, "She was lovely, personable. . . . She was the most generous person I have ever known, and the least prejudiced." Ned said, "She was an outgoing person. Regardless of what was going on, when it was time for me to be home, the house was ready for me, and supper was ready for me, and the kids were ready for me. She just was a wonderful wife." A few of the men noted that their wives were not outgoing, using these terms: quiet, shy, secretive, not sociable, and reclusive. Garrett said that his wife was "a very quiet, secretive sort of person. You never knew how she felt." He described her two sisters as being the same. He also said his wife was "deeply religious, very spiritual."

Many of the women were praised for being religious or having strong faith. Their caring natures were often described in the context of their volunteer work at church or their informal attention to the needs of people in their family and in their church congregation.

Intelligence was a quality noted by 12 of the men who described their wives as "smart" or "intelligent." Other similar adjectives included: competent, independent, practical, problem-solving. Several adjectives related to their jobs outside the home: ambitious, conscientious, hardworking, workaholic. No one described his wife's intellect in negative terms. Some of the men said their wives were not interested in or involved in things that the men wished they would do, but that was never attributed to the wife's lack of intelligence or ability. Men spoke readily about the strengths they saw in their wives; those comments appear later in this chapter.

Other positive personal qualities mentioned by the men included: always laughing, balanced (stable), brave, bubbly, caring, cheerful, down to earth, easy going, firm, generous, gentle, gracious, happy, kind, lovable, lovely, loving, loyal, mild mannered, noncomplaining, nonjudgmental, optimistic, personable, pleasant, real (genuine), relaxed, spontaneous, stoic, sweet, thoughtful, upbeat.

Some of the descriptors were not positive, and yet they were embedded in marriages that were described in a positive light. For example, Clarence was a bit mysterious in describing his wife. He described her as "inclined to be a bit somber." At one point he said, "I don't think she was the happiest person in the world." Later he said she was happy but "not an exuberant person." Still, he said he could not imagine being married to anyone else. Al and Craig described their wives as "hot-tempered." Al said, "She was always jolly and easy to get along with until you kept pressuring her to the place [where] she would get fired up." Craig said, "Every once in a while she'd fly off the handle and she'd knock me back a few steps. . . . She hit me with a lamp one time. Boy, I had a bump on my head." But he also said about her, "She was such a person. Everybody loved her." Clyde described his wife as "nervous" and said she was "scared" of taking financial risks. An excerpt from the interview with Clyde is presented in the Remarriage chapter to show his strategy for dealing with her.

There were a few other "not" descriptors: not always loving (sexually), not bubbly, not outdoorsy, not sentimental.

Wives Described in Role Performance

Good Mother

Being a good mother was the most commonly mentioned characteristic. Nine men used that exact term, while many others also spoke positively of their wives as mothers and grandmothers. Feeling sad that grandmothers and grandchildren had their years together cut short was a common theme. Stuart, for example, said his wife was a good grandmother for just a very short time. Their grandchildren were very young and probably would not remember her. Earl said, "I don't want to lose those memories because they are good memories and they're all associated with what I have left with my kids. No, I don't want to lose that." Stuart and Earl were among the youngest respondents; they keenly felt the untimely absence of their wives in the role of mother and grandmother within their families. When Kenneth remarried, his father told him never to forget his first wife, as she was the mother of his children. Kenneth said he responded, "I never will."

Several of the men praised their wives for emphasizing the importance of education for their children. Clyde and Russell, both men with little formal education, credited their wives with having seen that the children at least finished high school. Cordell said his wife was not judgmental about those of their children who lived together without being married, even though she believed it was not the right thing to do. "She probably had greater compassion for those who were having the most difficulty," he said, like the parable of the lost sheep, "you leave the 99 and go for the one that is lost, wherever that one is."

Good Cook

Apparently the way to a man's heart is through his stomach. Seven of the men described their wives as good cooks. Carlo was effusive:

> She was better than good! You never ate a meal that she didn't have one or two side dishes on the table. When I was young you would be lucky to get one dish at a meal. . . . It was so very good. I thank the good Lord for my memory every hour of the day that I can remember these wonderful things.

Jerry was more practical. He remembered his wife as a great cook and said he missed having salads at every meal. Yussef described his wife as a good cook. He was the only man in the study who had a friendly cooking competition with his wife. In widowhood, when he looked through a cookbook, mention of certain Middle Eastern cooking spices would stir his memory. "I'll say, 'Well, I never used [that spice], but she did.'"

Good Housekeeper

One man said that his wife was not a good housekeeper, but most men were emphatic about how well their wives kept the house. Arnold said, "My wife was the kind of woman, if I got up at 4 a.m. to go to the bathroom, when I came back, she had the bed made." Robert recalled an occasion when he observed his wife scrubbing the same frying pan for half an hour. He said he told her, "If you're still working on that one pan the next time I come by, I'm going to come in and take it away from you." He said, "She was that kind. When she cleaned, she cleaned. She always had it done when I got home." Most of the men compared themselves very unfavorably in their efforts to do housekeeping themselves. They were accustomed to the level of housekeeping provided by their wives, could not duplicate it themselves and, in many cases, hired someone to come in and clean a couple times a month.

Working Outside the Home

Determining the employment history of the women was difficult. Many had never held a paying job. Others worked part time at certain times, full time at others, and usually not at all while the children were young or while the children were living at home. Some wives worked in their husbands' businesses, often filling in when paid help was out. With all this complexity, the husbands could not recall dates or other details about their wives' working careers. Eleven indicated that their wives had worked before marriage. It was typical for the wife to quit working when she married; that was the custom and sometimes the rule, as in the case of schoolteachers early in the twentieth century. Yussef's wife continued teaching, as he described her work and her continuing education as the driving force in her life. Art's wife was not employed, but he said she was a leader in social and civic organizations.

DESCRIBING A MARRIAGE

"Good" and "happy" were the most commonly used descriptors for the marriages. Overwhelmingly the men remembered their marriages in a positive light. Al told the interviewer, "You know, my mother died when I was two years old, and I never had a home until I got married. I really appreciated a home, where I could say that was my home and that was my wife and the children we had, those were my children." A few referred to some bad times in the marriage, but none of the men said his marriage overall had been bad. We discuss the negative experiences in the marriages later in this section.

Courtships

We asked each man about courtship and got a great variety of answers, from the spectacular falling-in-love-at-first-sight phenomenon to finally getting together with someone who had been known for years. We provide examples here from the spectrum of responses. Conner immediately fell in love with the "gorgeous creature" who, mentioned earlier in this chapter, walked into his office one day. He found out her name, walked up to her and said "Howdy, stranger," and she laughed. They went out for dinner and married after a year's courtship. Richard met his wife through a friend, invited her to a movie and then they did not see each other for almost a year. He called her again after that long hiatus. "From then on, we knew we wanted to be together." Art spoke of stealing the date of his best friend's brother at a beach party:

> She was never his date again after that. I snuck off with her. People don't talk about falling in love today. I only know by my own experience. . . . My dear sweet companion in life, that's the way we lived.

Jacob, however, objected to the term "falling in love." To him it signified a haphazard, mindless act that was not befitting the kind of attraction that had led him to the heartfelt and enduring commitment he felt toward his wife. He spelled the word "luv" and said it was all about sex and was an artifact of American pop culture; in essence, it wasn't real. Jacob was in the minority with this opinion, as many of the men referred to their wives' good looks and the instant attraction that they felt. Carlo said, "She was the prettiest girl in the world." When the interviewer asked Clyde what it was about this young woman that made him decide she was the one, he replied, "She was pretty." Al recalled meeting a woman a little older than he who was visiting his cousin:

> She was a nice looking woman, as far as I was concerned , she was beautiful. And I says, 'Hey, do you have any more at home like you?' She says, 'Yeah, I got a kid sister at home.' I says, 'I'd like to meet her.' . . . So I met her and we hit it off right away.

Bert said, "Who the heck knows [how he got attached to the woman he married]? She was a nice gal and she felt sorry for me. She thought she could change me probably."

Describing the Marriage

Some men spoke in superlatives. They used these phrases: best marriage, excellent marriage, luckiest person in the world, marriage couldn't be better, wonderful marriage. Eldon's comment was a good example of how some of the men's memories had put a glow on everything:

> We got along. She was a wonderful, wonderful woman, wonderful family, wonderful neighbors; everything has just been great. Couldn't ask for anything any nicer. Now, what was the question you asked to start with?

Conner said that he and his wife "lived on Earth. We didn't just exist."

Negative Memories from the Marriage

The men who had negative things to say about their marriages were in a small minority. Don said he loved each of his first two wives; the poor experiences in those marriages seemed to result from the abuse of drugs and alcohol by both partners. Robert and Curly both expressed intense guilt relating to their insensitive treatment of their wives. Curly was verbally abusive; Robert was neglectful and at one time unfaithful. Robert pointed to a span of years that he described as happy, and Curly said the couple had lots of good times through the years. Craig said the marriage did not start off well, but got better. Jim said they fought some in the early years because his wife could be a bit volatile. He gave an example of a time when she hit him in the nose with a loaf of bread while he was driving home from the grocery store.

Common Interests and Activities

Some of the men talked of common interests they shared with their wives. Charles and his wife went to square dancing conventions and traveled around the world. Jerry said he and his wife were best friends. He said they would watch TV separately, and yell from one floor of the house to the other when there was something on a certain channel that the other should see.

Arnold said he got his wife involved in a singing group, but he could not get her interested in golf or bowling. Rain on the golf course spoiled her hairdo and she broke a couple fingernails handling the bowling ball.

Sharing Responsibilities

Richard's wife did not want to do any of their financial paperwork and he did not mind doing it, but he thought perhaps he should not have done it all himself, because she was shying away from it more and more as she got older. All through the years he helped do the dishes, the washing, and the marketing. Cordell told the interviewer:

> I don't want to give you the false impression that I was a super husband, but I was. I bought the groceries. I did the cooking. I helped with the cleaning until the kids got old enough to do it. I was good; I was easy around the house. I was comfortable. I didn't have to go golfing. I didn't have to do these various men's things. I didn't have poker parties. My family was primary.

Parenting

Cordell gave his wife credit for the parenting, as most of the men did. Russell and Clyde said their wives made sure the children studied and got through school. Ned said his wife always had the children "ready for me." Jerry said, "I was really kind of a taskmaster. I really didn't like the kids to sass back," indicating that as a difference between him and his wife. Bert said he did not get along with his wife's adolescent daughter and blamed the girl for causing their divorce. They did get back together after they split up.

Decision-Making and Strong Women

When we asked the husbands about decision-making within their marriage, two types of answers were common: (a) we were equal partners, or (b) she made the decisions about this and I made the decisions about that. In addition, their answers revealed quite a lot about strong wills, competence, and resolve in these wives. Malcolm said his wife almost always agreed with him on decisions. But she could be very assertive when she needed to be; that was usually in situations outside the family. Ned said:

> [My wife] was a strong-minded person. She never used her power, she never confronted me with anything. . . . She just quietly went about it and did what she felt was necessary, whether I would have approved or not. We did have some financial binds as a result of that from time to time.

Bapuji described his wife while they were with their families in India:

> Of the three daughters, my wife was very competent, and she had the final word in that family, in her father's family. In my house also, her word was final. Her control over the house, her control over my brothers and sisters, even over my father, was greater than mine. So many ways, I tell you, so balanced, so practical.

Charles described his wife as a very gracious southern lady, but he also said, "I never did much to make her mad, I didn't want to. I tried to please her if possible. She did not like to be imposed upon by anybody. That would infuriate her." Alvin expressed similar feelings, "I often gave in to her, for example, around the dwelling here. Mama makes the rules about what house to buy and all that, or God help you."

Curly described his wife as "dependent" and not willing to make decisions. This quality may have been an adaptation to Curly's overbearing and controlling behavior, which he admitted to, but which he did not connect to her behavior.

Disagreements

We asked each man how he and his wife had handled disagreements. Seven men said they never disagreed, but even they talked of situations were there obviously had been disagreement. A couple of these men had very forceful personalities and might not have recognized disagreement when it arose. They also may have intimidated their wives with their forceful personalities, thereby eliminating open disagreement. We found that disagreements existed in all marriages and were acknowledged in most. For example, Clarence commented, "We didn't quarrel a great deal. I can't remember many times when we did, but I suppose there were more times, some that I chose to forget. But, we got along well."

Husbands used these phrases to describe how they and their wives handled disagreements: I (always) gave in, I made up to her, I walked away, I would not argue because it wasn't worth it, we met half way, we reached mutual agreement, we separated after an argument to cool down, we talked it out, we worked it out in private, she always made up, she gave me the cold shoulder, she made me talk it out, she would retreat when mad—go into a shell, she had to prod me into talking.

Bruce said he and his wife had some disagreement over one of the children in their blended family. But Bruce had a general philosophy of not arguing with anyone, and he used that philosophy with his wife as well:

> Somebody ought to just walk away and let them think what they want to think. Eventually it worked out all right. We had our differences, but I won't argue with anybody. . . . It's not worth it to get mad. Life's too short.

Yussef said that he would try to joke about something when his wife would want to be serious and that would get him "in the dog house for two or three days, all day." He said they gave each other space until everything had cooled down. "Later you come back and you see a different view and that would be a different picture altogether," he concluded.

Richard said they would not argue about a child-rearing matter in front of their child, although "we might have a knock-down-drag-out after he was in bed." In the rest of the interview, he said that he and his wife saw eye to eye on most matters, especially on how to spend or save money and how to handle their social life. Handling money was the sore point for Russell and his wife. He said all of their many arguments were about money—spending vs. saving.

Clyde said, "We got along good. We weren't perfect, but we got along good. She'd give and I'd give. It wasn't no problem." Jerry said that many people had told him that he and his wife were a perfect couple, but he said they had their ups and downs just as all couples do. He described them both as being "kinda hot-tempered." He said they would holler at each other but never got physically violent. He considered it "a defect in my personality" that his wife always had to make the first move toward making up. He recalled her saying that he would regret being so stubborn, and said that she was right about that.

Domestic Violence

The incidents of hitting were all initiated by the wives, according to the husbands' accounts. In these cases, every man said that he never hit his wife. Earlier we mentioned Craig's wife hitting him with a lamp and Jim's wife hitting him with a loaf of bread. Cordell said his wife slapped him once when he had done something that hurt her emotionally. Carlo said that his wife once grabbed him by the shirt and shoved him roughly, in a way that would have caused a fight between men. He said that he never hit her, but once he put his fist through a wall in anger over a money matter.

Fondly Remembered Wives vs. Sainted Wives

Two interviews were similar: men who were unkind to their wives remembered them as perfect or "sainted." The two men were very different in their approaches to the interview situation, but they both idealized their deceased wives after having been controlling and verbally abusive toward them during their lifetimes. Curly was depressed and tearful, saying how much he loved his wife and how much he regretted not being good to her. Family members confirmed his verbal abuse as a pattern throughout the marriage. Karl claimed that he and his wife had been equal partners and that they always got along well—and that she was perfect. He avoided every question that dealt with emotional content; sometimes he looked at the interviewer with a blank face, other times he gave an answer to something other than the question asked. Finally, in response to a very general question of how he would express feelings of anger, he terminated the interview. A family member said Karl had been verbally very harsh with his wife throughout the years and that he allowed her very little access to money.

Other men spoke in very positive ways about their wives, but they did not claim perfection. They spoke of a real person who had strong points, pet peeves, and idiosyncrasies. According to Garrett (1987), this ability to remember both positive and negative qualities of a deceased loved one is an indication of healthy progress through bereavement. Al described his wife in glowing terms, but he conveyed a picture of a real person when he spoke of how she would "get fired up" in certain circumstances. Speaking of his wife, Louis said, "I felt I couldn't duplicate what I had." He described a disfigurement from surgery and said that it bothered her but "she never let anybody know it did. She was an outgoing individual. . . . She would entertain, very funny." He laughed heartily at his memory.

Other men had significant differences with their wives, but they did not try to camouflage them with summary statements of the wife's perfection. For example, we knew that Clyde and his wife had some differences of opinion. He seemed, in fact, to be shaping his life in the present by thinking of how she would respond to situations. He was not fully open about their disagreements or power struggles, but he did not deny them either. He just muted them. In other words, the disagreements were there in his mind and he tried to phrase them in a way that wouldn't sound too bad or be too revealing. He did not seem to carry guilt for the way he had treated her. If anything, he might have felt a bit embarrassed that he was not able to prevail against her and would not have wanted to explore that power dynamic with the stranger who came to interview him.

However, for the man who "sainted" his wife, it seemed that he could not describe the woman's qualities in such detail. Perhaps for each man in his own mind, her goodness had grown to override the images of sad faces and angry voices that he otherwise might have recalled. From an interviewer's perspective, sainting a wife moved her out of the realm of a real person who could be known to someone inquiring about her. Telling someone she was a saint or perfect was a summary statement that neither invited nor allowed further questions.

The "sainting" of a wife seemed to come from the man's knowledge that he behaved badly but she stayed with him, thereby proving that she had qualities that an ordinary woman would not have had. That was probably the dynamic working for Curly, who was so open about his shortcomings toward his wife. He could not hide his regrets, so he admitted that only a perfect woman would have put up with his treatment. Karl was probably hoping to avoid paying a price for what he had done. Fortunately, his son still cared for him, but if the way Karl had acted toward his wife would be known to others, he might be judged harshly and so he had to convey a peaceful and perfect home scene.

Here are some other ways that the "sainting" of a wife might work for the man who depicts his deceased wife that way: (a) if she were perfectly good and stayed with him, surely he was not perfectly bad, (b) if he told someone that she was wonderful and she lived her life with him, then he would be seen by that individual as a person worthy of her, (c) if she remained so wonderful all through her life, then she was not damaged by anything that he did. We were not able to discuss these dynamics with the two men, so they are simply intriguing conjecture at this time. These dynamics would be interesting to study with a research design more suitable to delving into personal motivation.

Findings

Almost all of the men gave positive descriptors of their wives and marriages, although they did speak of qualities and patterns of behavior that were not positive. The overall memory of the marriages was positive. These women grew up and married at a time when women did not have much power in any public realm. They did not participate much in political life. Most of them did not work outside the home. But these women had strengths that gave them power within the family and earned their husbands' respect.

Most of the couples had a traditional division of chores. Their husbands remembered them as very good housekeepers and very good cooks. The women were described as reaching out to others and doing good for others. Some wives used physical aggression to express their feelings toward their husbands. The husbands said they did not return the violence. The inability to describe a wife in realistic terms may indicate a problem in the relationship that could be further investigated.

REFERENCES

Garrett, J. E. (1987). Multiple losses in older adults. *Journal of Gerontological Nursing, 13*(8), 8–12.

4

Illness and Death of Wife

The natural continuity of a wife's illness and death pulls together many themes, which become difficult to consider separately for analysis. The type and timing of illness, the need for caregiving and the course of that process, the type of death (accidental or illness, sudden or prolonged), the impact of the loss upon the husband, the support he receives during the illness and death, the final arrangements, the disposal of property, memories of wife and marriage, the grieving process, beliefs and attitudes about the future—all of these factors merged as a man talked about the death of his wife. In this and the following three chapters, we examine some of the patterns that emerged as we studied the death stories that we were told. We also look at some exceptions to those patterns in order to acknowledge the uniqueness of the death experience for each couple. Using a thematic approach to analysis allows for gathering together related content from the stories of different men. It also means that a story is told here and there instead of all together. The risk in this approach is that the continuity of the story is jeopardized. These very brief episodes told by four respondents are a reminder that each death story was the center of a powerful emotional experience uniquely experienced by the man who told it.

The story told by Sy:

> I knew I was the main person to help her out in all of that. Nights she would be up or else she would lose control. I'd have to take care of it all. I called 911 in cases where I couldn't take care of her. Many a night. . . . When she went to the hospital the last time, when she was very bad, a woman that weighed 160 or more pounds, she was down to about 90 or 80 pounds. Finally she couldn't eat. . . . I called 911 and they took her to

the hospital; then they kept her there. They said to her, said to me, that she'll have to go home. There's nothing they can do for her. It's a heck of a thing to say, the fortunate part is that, when I was supposed to take her home . . . she passed away.

The story told by Arch:

She was actually diagnosed [with multiple sclerosis] about 9 or 10 years before she died. She first lost her eyesight, but then it improved. . . . Then it got so her legs got weak and it worked from her legs up. She went to a wheelchair and that's when I had to leave the office so I could be here during the day. [Our son] had the night time to look after her [while I worked]. I did that for about 8 years. Then she died.

The story told by Russell:

She had a massive heart attack. She got up that morning, went to my grandson's football game and came back home and washed a load of clothes. Then she went shopping to the store for groceries and stuff, came back, she put them away. She went in, sat down in a chair, and 10 minutes later she was gone. I walked out of the house into my mother's, and I came back. . . I thought she was sleeping.

Interviewer: Did you call the emergency squad?

Russell: Yeah. 911. My son tried to get her back too. We called 911, and they tried. They took her to the hospital, and they tried for three or four hours but they could not. Finally they came out and said they'd lost her. Two doctors told me that if they'd been right there they couldn't have saved her. They said that their heart just explodes. That's what my family doctor told me. And the doctors at the hospital, both of them told me that no matter who was there they couldn't have saved her. It just happened so fast.

Interviewer: She didn't say she hadn't felt well?

Russell: No! Like I say, we were joking around after she came back from the store. I was back in the garage and she blew the horn for me, but I didn't hear her. So when I came up to the house, she told me that she had blown the horn. I told her that I didn't hear it. She was joking around. She said "Aw, you heard it!" and she wasn't sick or nothing! Just like that, she was gone!

The story told by Jerry:

The two kids, my sister and I were there. . . . We were holding onto her. My daughter was sitting on the floor and she had my wife's hand and she

> had her cheek on her hand . . . we just held on to her, she breathed her last, the sun was shining through the window, that was incredible, it really was. . . . My wife was a very spiritual lady and we both believe in God and the hereafter and I knew she went straight to Heaven because if that woman didn't go straight to Heaven, you know, she was just a good person, she really was. And so we celebrated that.

After reviewing all of the death stories, the statement we can make most confidently is that the death experience is highly individualized. Ours was a fairly homogeneous sample—men over age 60 (most of them white) who had outlived their wives. Aside from the occasional accident or heart attack, one might have expected to hear the same story again and again: woman is diagnosed with cancer and receives treatments, husband helps her when she is not feeling well, her condition declines to the point where she needs care, husband with help of adult children provides care until either hospice care or institutional care is needed, she dies.

In fact, this was the story outline in 20 of the 56 death stories that we heard. However, in reviewing these stories, one is struck by the value of the ethnographic approach to collecting data. Sifting through the details provided by each man, the researcher sees that these stories are not the same. One man was distraught because he had already lost one wife to cancer, while another was losing the only love of his life. One man would not allow himself to believe that his wife was dying, while another prayed for her release from suffering. One watched his wife die in a matter of a few months, while another gave care for years. One talked with his wife at length about her dying, while another couple never mentioned it in words. One found his children ready to help when their mother died; another found that earlier alienation continued in spite of their mutual loss. Death stories became individualized in the telling of the details.

Studying Death Stories

Every death has a story (Moore, 1989). Telling the death story allows the survivor to organize events and feelings, and to hear them being spoken in a way that confirms the reality. Further telling of the story long after the death may honor the person who died and is a way of sharing intense feeling from the less emotionally involved perspective of narrator.

The heart of our inquiry for this study was the death-of-wife experience and its aftermath for each man. We interviewed 51 men who had lost a total of 56 wives. A couple of men had lost first wives when they were much younger. We focused for this study on the loss of the wife that occurred when they were older.

We asked each man to tell about the death of his wife. By doing so, we hoped to learn about the specific circumstances of the death, to hear about the impact of the death on the husband, to find out what kind of support system was available at that time, and to observe the emotional tone that the death elicited with the current telling of the story. We hoped to find patterns and relationships. These are some of the questions we explored: Were most of the men present with their wives at the time of death? Did long caregiving prepare a man for his wife's death? Had the couples discussed the wife's impending death and/or the husband's future after her death? Did older men find it easier to accept the death of their wives because they were at the time in life when people in their age group were dying?

In the style that we had adopted for our interviews, early in the process we allowed each man to bring up topics that he wanted to speak about. Later, we would introduce topics that he had not. Also, we delayed introducing topics that might evoke an emotional response until the respondent had become comfortable in talking with us about his life; usually that would be late in the first interview or in the second. We found that most of the men did not bring up the topic of the wife's death on their own. They often made references that allowed us to ask a question to elicit the death story. Usually though, we had talked about many other things before that. Our respondents knew that they were taking part in a study of widowed men, so they were prepared to talk about the death. (Bert was an exception. He apparently misunderstood the intent of the interview; he terminated it when asked about his wife's death.) We had been turned down by several widowed men who said they did not want to talk about their wife's death. Our sample therefore consisted of men who were willing to discuss this subject. Nevertheless most of them chose other subjects to talk about early in the interview. There were exceptions. Alvin opened his interview by saying: "I have a few things I can volunteer to you. I've been seeing a psychiatrist since before my wife died because we knew in no uncertain terms her condition was terminal."

Types of Illnesses and Deaths

Cancer

Most of the deceased wives experienced an illness of some duration, which involved need for care. By far the greatest number of wives had died of cancer, a total of 18 out of the 56 women who had been married to the men we interviewed. Within the U.S. population, malignancies are the leading cause of death for women ages 35-64 and the second most frequent cause of death for women age 65 and over (Centers for Disease Control and Prevention, 2000).

Jerry cared for his wife for four months as she quickly succumbed to colon cancer that had spread to other sites. Don and Daniel lost wives to lung cancer and to pancreatic cancer, respectively, in a year. However, the caregiving period for a cancer-related decline was more commonly two to three years and sometimes longer. Sy spent two years caring for his wife as she died from breast cancer. Terrence's wife's cancer was caused by asbestos; the illness had a two-year duration.

Jacob's wife and Daniel's second wife had cancer illnesses lasting three years. Kenneth and Craig lost their wives to breast cancer after four and a half years. Conner's wife was ill with cancer and heart disease for six years before dying of a stroke. Garrett's wife had lymphoma for 14 years. As with other types of illnesses, it was difficult to delineate a caregiving period for those couples dealing with cancer. Yussef's wife had breast cancer for 17 years, but maintained a busy schedule until just a few weeks before her death. Richard's wife had a brain tumor and Alzheimer's Disease; he stated that she had been in poor health for 15 years. When did caregiving begin in such a case?

Heart Disease and Stroke

Heart disease and strokes claimed the lives of 11 of the 56 women. Heart disease is the leading cause of death for women above age 64 and the second leading cause of death for women from 45–64. Cerebrovascular conditions are the fourth leading cause of death for women 45–64 and the third leading cause of death for women 65 and older (Centers for Disease Control and Prevention, 2000). Heart attacks and strokes may be instant killers or they may lead to debilities that last for years. Russell's and John's wives died suddenly. Bill's wife lived for three years following her stroke. Charles' wife broke her hip, then suffered pulmonary and cardiac arrest. After years of poor health, Al's wife succumbed to congestive heart failure. Heart disease and cerebrovascular disorders are intertwined with other health problems, complicating an analysis that looks at the course of illness and caregiving needs. Stuart's wife's thyroid and heart problems led to death from stroke. Arch's wife had multiple sclerosis, then died of blood clots that suddenly hit her heart and lungs. Hospital personnel restarted her heart, but she never regained consciousness and died soon afterward.

Claude's wife was in serious decline with diabetes and then died of a stroke. Joe's wife had asymmetric septal hypertrophy, a heart condition in which the abnormal thickness of the heart muscle causes an obstruction of blood flow; she died of a stroke after 12 years of decline with the heart condition. Some of the surviving husbands did not have a specific diagnosis for heart disease or other systemic weaknesses. Eldon, for example, said his wife's heart and kidneys were weak.

Diabetes

Five of the women suffered from diabetes and its complications. Claude's wife, mentioned earlier, was typical in the debilitating course of her illness, but also typical in that she died of something else, in her case a stroke. Jim's and Frank's wives had diabetes but died of pneumonia. Diabetes is the sixth leading cause of death in women over age 65. Pneumonia and influenza killed more than 43,000 women over age 65 in 1997, the fifth leading cause of death in that age group (Centers for Disease Control and Prevention, 2000). Frank said his wife got double pneumonia, after never having had a cold in her life. "She wasn't feeling good; I took her into the hospital and they were going to keep her overnight and check her out. . . . I came home, got a phone call they put her in intensive care, started pumping her lungs right now. . . . The lungs filled faster than they could keep them pumped out. I think it was only about eight days and that was about it." Curly's wife had diabetes and Alzheimer's Disease, leading to an elongated decline that ended with a year in a nursing home. The final stage of her illness is described below in the discussion of dementia.

Respiratory Conditions

Respiratory illnesses were less common among our respondents' wives than cancer, heart disease, and strokes, but they were factors in the poor health of several women. For American women over age 65, they are the fourth most common cause of death (Centers for Disease Control and Prevention, 2000). Walter reported that his wife had spent a lingering decline with emphysema which was related to her smoking; he also had emphysema which the doctors related to second-hand smoke. Will described his wife's decline with emphysema, then a stroke, and finally dying of pneumonia. Russell's wife had asthma all her life; she died of a heart attack. Bruce said his wife had "dry lungs" and Clarence said his wife had "weak lungs."

Dementia

Dementia deaths were characteristically preceded by long periods of decline and need for care. Alzheimer's Disease enters the Center for

Disease Control and Prevention's (2000) ten leading causes of death in the 70-80 year old age group, where it occupies position 9; it grows steadily as a cause of death with advancing age. Ned, Carlo, Clarence, Richard, and Curly faced caring for a wife with dementia. In these cases, the man would take on more and more responsibility for care. These deaths involved their unique experience of sadness, for the husband would "lose the person" even while she was physically still present and needing care. Ned said, "I think when she died, I felt relieved for her. Before that, as a person she had left me. She would talk, and we would talk about this and that a little bit. But she wasn't herself. Pretty much, as a personality, she had disappeared." Typical of Alzheimer's patients (Mace & Rabins, 1999), these women would be confused and sometimes difficult to deal with in a way that was very stressful for the caregivers, who no longer received the compensating benefits of congenial companionship. Our respondents did not complain about the care that was required or the stress that it produced. Ned's daughter-in-law said that he was always very patient with his wife, but that she would become frustrated and contrary with him at times. Ned did not complain about her moodiness. He described her as withdrawn. "As time went on," he said, "she was just less active in whatever we were doing or whatever we were planning and so on."

Curly took care of his wife until his son and daughter-in-law decided he could not manage any longer. He spoke of her final year:

> She was in [the nursing home] almost a year until she passed away. But I guess it was a good thing she did, because everything was wrong with her—her heart, her eyes, her ears. There wasn't anything that wasn't wrong with her. She'd been lonely half of the time. The only way I knew she knew me, she'd grab me around the neck and hug me and kiss me and tell me, "Where have you been, honey? I've been looking for you." Well, I've been here because I came every day, every single day to see her. But she just couldn't remember.

Vague, Less Common, and Multiple Conditions

The longest periods of declining health usually were experienced by women whom their husbands described as having been unwell or "not strong" even as young or middle-aged women. Cordell said his wife has been ailing for years. "After the rheumatic fever, she never had much energy. For the last 20 years she was just too tired, didn't have the energy. . . . She took care of the children, that was her. So I'd come home from work and she'd say, 'Okay, I'll take care of the kids, you get supper.'" They had a very large family; Cordell did not attribute her early decline in health to childbearing and child care responsibilities, but they might have been factors.

After his remarriage, Stuart admitted that he had not realized what a difficult time his first wife had with her many health problems until he married a woman who was healthy. "Now I realize it," he said.

Some wives experienced multiple health conditions, leading to increasing frailty and physical breakdown in their old age. Often in these cases, the husband was able to describe the disability, but could not name a specific diagnosis. Harry said that his wife would fall. "It was, I don't know, rheumatism or whatever you call it, got worse. . . . it settled in her knees. . . . just quick, down she'd go!" He went on to describe her death at age 86, "She developed something on her throat, kind of pouch thing. I don't know what it was. Anyway, they couldn't do anything about it. Around midnight, why, she died." Harry's daughter told the interviewer that her mother had arthritis in her legs and hips and would fall because she was not willing to use a walker. After one fall, her back was x-rayed and an infection discovered. She was put into a nursing home while the infection was treated. The infection caused the swelling on her jaw, but the official cause of death was pneumonia.

Arch's wife had multiple sclerosis, Art's Parkinson's Disease, and Henrik's wife kidney disease. These are not exotic or uncommon diseases, but they severely tested the physical and emotional stamina of the caregiving husbands. Their situations are described in the Caregiving chapter.

Arnold's wife had myasthenia gravis, an autoimmune disease characterized by muscular weakness. "She had the other things that go with it, chronic syndrome. . . . She picked up diabetes. And I think she overmedicated herself too." Arnold was referring to her use of steroid drugs which were effective in relief of symptoms, but had serious side effects.

Alvin's wife had scleroderma, a chronic, autoimmune disease involving unbridled growth of the connective tissue; it is classified as a rheumatic disease. The systemic type, which she had, may affect the connective tissue in many parts of the body (skin, esophagus, gastrointestinal tract, lungs, kidneys, heart and other internal organs, blood vessels, muscles, and joints). Alvin's wife's condition also involved Raynaud's Phenomenon, an abnormal sensitivity to cold in the extremities.

Husband's Feelings About Wife's Medical Care

Some of the men offered opinions about the medical care their wives had received. Joe praised his wife's care, even though the blood thinner that had been prescribed contributed to her fatal stroke. He said they knew it was risky. "One minute you call a strike and the next minute you call a ball." He said she didn't want to suffer. "We had excellent care, very good cooperation." Jerry said he felt reassured when "this high-priced cancer doctor [in the big city] told me that the doctor [in the small town] had done a fine surgery. . . . Sometimes we look at small towns and think you're getting second rate. This guy said, 'I couldn't have done it any better than what he did.'"

However, Jerry complained that her gynecologist had not ordered a sigmoidoscopy when she had her full gynecologic exam. Jerry told him, "If you don't want to do that, I really think you have an obligation to your patients to tell them to go back to their regular doctor and have that done." Malcolm said his wife had been diabetic and "the doctor just didn't pick it up." Stuart also faulted the doctors for not recognizing his wife's ailment. The women in his family were nurses, but he was still disillusioned by his wife's treatment. "I guess it kinda surprised me the way things turned out. It just always seemed like the medical profession was a step behind." However, Yussef said of his wife, "She could be alive today if she'd listened to the doctor."

Bill complained of the ambulance staff acting slowly and taking his wife to a hospital farther away than the one where her doctor practiced. "I am teed off to them yet. . . . I wrote a little dissertation on that thing and I should have given it to them." Walter said that his wife's doctors had made a mistake in giving her a tracheotomy, which prolonged her life for four more years of existence in a nursing home. The tracheotomy prolonged her suffering "from weeks to years," he said.

Ned was also critical of his wife's treatment. He said, "We got the best surgeon that we knew about. He operated and found the ulcer. . . . but apparently he did not leave enough room for passage of food because she couldn't eat anything afterwards. . . . She had to go back in the hospital after about six days. He opened up the lower end of her stomach, but I didn't think that was a very good job. She never after that got over the stomach thing."

Alvin said he had taken his wife out of state to a specialist for her disorder. Alvin knew someone who had the same condition. "He bought quite a bit of time by going to that doctor. But it didn't help us." Art said, "This Parkinson's can be a terrible, terrible thing. She used to get rigidity so bad that she was unbearable in pains. . . . My son-in-law a couple of times, he said we would go across the street to the hospital. He said, 'I'll raise hell and I'll try to get a narcotic.' It's illegal, OK, so it's illegal. So what?"

Medical treatment had a sad ending for the men who lost their wives, so complaints would be expected as part of their regrets over the outcome of their wives' illnesses. It was beyond the scope of this study to examine medical records or interview medical personnel, so no assessment can be made of the medical treatment that was given.

DEATH

"Almost Died" Episodes

Some of the men had experienced episodes in which the wife was extremely close to dying or had died and somehow returned to life. We wondered if such episodes prepared a man for the eventual death of his wife. These situations were uncommon, very individual, and filled with meaning based on personal values and beliefs. Our few examples of such events yielded no particular patterns. We will tell these stories and assess their impact upon each man.

Al described a wild ride to the hospital holding his wife in the back of his grandson's van. He said he did not know at the time that she had died, but the emergency room staff asked if Al wanted them "to bring her around." He said yes, and they revived her. Al's wife, having battled cancer and heart trouble, responded to the reviving by asking him, "Why didn't you leave me dead? What was the use of bringing me back? I'm no good here." But Al assured her that he loved her. "I want to keep you as long as I can," he told her. "And we did," he said to the interviewer, "we kept her as long as we could." He described her death with this story:

> She was in the hospital eating her supper and feeling fine. She was laying there in bed, kidding us and talking to us and I said, "Well, Jim and I need to go home and get a bite to eat. I'll come back in the morning and bring your glasses over. She didn't have her spectacles. . . . We got home, ate our supper, and I was listening to the TV. Jim's wife [was talking on the phone] for a long time. Well, somebody knocked on the door and here it was the police come out to say, "They are trying to get you on the phone; your wife is dying." So Jim called the hospital and they said she's already dead. . . . We went back over to the hospital; she was laying there on the bed dead."

Al narrated these episodes in a way that recounted how he was getting prepared for his wife's death. They both were very old. She had many ailments. Her close call with death was a signal of her precarious condition and it had given her the opportunity to tell Al that she was ready to die. Living wills had been discussed, decided upon, and put into place. In spite of his reluctance to part with the love of his life, he was preparing to lose her. However, when she actually died, he was greatly distressed, probably depressed. He had to move a couple of times, seeking a relative's home in which he could live with minimal friction. When he finally got his own apartment in a retirement building, he seemed more settled and content.

Malcolm, age 74 at the time of the interview, was about 20 years younger than Al when he faced widowhood. He wept during the interview, saying that this was the first time he had spoken of the death of his wife. He had been widowed for four years at the time of the interview and had been remarried for three years.

Malcolm: [My wife] went into the hospital and I'm going to tell you something that's going to make you wonder. . . . The doctors said, "If you have anybody that you have to get hold of, you'd better get hold of them because your wife's not going to last the night.". . . She was in the hospital there, and she was sitting up in a chair, she wasn't laying down. . . . She was like that for a week. Just sitting there, all of us were around.

Interviewer: Was she aware of you?

Malcolm: No. I'm going to tell you something. So when she came home, she surprised us all one day; she came out of it. She wasn't in a coma, because they said she wasn't. . . . So one day she and I were talking and I said, "I want to ask you something. Where were you?" She said, "I was with my mother in Heaven." And He sent her back. . . . That's all she said. She was back here until August when she died, about six months. . . . Knowing my wife and knowing her love for the gospel, it was true.

This crossing-over-and-return experience is based in the strong religious belief in the hereafter shared by the two spouses. Whether it prepared Malcolm for his wife's eventual death is questionable. He did not say that he had thought she might recover, but with the astounding news of her journey to Heaven and back, he might have nurtured that hope. As stated earlier, he wept bitterly while telling of her loss. He seemed to be a man who had tried to get on with his life by remarrying, but had not gotten free from the active grieving for his first wife. The bitterness of his grief was intensified by a feeling that people where not kind enough or attentive enough to his wife when she was ill. His stories in general conveyed a theme of feeling at odds with others; this one was particularly emotion-laden. It mattered a great deal to him, and amends could never be made.

Bill recounted a time when he thought his wife had died. He said, "I was just destroyed . . . I cried and just was terribly out of control and I was ashamed of myself really. That was when I got her in there [to the emergency room]. I thought one of two things: that she was dying then or she would come out of that a vegetable. But neither one of those things happened." When she actually died, Bill was much more composed. This episode seemed to have allowed him to acknowledge the terrible loss he was facing, saving him from that painful recognition at the actual time of death.

Knowing the Time Had Come

Some men told of their awareness that the time of death was at hand. Sam said, "We did [know the end was close]. She lost her hearing. She stopped eating. I used to come out and take her and feed her and everything else in the nursing home, try to spend time with her almost every day."

Clyde recounted:

> [My son] came home that night about 2 o'clock and says Mom passed away. And I was expecting it. It was not new to me. When I took her away, called the ambulance, I says, I'm taking your mom away, kids, she's sick. I says she ain't going to be back, she's gonna get worse. Sure enough she did. In a week's time she was dead. And I heard [my son] make a comment to somebody about how well I handled that, knowing that was going to happen. And I did. She's not going to be back. . . . We have to make out the best way we can. . . . There is nothing you can do about it. That's one of them things that's beyond our control.

Jerry remembered:

> I told her, "We [the family] think you ought to let us take you off this [nutritional supplement]. You know they can't do anything more for you." She wasn't ready to make that decision right there, but later, I don't know if it was the same day or the next night, she told us, "I'm ready." I crawled up in bed with her and she opened her eyes and our faces were this far apart. I looked at her and I said, "Do you love me?" She looked at me and she said, "With all my heart." Closed her eyes and she died the next afternoon; we never said another word to each other. You know, I'll cherish that for the rest of my life.

Were You There?

Commonly in qualitative research, when respondents are asked to recount an event, the compiled stories do not fall into neat categories.

Rather, they tend to lie on a continuum. We thought that a simple question—were you there when your wife died?—might be an exception. However, some of the responses challenged our simple yes/no possibilities. Benjamin had stepped out of the hospital room to call his children from the waiting room and missed the moment of his wife's passing. Robert was keeping vigil outside the bedroom; his wife died in her sleep and he does not know exactly when.

By far the most common situation was the husband not being present at the moment of death. Usually in such cases he had been attentive in visiting her in the hospital or nursing home or was still giving her care in the home, but was away to get some rest when the death occurred. A tone of regret and sadness accompanied such a story, thinly veiling the man's feeling that "I should have been there." Benjamin described the death of his wife in this way:

> I walked into the room and she opened her eyes. She had been in a coma. Just for a second, she saw me and called out my name. I sat and held her hand and they told me it would only be minutes. My children were still out in the lobby. I had told them that when the end was near I would call them. But it happened so fast. I thought I would have time to call them. But while I was on the phone she, I wasn't with her when she expired. [I came back] about a minute after she passed away and that always bothered me. But she knew I was there. Because just for that fleeting moment. . . .

Earl said:

> All my family had been there and her family as much as was able was there the night that she died. . . . My oldest son and his wife, we went out to eat and I had decided to just go home and get some sleep. About 4 or 5 o'clock that morning they called from the hospital that she had died. So at the time that she died, there was really nobody there. I've had some feelings about not being there when she died. It bothers me some as I think about it—that I wasn't there. I guess I justify it by knowing that she wouldn't have known I was there. While she was semiconscious I had opportunity to be with her and give her up and give her to the Lord and say that the inevitable was here. And so I could do that; it was a difficult thing. I have kind of mixed emotions about that time.

Jim had been with his wife, but had gone home to make some phone calls when she suddenly took a turn for the worse. She passed away just before he returned. He said, "I would have preferred to be there at the time, but I wasn't, and there's nothing I can do about it. I spent lots of time with her. I don't feel guilty about not spending time with her." But

Art said, "This is the most terrible thing. No, I was away for 20 minutes, left her, or maybe it was 30 minutes, but no, I wasn't with her."

There were exceptions to feeling regret about not being present, but they were certainly not devoid of emotion. Two of the men decided not to be present at the death. Cordell had to make the decision about turning off life support. "I knew that's what she wanted," he said. "I was not with her. . . the doctor or the nurses said, 'Unless you have some strong reason.' And so we did everything by phone at the last day." Joe kissed his wife goodbye and left, making the decision not to be present at the time of her passing.

Joe:	They gave her a CAT scan right away, and the doctor showed me. I said, "Well, just make her comfortable." No life support. She didn't want life support.
Interviewer:	What were your feelings at that time?
Joe:	It's hard to explain. . . . "Well, this is it, man." I kept saying, "Well, this is a real kick in the ass."
Interviewer:	Who was saying that?
Joe:	I was saying that. This is the only way I could explain it to myself. I just kept going at it. Gritting my teeth and face it. . . . I didn't stay with her. I kissed her goodbye. I knew this was the end. I didn't stay with her. I went back and I made some phone calls, and then I kept myself busy. . . . Then I got the phone call and I kept myself more busy, getting rid of her medicine and stuff like that. I knew it had to be done. I went right at it. I'm that type.

Being present for the moment of death seems to be a matter of personal choice, and most of the men wanted to be there. Joe needed to keep moving, to keep busy. For both Joe and Cordell there seemed to be a sense that the wife was already gone. Being elsewhere at the moment of death probably allowed them to go on with that level of awareness, without having to witness the exact moment of passing or feel the fresh pain of finality.

Thoughts of Long-Term Caregivers at Death

Those men who had given care during a long illness experienced different thoughts and feelings when the death finally came. For some, the death seemed to bring closure. Others simply acknowledged the end. For some, the time of death brought overwhelming grief. Some were depressed, some were anxious, and some were devastatingly lonely. We consider all of these responses more fully in the Grief and Adjustment chapter.

RELIGIOUS CONTENT OF DEATH STORIES

Some of the death stories had religious content. Especially for Christians with a sure belief in life after death, the time of death brought comforting assurance that this physical end was not truly the end of existence. Our respondents differed in their conceptualizations of what Heaven would be like. (Their ideas about the nature of Heaven are presented in the Life Values Carried Forward chapter.) Simply stated at this point, believing in a nonearthly existence after death—whatever its form—helped the men cope with the physical death. Jerry, who was Catholic, explained, "I've always been very comfortable in my faith. We are all going to die someday and this is really a small part of eternity, so that was always a comfort to me because I believe that, and when my wife died, I knew she went straight to Heaven. . . . so that helped me." He described his wife's dying in the midst of family; his story was in the opening to this chapter. Craig, a Protestant Christian, also described the last minutes with his wife:

> I don't know. It looked like she'd met opposition and she was fighting. . . . The nurse said, "Get so she can see you." So I got over the bed and got right in front of her and got her attention and I told her that it was all right now, she could go, that I loved her very much, and she seemed to just settle down after that. Then she was saying, well, she kept asking for her grandmother and her mother and her grandfather, and then all of a sudden she started saying it was all right, she was talking to Jesus. And she was real quiet and just laid down and went back to sleep.

Sudden Deaths

For those whose wives died unexpectedly, the death was a matter of living through shock and horror, whether or not they were present at the exact moment of death. Russell's wife's sudden death by heart attack was described at the beginning of this chapter. Frank's wife, as previously noted, was hospitalized for pneumonia, took a turn for the worse, and the family was suddenly faced with the realization of death. George came home from work to have lunch with his wife. She collapsed with a brain aneurysm and died three days later. Don said that he wondered if he was a murderer when his second wife, like his first, died of a drug overdose during their mutual drug-using lifestyle.

The interview with Bert ended when he was asked about his wife's death. He explained that she had been killed by falling to her death. She had pulled the car to the side of the road to get out and fasten the latch on the car's hood when it had come loose, not knowing it had a safety catch. For safety reasons she had climbed out the passenger's door rather than the traffic side of the car. The wind was blowing hard; the police believe the car door was blown into her body and she fell to her death. Bert said the police came to his apartment and told him. Telling the interviewer this, he then said that was all, and walked away from the interview.

John said his wife had felt unwell suddenly the day before. Then she woke up about 5 a.m. the next day and said she felt better. He went on, finishing this statement in tears:

> I don't suppose it was an hour after that you could see the change in her. She wasn't coherent like she was, and I kept asking her about calling the emergency squad, and when it sounded like she said no, I said, "I'm going to call them." Here she had a heart attack, and you see, through all of this was a total of about four hours and she was gone.

Bapuji said he drank tea with his wife, said goodbye and left for a typical workday, only to be notified a few hours later that she had suffered a serious collapse (from which she was destined not to recover). She was in a coma for 32 days and passed away. He said:

> I think [it was a] stroke. I think she must have had low blood pressure (crying), but she did not complain. It was not in her nature to complain about her health. It was a terrible time. . . . It shocked me so much that I did not adjust myself for so long. . . . At age 60 I had plans. . . . I would pass my life in India in a very good way. . . .Even today I don't feel adjusted.

The sudden deaths were a small proportion of the total deaths, but they stood out for the impact that they had upon the husbands. The subject of the wife's unexpected death still brought fresh emotions, no matter how long ago the event had happened. These sudden deaths were characterized by the lack of opportunity to get accustomed to the idea of impending loss. In the chapter on Grief and Adjustment, we look at the ways in which the type of death affected the husband's grieving and adjustment.

Findings

The causes of death for the wives in our study followed a pattern very close to that for women across America. Many of the wives had more than one condition. Some died of a condition that was not related to their chronic illness. Almost all of the husbands wanted to be present at the death, but most of them were not. They had been attentive, but typically were away from the bedside getting rest when the death occurred. Being there at the time of death was important for most of the men and was a cause for regret if they had not been there. Sudden deaths were very traumatic. Lingering deaths were heart-wrenching, although they provided some opportunity to get prepared for the loss.

REFERENCES

Center for Disease Control and Prevention. (2000). *10 leading causes of death, United States 1997, all races, females* [on-line]. Available: http://webapp.cdc.gov/cgi-bin/broker.exe?...c_age1=50&c_age2=60&Submit=Submit+Request

Mace, N. L. & Rabins, P. V. (1999). *The 36-hour day.* Baltimore, MD: The Johns Hopkins University Press.

Moore, A. J. M. (1989). *Life moves on: An exploration of motivation in elderly women.* Unpublished doctoral dissertation, University of Illinois, Urbana-Champaign.

5

Caregiving and Communication

Kaye and Applegate (1994) state that a significant number of older men are acting as primary caregivers, particularly to their spouses, and are devoting a significant amount of time, energy and emotional investment to the task. McCann, et al. (2000) surveyed community residents age 65 and older. They found that caregiving increased as age increased among married respondents. The probability of being a caregiver was greater for women than for men, but among caregiving respondents, the time commitment did not differ by gender. Kaye (1997) suggests that "there are unique dimensions to the older male caregiving experience that separate it from that of female caregivers" (p. 232). Therefore, in this chapter we look at the caregiving experiences of our widowed respondents, and explore those features that may differ from the female caregiving experience or that may be counter to the general expectations for men's behavior.

AN ALTERING MARRIAGE RELATIONSHIP

A serious illness in either spouse changes the routine and the ways of relating that have been in existence for a very long time in a long-enduring marriage. In this section we relate the ways in which husbands had to take on unfamiliar chores, administer medications and treatments, and relate to the growing dependency of their wives, while giving up many of the earlier comforts and pleasures of the marriage relationship. Kaye (1997) writes that male caregivers tend to keep a "stiff upper lip" (p. 232) about their caregiving. Young and Kahana (1989) had similar findings; they found men caregivers likely to downplay or deny the difficulties they experienced. We found that to be the case among the men we interviewed. Their accounts almost always minimized the stress and health burden of caregiving.

Loss of Helpmate/Doing Chores

Nearly all of the couples represented in our study had a traditional division of chores when the wife was well. Some of the husbands reported having helped with household responsibilities all along, but for most, the wife's illness meant husbands were doing something new and unfamiliar, then more and more, until eventually they were doing it all. Lund, Caserta, Dimond, and Shaffer (1990) and Lund, Caserta, and Dimond (1993) report that widowed persons' difficulties in managing household chores are identifiable with traditional gender-related expectations. Men have more problems assuming chores such as housecleaning, laundry, cooking, and shopping. Women have difficulty with auto maintenance, repairs, and handling finances.

The few men in our study who reported knowing how to cook and clean before they entered the caregiving period attributed those skills to childhood training or to military training. Garrett said he grew up cooking. Kenneth said he learned to cook and press his pants for wearing to school because his mother had been ill. When his first wife became ill, he took over the cooking and dishwashing. He joked with his father about needing to remarry because he was tired of cooking. But when his second wife became ill, he had to do it all again. Frank said he learned to do dishes and clean house as a youngster, but attributed his cooking skills to his time in the Marine Corps.

Henrik shared cooking responsibilities with his wife even before she became ill because they both held jobs. "Of course, me being a cook in the service, there was no pain for me to make a meal. . . ." When his wife had to go on dialysis, he did practically all the cooking. "The doctors told me not to baby her," he said. "Don't say she can't do anything. . . . Just be firm and get her to do what you think she can do. . . . She would go to the basement to do the laundry and I did all the cooking and vacuuming. So we had a really good arrangement."

Cordell's situation was typical of those in which the wife gradually needed more and more help. He explained:

> It developed so naturally I didn't even realize that I was doing it. . . . maybe the first thing she said was, "Would you mind doing the vacuuming?" "No, I don't mind doing the vacuuming." . . . I carried the laundry to the center and she would hang up the clothes and take them down

> and . . . I'd have to bring them back. . . . Gradually she said, "Would you mind doing the laundry?" I'd hang them out and bring them back. And she'd say, "Did you put them in the front room? I will sort them and fold them." . . . Towards the end she would insist that she would . . . do the dishes. . . . It took her half an hour to do what I could do in five minutes. But it was important to her.

Ned's wife had dementia, so they did not directly negotiate what he would do. When she couldn't think of what she wanted at the grocery store, Ned started doing the shopping and the cooking. He gradually took on more and more of the things that she had done while she would sit and read. He recounted, "[There was a] separation; she just kind of left me. I didn't realize how much it was true. I think the kids recognized it. But life just seemed to go on, and I seemed to get more and more involved in the details."

Richard said he did the cooking while his wife was ill, adding that they went out often even though "she hated to get out to the car and [hated to] sit in a wheelchair." Bill also admitted to a lot of eating out. "My cooking is not that great," he said, adding, "I like to bake." Walter did not take on the cooking duties, nor did they go out to eat. He and his wife were reduced to a meager diet, according to his report. "I guess we had cold cereal for breakfast. I don't remember much. My son had tried to give us a microwave for two Christmases, and we said we didn't want it. On the third year, the microwave arrived. . . . So it sat in the cellar for 6 months, and we got tired of Sears calling us every other week to say, 'How do you like the microwave?'"

For many of the men, doing household work involved a new relationship with the wife. This was clear in the way that some of the wives participated in the new arrangements. Bruce's wife called out directions for cooking from her bedroom; Bruce still had her recipes posted on the refrigerator at the time of the interview. Arnold's wife had him place her chair where she could command a view of three rooms of the house and thus could direct him as he worked on various chores. Arnold described the situation this way: "You see that chair there? I never really put it away. . . . It used to be right here where she could keep an eye on me and tell me to do things. Tell me how to run the washer and cook and give her shots."

A few of the men spoke of their failure to live up to the wife's standards. Clyde admitted, "Yeah, I cooked. I mostly did the cooking 'til she died, for 2 or 3 years, and cleaned house, all that. . . . She could tell me how and I'd do it. . . . She could do that better than I could."

Robert's story related the tension that developed:

> When she became ill, I took over [the housecleaning]. She'd sit there sometimes and she'd tell me that I missed this corner or I missed that corner and I'd get mad at her for telling me, but I took over completely when she couldn't do it. She liked it clean and she liked everything in its place. Of course, I was used to it that way too. . . . Cooking, she told me what to do, but I've just never been one to enjoy that kind of thing so I did what I was supposed to do, but then ten minutes later, I couldn't remember what I did.

Loss of the Marriage Bed

We did not ask our respondents about sleeping arrangements as the wife's illness progressed. However, several made comments indicating that separate beds and often separate rooms became the arrangement. In practical terms, a restless ill person could keep awake the person who needed rest in order to give her care the next day. However, there were surely some feelings about leaving the marriage bed, as such a move could have symbolized emotional and sexual distancing at the very time that the circumstances of final illness were drawing them together, as Sy described:

Sy:	I had to sleep in the same bed with her. If I didn't she would feel that I didn't care for her. Because she lost her breast, she would say, "How can you stand looking at me? I'm half a woman now." I said, "I'm not looking at your body, I'm looking at you, how good you are."
Interviewer:	Even when she was very ill, you were in the bed with her?
Sy:	In the bed with her, yeah. I took care of her.
I:	Was it hard for you to sleep?
Sy:	Yes, yes, yes, it was very hard because the pain was great and she couldn't control her bowels. I had to worry about this thing and the other thing and medication.

Carlo said that he would put his wife into bed at 8 p.m., as she would ask him. Then he would watch TV until 10 p.m. When he got into bed, she would put her arm around him, still awake after two hours. "She was waiting on me every night," he said. So he decided to go to bed at 8:00 with her. "I would be there two seconds, and she would be asleep. Two seconds! She would just wait to sleep until I came there!" he exclaimed.

Curly and Richard both recalled sleeping "on the alert" in separate beds. Curly would listen for his wife's breathing. Richard slept "with one eye open to see what she was doing." Robert described the stressful nights with his ill wife:

> She wanted the TV on all night, practically all night. I couldn't sleep at all with the TV, so I moved into the other bedroom. But she tended to call out to me quite often during the night. . . . so it wasn't what you would call solid sleep. I was on my feet in two seconds flat when I'd hear her holler. . . .We had a potty chair right next to the bed and she could use that, but it was even getting difficult for her to get on that. But I didn't move in there because I just couldn't handle the TV. She thought she was awake. She'd say, "Don't turn it off, I'm listening." She was sleeping, but she thought she was awake.

Husband To Be in Charge of Care

When the ill wife could no longer manage her own medications and treatment, the husband had to take responsibility for that management. Clearly it was stressful for the men to have to be in charge of these regimes; however, as with the housework, they took on the tasks of managing medications and giving treatments as they were required. The following stories convey the stress that could develop in these caregiving arrangements.

Carlo recalled:

> I had a hell of a time trying to get her to take her medication here at home. . . . One night I was sitting down after giving her the medication and I felt something hit me. I looked, she had a pill in her mouth and she spit it up against my neck! . . . [After that] the doctor told me to hold her nose. . . . She probably thought I was trying to kill her. It's been almost ten years since that happened. I'd kill myself before I'd lift a finger against her. But I know that she must have thought that.

Ned said, "Toward the end of her life she didn't want to eat. We had several bouts of trying to force feed her. . . . It just went on and on and she was uncomfortable, and we couldn't find any way of making her comfortable. So it was really, really a bad time." Claude also had a stressful time with his wife's eating. He said he felt she declined because he did not follow her diet properly. He too had difficulty getting his wife to take her medications. "People get tired of taking medicines," he said. "I had to watch and see that she would actually swallow it. She'd take it in her hand and probably put it down. . . . She just got to the point where she couldn't see evidently. She'd wake up and say, "I can't see." I said, "I'll see for you."

Several of the men recalled a certain place where the wife would sit or lie during the day. Her illness and his caregiving were centered in that location. Curly explained that he would feed his wife breakfast, and then see that she got her insulin and other medications. "I'd see that she got her clothes on and situated her in the davenport in the living room. And that's where she was most of the day because I couldn't leave her alone."

Henrik explained about the six weeks of training he had for running a dialysis machine. He was operating his business at the same time that he was managing his wife's dialysis regime. As he explained, "At that time she had to be on dialysis three days a week, eight hours of circulating. It took an hour to get ready and an hour to clean up afterwards so it was a 10-hour circulation." He did that for five years and said it "got the best of me." Garrett also had training for an occupational therapy routine: . . . "how to pick her up and set her down, how to turn her over in bed, because I was going to be the number one caregiver. . . . I didn't realize what an art there was to that sort of stuff." Bruce told of a harrowing experience when he had to locate the backup oxygen supply in the dark when the power failed and his wife's usual oxygen machine did not work.

Another variation on being in charge was making the decision about terminating treatment. The oncologist treating Michael's wife told him they would have to move her from the hospital because no more could be done for her there, and he said, "You can't make a hospital of your apartment." So Michael's wife was moved to a nursing home, where Michael hired an additional private duty nurse. He consulted with the children and then told the doctor they did not want her to have "a nothing kind of existence for an extended period of time." He told the doctor, "I want you to stop. All the medicines and everything." That's what was done, and she died shortly thereafter. It appears that Michael and his children did not discuss the decision with his wife; we do not know if she was capable of having that discussion. We do not know if there were other cases among our respondents in which a decision to end treatment was made without consulting the wife. Cordell said the doctor recommended "pulling the plug." He said his wife was not able to speak because of a tube in her throat, but he knew that is what she wanted. Jerry recounted the story of having asked his wife if she was ready to be taken off the nutritional supplement.

EFFECTS ON CAREGIVER

Gaining an accurate picture of the effects of the caregiving experience on the older male caregiver is not an easy matter. As Kaye (1997) indicated, the caregiving man is likely to be stoic about what he is going through, unlikely to report feeling burdened, and unlikely to ask for help. In our interviews, we often had to probe to get any details about the experience, and then had to probe still further to elicit comments about the feelings that went with the experience. The comments presented here may appear to be open and explanatory, but most of them were shared only after considerable interviewer encouragement to discuss the caregiving more fully.

Stamina

We found that the men in our study varied greatly in the length of time they had given care to an ill wife. Those whose wives died accidentally or from a sudden health crisis spent no time giving care, while some gave care for decades. One can count months or years of caregiving, but time may not be the most salient factor in looking at the effects of caregiving on a man's life in widowhood. As already stated, it is difficult to pinpoint when caregiving began. Also, caregiving would be defined subjectively; one man might view fixing lunch for himself and his wife as the beginning of her needing care while another man would not.

More importantly, we must remember that the interviews were conducted after the caregiving had ended. The stories were related from a perspective of looking back on the entire process. However, when one is within the caregiving experience, one does not know when it will end. With cancer deaths, the doctors would give predictions and the deaths often would come within the predicted range. In some cases, however, the ill person would live beyond the prediction. Other illnesses did not lend themselves to predictions; a terminal diagnosis would bring the weight of a death sentence without much clue as to when it would be carried out. It would be very difficult for a person who knows the ending to a story to tell the story as he experienced it during the time of uncertainty. It was left to us as researchers to try to understand the impact of the ongoing caregiving experience on the man who was living it. We decided that an important consideration was the stamina of the caregiver. Some of the men who had given care gave detailed accounts of the exhausting regimes they followed. None of the men reported health problems as a result of caregiving, but some finally placed their wives in nursing homes, others needed assistance at home, and still others managed everything by themselves until the end. We expected that the group of men who had maintained stamina throughout the caregiving period would have experienced a shorter time of caregiving, less demanding care needs, and were themselves healthier and younger than caregivers whose energy and resolve wore out.

Several studies report that women caregivers perceive more stress from caregiving (Borden & Berlin, 1990; Fitting, Rabins, Lucas & Eastham, 1986). Some possible reasons for the differences include (a) the nature of the care given, wherein women often give more personal care, while men may provide transportation and do handiwork (Miller & Cafasso, 1992; Young & Kahana, 1989), (b) the men being more emotionally detached from the caregiving (Hinrichsen, 1991), and (c) men being stoic (Kaye, 1997; Kaye & Applegate, 1994). As mentioned earlier, we felt our respondents were probably quite stoic during the caregiving. In speaking of that time, they minimized the stress that they had felt; they had done most of the caregiving, but did not describe it as a burden. As they were encouraged to give more details, the picture of a caregiving burden did emerge in the illnesses of long duration. They did not seem emotionally detached, but may have been better able than women caregivers to put their emotions aside and just do what needed to be done. Some of the men spoke of the loving attention they had given their wives, and some regretted not doing as much as they wished they had done, both of which would indicate emotional involvement in the process. Pruchno and Resch (1989) found that husbands in ill health are more likely to become depressed as they attempt to give care. Gallagher, Rose, Rivera, Lovett, and Thompson (1989) found that nearly one-third of caregivers seeking help to increase their coping skills were depressed.

Keeping Wife at Home

Those men who kept the wife at home and took responsibility for her care up until her death or very close to her death expressed in their stories the very tiring nature of that care. Henrik, mentioned earlier, had an arduous dialysis routine to maintain. Benjamin got relief from Hospice workers and was very grateful for the opportunity to "get out of the house for a while. . . . It's a 24-hour job. There's no question about it. But it's the least I could do."

The demands of a very ill person were stressful. Craig responded with resignation to them, Sy with a sense of honor and duty, Claude with regrets about his own exhaustion, and Arch with faithfulness to a commitment.

Craig told this story:

> I'd go in the other room and she'd want me back right now. If I went to fix her dinner or something. It went on like that for about two months, that I couldn't get away from her. [The neighbors took me] out to dinner one night and I said we'll be back in 45 minutes and we were gone a half hour and she said we were gone too long. So we decided that we wouldn't do that again.

Sy remembered his wife saying, "I'm sorry for what I'm putting you through, Sy." He told her, "It was vice versa, you'd do the same for me too." He said to the interviewer:

> All I know is that I'm glad that I was able to take care of her. That I did my duty and had to be very understanding. Because the [ill] spouse says things that would pick on you and don't mean it, and you have to be understanding why she is the way she is. You have to close your eyes, mouth and everything like that and just say good things to her.

Claude said sadly, "Sometimes I just figured, I had to have some, you have to have some time off to yourself." Claude and his wife were childless; he had no informal support system to call in for help when he was tired. Arch's religious faith and commitment helped him deal with his wife's need for care. He said:

> I didn't feel frustrated. I just felt like it was something that I needed to do to take care of my wife. Family comes before everything else. In sickness and in health, in poverty and in riches. You're supposed to do those things. . . . I didn't feel hurt or deprived. I just didn't think about it. . . . You did it in the name of God, and you should be willing to go through with it as much as you can.

Accepting Help

Caring for a spouse with dementia puts the caregiver in a population at great risk for wearing out. Kaye and Applegate (1994) suggest that caregiving takes a health toll on husbands whose wives have Alzheimer's Disease, thus undermining their ability to give care. Enright (1991) found that both men and women caregivers to spouses with dementia give large amounts of time to caregiving. Husbands received more assistance from family and friends than did wives, but most did not receive much assistance. Harper and Lund (1990) found gender differences in the types of burdens felt by caregivers to dementia patients. Husbands were better able to cope with aggressive behavior, but were more bothered by their wives' deficits in orientation and daily-living functioning. The husbands also were stressed by conflicting demands on their time, particularly if they had to watch out for the person's safety at all times. They also seemed to be bothered by having someone else living in the house to observe the decline in their wives' condition.

The "wearing out" of the caregiver presented an emotion-laden problem of how to arrange for others to help with the care or take over the care. Such a situation led to problem-solving activity, often with the family involved.

Curly's son and daughter-in-law told him that the caregiving was getting him down. They had already arranged for his wife to be moved to the nursing home. He said he thought at the time he was getting along all right, but admitted later that he was not. Louis found he could not manage getting his wife into and out of the bathtub any longer. "So I called my son and said, 'I can't lift Mom anymore.' He came over and took her home. She was there about a week and went to sleep." He added, "My wife kept telling friends that she wouldn't have lived this long if it wasn't for me taking care of her."

Jim said his daughter moved back into the house to help him. "I just couldn't have handled it for that long," he concluded. Malcolm arranged with a friend to come in and assist his wife with personal care, such as bathing, while he did odd jobs in the neighborhood. "That kept my mind off everything and she [the neighbor] stayed right up to the last," Malcolm said.

Support Systems During Caregiving

Adult Children

Ned and Louis had help from their children as they in their own old age cared for a wife in failing health. Louis' son moved his parents into his own home. Ned's children had the parents move close by so they could help tend their mother who had dementia. Carlo's daughter quit her job as a nursing assistant in a nursing home to help Carlo take care of her mother. Then she stayed home to take care of him. Carlo exclaimed, "I thank God for sending us her, for her taking care of her mother. She kept things spic'n'span, believe me, spic'n'span."

Wife's Relatives

Jacob praised his mother-in-law and sister-in-law for coming and staying for extended periods of time. "I could go to [work which provided] psychological help, I could get away from it. . . . I knew she was in safe hands."

Relatives Who Were Nurses

Five men spoke of relatives who were nurses. These women were in every case viewed positively and described as very helpful during the wife's illness. Indeed, it appeared that whenever there was a nurse relative, particularly a sister, she stood ready to become a caregiver, and in some cases the primary caregiver. Sam's wife's widowed sister took Sam's wife into her home to give her care. Garrett commented, "We finally called her sister who's a nurse. I told her that [my wife] had been getting real bad, that she had better come up. And she came up." Jerry said that his sister, a hospice nurse, had been "a real advocate for my wife." Bruce's daughter-in-law, a retired nurse, visited his wife often during her illness and was still helping Bruce talk through his feelings of loss.

Neighbors

Craig described his neighbors as "the best you ever saw. They brought dinner in for us, washed clothes and stuff like this, all kinds of them up and down the street." He mentioned one neighbor in particular who would drop in to visit his wife every day. "She looked forward to it and they'd talk as well as they could and he'd get her stuff and give me a rest. And he'd sit and talk and hold her hand. . . ."

Friends

Jerry said that his wife's friends brought food and one time they cleaned the house. Sam's wife's friend wrote her a card every day or every other day. His sister wrote often too. "That not only helped her, but it helped me too," he commented. Stuart mentioned both neighbors and friends who would stay with his wife while he was still working. Also, two of the pastors from their church came to the hospital (60 miles away) whenever the family called. Richard, a childless widower, named a long list of friends, neighbors, and former work colleagues who helped during his wife's decline.

Support Groups

Only one man mentioned attending an illness-related support group with his wife. None spoke of attending a caregivers support group of any kind. Miller (1987) noted lack of male attendance at support groups, and Kaye (1997) wrote that it was rare for group facilitators to reach out to men. Kaye and Applegate (1993) suggested these benefits for male caregivers who do attend support groups: (a) social support to buffer the caregiver from the mental health stress of caregiving, (b) satisfaction from group association, and (c) gratitude for the chance to share experiences with other men and receive support. Harris (1993) advised that groups for male caregivers should be time-limited groups and led by a male caregiver and nurse. Other ideas that might attract men would be putting caregivers in contact with each other via a computer bulletin board or a telephone network.

Use of Hospice

Eight of the wives had services from a hospice, six in their own homes, two in the hospital. Six of those wives had cancer, one had heart and lung problems, one lingered from a stroke. Two of their husbands became hospice volunteers after their deaths. One had been a volunteer along with his wife, he volunteered again after her death. Sy's wife died of cancer in the early 1980s; he spoke at length about what hospice could have done. He said he did not call them himself; he was in "such a mood" at the time that he would ask no one for help. He expected the hospital to connect him with available services when they told him they could do nothing more for his wife. As it was, no one made a contact and he was left on his own with an exhausting care routine. He did not know what might have been available at that time. However, knowing what services hospice would offer now, he recognized how beneficial they would have been in his situation.

The surviving husbands spoke of hospice nurses coming to the home to deliver direct care to their wives and of hospice volunteers who gave them [the husbands] some respite from being at the call of their wives. Some of the men were filled with praise for hospice. Benjamin said, "My experience with hospice, I cannot speak enough. I had people who came from hospice just to relieve me so I could go. . . ." Craig described the hospice services his wife received: "They furnished the bed and oxygen, her medication. They furnished us everything and she had three nurses who would come in to see her. They'd come in just about every day. We had a doctor. He was in here quite often and we did fine."

Others appreciated hospice services but would refer to hospice workers coming "only" once or twice a week, leaving them with most of the care. Robert said, "Hospice came in from the standpoint of just having a visiting nurse come once or twice a week and administer medication, pain medication, but not on a daily basis, not on a regular basis."

"Caregiver stamina" was sorely tested in a cancer death. Sy looked back on his expectations and his decisions at that time, and knew they were probably not reasonable. But that's where he was at that time—extremely tired, extremely worried, not thinking very clearly. The respondents who did use hospice reflected these same caregiving strains. For some, any relief was seen as a blessing; for others, it was seen as helpful but very limited.

After becoming a hospice volunteer, Robert commented on hospice's role in his own experience as a caregiver:

> They brought up a point at hospice [training] that hit home with me; they were talking about some of the things that you say and do in that kind of a care situation . And I said to them, "We should be talking to the caregivers before [the patients] die, instead of after they die. . . .You're telling me all these things and much of this information would have been helpful at the time. If you had told me this six months ago, I would have said things differently than I did." And it's true, that time when I told her she wasn't trying hard enough, and she got really mad because she was trying, she was trying as hard as she knew how. . . . I think I'm helping her, but I'm not.

Regrets About Caregiving

None of the husbands complained of loss of emotional support from their wives during the illness. Only Jerry said that he wished his wife had been able to understand his need to process his feelings of impending loss, but he knew her illness was proceeding rapidly and that she could not attend to his needs. There must have been times for many of the men when they felt very lonely and exhausted and were not able to express their feelings honestly. Some men regretted things they had said or things that they had not done, but they did not complain about failing to receive sympathy and understanding from their ill wives.

Robert would advise other men to be "awfully, awfully careful what you say, because you live with a lot of regrets afterwards about what you said and shouldn't have said. Be a lot more patient and attempt to understand the situation." Claude said, "Sometimes I think that I didn't do enough for my wife. . . . I had a feeling I did not go to her enough to console her. That's what bothers me today."

By all descriptions, Ned had been a patient and attentive caregiver; yet his list of regrets was long:

> I might have told her more often that I loved her. I might have read to her. I might not have been so contentious when she didn't want to eat. I

just could have let her know more how concerned I was. You just sort of go on from day to day. And God help the next day be better. . . . I'd like to have made more effort to entertain her. I'd like to have taken her out more often. The last few years I'd give her flowers on her birthday and anniversary. But we'd always been conservative on entertainment (chuckles). I never thought of loosening up and giving her some fun. . . .We had a long time of visiting her mother in a nursing home, and I was anxious for her not to have to go through that environment. I was glad that she was home.

Costs of Caregiving

Curly said he had spent $16,000 up until he was able to get his wife qualified for Medicaid and settled in a nursing home. Walter said he had sold their home anticipating the ongoing expense of the nursing home. Henrik explained, "When she first developed her trouble, I thought sure I was going to go broke. There was just nothing I could do. I had a $20,000 calamity insurance, and that lasted 3 months." He went on to say that Medicare began to pay the expenses, except for traveling and housing. When those expenses began to be a burden, a community benefit helped him out. He recalled:

> Some good friends of mine, our preacher and American Legion members, the whole community put on a tremendous benefit for us. . . . And they raised at that time $5000. . . . If it hadn't been for that, I don't know what I would have done. That bought the gas and hotel bills and to pay an extra person to run the store because I was gone so much. . . . So when they say community support, I have really had community support. Even to this day, when somebody is having a rough time, I give them $10 or $20 because so many people did that for me.

Richard said he had thought about having round-the-clock care at home for his wife, but getting reliable help was difficult and the cost was prohibitive. Sam had a new bathroom put in on the first floor. His wife was only home for two weeks, and then he was not able to take care of her.

EFFECTS ON WIFE

From the stories of caregiving reflecting the husband's perspective, it seemed that there was a "dance" between husband and wife, a give-and-take in terms of power and in terms of getting things done. Henrik's wife's doctor told him to "let her do things." Cordell's wife decided what to ask him to do and what to say she wanted to do by herself. Several of the wives directed housecleaning so it would be done to their standards. The stories revealed a lot of variability in the power dynamics of the couples relationships, depending on the personalities and the illnesses.

Asserting Independence

Yussef and his wife had very independent lives, leaving an interviewer to imagine how much she would have chafed at the notion of needing care. "She didn't want nobody to take care of her. Very independent," Yussef said. She scheduled her surgeries around her schoolteaching vacations, and ended a 17-year illness with only 2 weeks of receiving care.

Craig said his wife fixed the meals and washed the dishes. She turned away his offers of help. "The doctors told me, 'Anything she wants to do, let her do it. If she wants to drive the car, you get up and go around and get in the passenger's side.' So we went that way and there was a lot of things I could've done and I didn't do."

Terrence's wife, by family members' unanimous agreement, was an assertive and competent woman. She managed the details of her illness and treatment and even attempted to arrange new intimate relationship possibilities for the man she would leave behind. Earl told this story of his wife managing the circumstances of her own death:

> She didn't want me to be, I think, around or having to take care of her while she died. She just knew intuitively when her days were limited. She was getting weaker and weaker. She decided she wanted to go to a hospital, and I knew why she wanted to go. She made that decision to spare me that difficulty.

Losing Independence/Needing Care

Loss of Mobility

Alvin said that his wife's lack of independence was her main suffering. He said that he told her that he loved her and would be happy to take her wherever she wanted to go. He had ordered a power scooter for her. "It was going to come the following Tuesday and she was so happy because it meant that she could get anywhere here on the cart paths, or inside buildings on her own. That was on Thursday, and Saturday she died. But she was on a high on account of that."

Needing Personal Care

Arnold said that his wife was "a vain person." When she became "involuntary," that bothered her a great deal. "I don't blame her for that. When I'd have to help her, you know . . . What you have to do you have to do. It's not easy." Bruce said, "That was a tough year because I had to look after her, and she didn't want anybody else to look after her. I had a nurse, a couple of nurses, and then she said, 'I don't want those nurses here, Bruce.' She said, 'I want you to look after me.' I said, 'Okay.'"

COMMUNICATION WITH ILL WIVES

The question is not whether husbands and wives talked about her death, but at what level did they communicate their feelings about it? Unless it was a sudden death, there were two people in close proximity sharing the "knowing" of a serious health condition. Whether or not they used words, they did communicate. How did they do that?

Indirect Communication

Communication that acknowledged impending death without saying so directly seemed to be, in many cases, a way that couples could deal with the reality in a less threatening way. Joking or "smart cracks" sometimes seemed to serve that purpose. Stuart, who said he believed he would die first, joked, "Some young guy will be interested in you for your retirement money." Arnold's wife said, "You'll probably be married in about 3 weeks." Malcolm's wife said she would not remarry. He joked that he would remarry in six months.

Conversations With Ill Wives

From what our respondents conveyed to us, we see that it is easier to talk in advance about concrete details of preparing for death, such as wills, living wills, and prepayment of funeral and burial expenses. It is not so easy to talk about dying and death when the process is actually happening. Even when both husband and wife knew the wife was dying, it was easier to talk about details than to have conversations with emotional content. "We must make certain that our wills are in order" is an easier conversation starter than, "I know that you are going to leave me soon and I feel so bad, I don't know how I can go on."

We identified some barriers to conversation when the wife's terminal condition was already a fact:

1. Husband did not want to face the reality and therefore kept himself in as much a state of denial as possible. Ned said simply, "I didn't want to face it." Robert explained:

> I say there is a lot of psychology goes into what you say and what you don't say. You're trying to paint a more rosy picture and you're trying not to worry, [thinking] things will get better, you know. And she knows damn well they're not going to get better.

Joe said of his wife at her death, "I'd gone through all these years of her being in this state." However, they had not talked about death, he said, because "she was not that ill."

2. Both husband and wife would have to want to participate in the conversation. We saw some mismatches in willingness to talk about the impending death. For example, Jerry wanted to talk more than his wife did; when Jacob's wife spoke to him, he hurriedly left the room. Benjamin knew his wife wanted to talk about her illness and death, but he could not talk about these subjects; they did talk about giving away her possessions. Jacob had walked out of the room when his dying wife asked him what he would do [after she was gone], but he also reported that she did not bring up the subject of her death because "she didn't want to make my heart heavy."

3. It was difficult to find the words for such a conversation. In a following section, we will point out some of the terms used to mention remarriage without actually using the word. Some men, such as Louis, used the term "went to sleep" to refer to the death. It is very likely that some of the couples did not discuss the wife's impending death or the husband's future after it because they did not know how to begin talking about these subjects. One man said directly, "I wish we would have talked about it."

4. Wife's condition would not allow her to take part in a conversation. This would happen in cases of stroke, coma, and dementia. Curly's wife had dementia; he said, "She wasn't able, and I never said a thing to her about it." Sam's wife had a brain tumor; he said, "She wasn't comprehending this." Also, of course, the sudden deaths did not permit time for conversation.

Conversations About Tangible Aspects of Death

Buying gravesites and gravestones, prepaying funerals and cremations, making wills—these are activities which older couples often do without the immediate likelihood of death. Several of the men reported taking care of such details prior to the loss of their wives. Some made additional arrangements because their wives were very ill. In addition to prepaying her cremation, Cordell and his wife decided where her ashes would be scattered. So did Alvin and his wife. Arch took out insurance on his own life in order to provide for his wife, thinking that she would outlive him with her multiple sclerosis but would need a great deal of assistance. Al's wife signed a living will after her near-death experience; she did not want to be revived again and he wanted to be clear about her wishes. Benjamin's wife talked about dispersing her possessions and Sy's wife gave away her jewelry. It is important to note that handling such details did not necessarily mean that the couple discussed their feelings about the impending death.

Conversations About Feelings

Conversations that revealed the awareness of death and parting were usually brief and indirect. Stuart reported:

> She would [tell visitors] we had a good marriage. We tried to be good communicators with each other and we were close. We still liked to hold hands and we still liked to hug and when she was ill there at the end, I would say, "I need a hug." . . . It was very difficult to part.

Charles described a brief comment that revealed his wife's final step toward death. The occasion was an outing to their daughter's place for Thanksgiving dinner. The nursing home staff had "fixed her up so nicely, just as pretty as a picture. She told me which jewelry she wanted. . . . They powdered her up and combed her hair. Just as pretty as a picture." Managing her wheelchair and getting her in and out of the car was cumbersome, she thought. As they got her back into the car after dinner, she said, "Is it worth it?" "That's the first time she'd ever expressed herself along that line. 'Is it worth it?' The next day she died," Charles said.

It appears that direct conversation about the emotions that accompanied the dying of the wife was difficult or impossible for most of the couples. We expected that those couples who were able to talk about their feelings would have experienced more closure as the death occurred. Yet we found no pattern in the stories of the death event that would support that expectation. Jerry's wife and Garrett's wife both died amidst family vigils that were religious and caring. Jerry and his wife had talked about feelings, but not specifically about how Jerry was affected by the impending death. Garrett's wife had not been willing to talk about the dying. Earl's adjustment to loss seemed no easier than those of husbands who had not had the chance to grieve openly with their dying wives. Malcolm and his wife had talked about her cross-over experience to Heaven; he had gone on with his life by remarrying, but he sobbed with renewed waves of grief when interviewed about his first wife. We are left with the possibility that talking about dying and death may not relate to the way in which the couple make that final parting, or to the husband's adjustment after the death.

Wife Wanting to Die

The wife wanting to die and conveying that to her husband was a particularly painful circumstance for the man. Some of the men dramatically described their difficulty in letting go:

> Terrence: There got to be a point . . . that she knew she was dying and wanted it over with. She prayed to the Lord to take her. She's praying to the Lord to take her and I'm praying so not to take her, to come up with a cure. . . . I would sit there and talk to her as long as she wanted to talk every night until I would fall asleep in that little chair there in the room. One particular night I woke up and she's standing on the window sill trying to figure out how to open the window. . . . Then I knew that she was in enormous pain and she wanted to get it over with. I couldn't see her jump five floors to her death.

Craig said his wife came to the point of feeling it would just be a week or so until she would die and she wanted to die. "That's where it hurt me because I didn't want her to go. And I wouldn't let go and she had her ten radiation treatments. . . . She even asked me to kill her and I wouldn't do it." Craig's wife was so deeply asleep one day that he thought for hours she was in a coma. Finally, when he kissed her on the forehead, her eyes popped open, and he said in surprise, "Well, where you been?" Then he told her what had happened. He said to the interviewer:

> So we had a long talk and we both cried and I mean wept. I was laying on the chair next to her and she was in the bed and I was holding her. She talked me into letting her go. So after that day, my whole attitude changed.

Craig was our outlying respondent in terms of the length of time in widowhood. We had been given inaccurate information about how long he had been widowed; he had lost his wife just four months earlier. The interview with him confirmed our earlier decision not to interview men in active bereavement. Craig was numb with his sense of loss at the time of the interview. He was lonely but stable in his surroundings and in his daily routine when we met with him two years later.

Al said his wife criticized him for having emergency room personnel revive her. She said she was no good anymore and should have been left dead. Richard said near the end of her life his wife "had given up by then. Could see no sense in going on." She made her resignation clear to him although her dementia prevented a conversation about it.

Expectations About Who Would Die First

Most of the husbands had formed some idea of who would die first. They knew that men usually die before their wives and that women on the average have a longer life span than men. Many men thought they would die first even when the wife's illness was serious. In such cases, they worried about who would take care of their wife.

The reality of a seriously ill and visibly failing wife could alter the stereotypical expectation. Clarence, Al, and Karl said they came to a point where the wife's impending death had to be acknowledged. Daniel had lost one wife to cancer, so he knew what the course of his second wife's illness would be, he said. Walter said, "I just knew it was a matter of time and there wasn't anything I could do about it." Bill explained in his colorful way, "Lou and I expected me to outlive her. Now I'm sure that there's people who say that anybody who thinks like that's a dirty rotten egg. But that's what I thought." In some cases, the husband who knew his wife was terminally ill was surprised by the death when it occurred. Don was unprepared for his third wife's death. She sent him away on a trip so he would not be there when she died. Curly said, "We all knew she wasn't going to get well, but it came so unexpectedly." Jim said:

> I never really thought I was going to lose her that quickly. When she contracted pneumonia, I said, what the heck, pneumonia is no big deal anymore, all the fancy antibiotics. . . . I didn't realize the effects of those other diseases on the healing process, so I guess right until the last week, I was sure that she was going to make it.

Wives' Predictions About Remarriage

Fourteen of the couples had some sort of conversation about the husband's future without the wife. In some cases the wives had verbalized predictions about the likelihood of their husbands remarrying. Four directly predicted remarriage. “Go on with life,” “difficult to live alone,” “need somebody,” and “get back in the race” appear to be phrases that allowed reference to remarriage without actually saying so. Six couples spoke of the husband’s future using such terms. Three wives expressed concern about what their husbands would do or how they would get along. One couple each stated a prediction of their own likelihood of remarriage.

Of these fourteen couples in which the remarriage of the husband was predicted or acknowledged, five of the men had remarried by the time of the interview but nine had not. One of the nine was seeking a new wife, one was in an intimate relationship, and two others had steady companions, but they had not remarried. Although some of the predictions were correct, it appears that the wife’s acknowledgment that her husband might remarry did not send him rushing off to another marriage. In fact, two of the men seemed to have responded to the wife’s prediction by refusing to let her be correct, even in death. Later, when we discuss the men who did remarry, we will see that they believed their wives would have wanted them to “go on with their lives,” even if the couple had not discussed the matter. It appears that having the wife’s acknowledgment relieved the man of uneasy feelings that she would not approve of his decision. In the two cases where the husband was vehemently against fulfilling the wife’s prediction, the predictions seem to have been made in a rebuking tone. To remarry would be proving her right. Clyde said, “I’ve heard her say that I’d be married in no time when she died, but she’s wrong about that. She is wrong. I’m not going to marry.” It is interesting that Clyde used present tense verbs in these statements, as if the argument were still going on.

Findings

Men caregivers are not uncommon. They seem to give care willingly and with love and respect for the woman. The husbands were personally involved in giving care to ill wives, although in some cases they found a female helper to give personal care such as bathing, toileting, and dressing. It was impossible in many cases to delineate the caregiving period, as it began gradually, probably as beginning to give assistance in areas that had been the wife’s domain—such as doing the laundry, changing bed linens, and vacuuming. These husbands minimized the burden that they felt during caregiving. Caregiving caused fatigue, but did not seem to cause health problems. They received some help from a variety of other people, but were the primary caregivers in most cases.

There was little, if any, involvement in caregiver support groups. Hospice was a resource for some of the men and their wives. Each couple developed their own patterns of handling power during the caregiving period.

Husbands and wives found it easier to talk about the tangible aspects of death than about feelings. There was little talk about impending death or emotions. Some wives did express wanting to die. Some wives made predictions about the husband's future. These predictions seemed to be a way of continuing the relationship, of taking care of the husband, or of controlling him. Making joking remarks about remarriage was perhaps easier than talking about emotions. Many husbands expected to die before their wives, even when the wives were ill. Some realized finally that they would survive their wives. Others were surprised when the death occurred even though they knew their wives were very ill.

REFERENCES

Borden, W. & Berlin, S. (1990). Gender, coping and psychological well-being in spouses of older adults with chronic dementia. *American Journal of Orthopsychiatry, 60(4),* 603–610.

Enright, R. B., Jr. (1991). Time spent caregiving and help received by spouses and adult children of brain-impaired adults. *The Gerontologist, 31*(3), 375–383.

Fitting, M., Rabins, P., Lucas, M. J., & Eastham, J. (1986). Caregivers for dementia patients: A comparison of husbands and wives. *The Gerontologist, 26*(3), 248–252.

Gallagher, D., Rose, J., Rivera, P., Lovett, S., & Thompson, L. W. (1989). Prevalence of depression in family caregivers. *The Gerontologist, 29*(4), 449–456.

Harper, S. & Lund, D. A. (1990). Wives, husbands, and daughters caring for institutionalized and noninstitutionalized dementia patients: Toward a model of caregiver burden. *International Journal of Aging and Human Development, 30*(4), 241–262.

Harris, P. B. (1993). The misunderstood caregiver? A qualitative study of the male caregiver of Alzheimer's Disease victims. *The Gerontologist, 33*(4), 551–556.

Hinrichsen, G. A. (1991). Adjustment of caregivers to depressed older adults. *Psychology and Aging, 6*(4), 631–639.

Kaye, L. W. (1997). Informal caregiving by older men. In J. I. Kosberg & L. W. Kaye (Eds.), *Elderly men: Special problems and professional challenges* (pp. 231–249). New York: Springer Publishing.

Kaye, L. W., & Applegate, J. S. (1993). Family support groups for male caregiver: Benefits of participation. *Journal of Gerontological Social Work, 20,* 167–185.

Kaye, L. W. & Applegate, J. S. (1994). Older men and the family caregiving orientation. In E. H. Thompson, Jr. (Ed.), *Older men's lives* (pp. 218–236). Thousand Oaks, CA: Sage Publications.

Lund, D. A., Caserta, M. S., & Dimond, M. F. (1993). Spousal bereavement in later life. In M. S. Stroebe, W. Stroebe, & R. O. Hansson (Eds.), *Handbook of bereavement* (pp. 240–254). New York: Cambridge University Press.

Lund, D. A., Caserta, M. S., Dimond, M. F. & Shaffer, S. K. (1990). Competencies, tasks of daily living, and adjustments to spousal bereavement in later life. In D. A. Lund (Ed.), *Older bereaved spouses: Research with practical applications* (pp. 135–152). New York: Hemisphere Publishing.

McCann, J. J., Hebert, L. E., Beckett, L. A., Morris, M. C., Scherr, P. A., & Evans, D. A. (2000). Comparison of informal caregiving by black and white older adults in a community population. *Journal of Aging and Geriatric Studies, 48*(12), 1612–1617.

Miller, B. (1987). Gender and control among spouses of the cognitively impaired: A research note. *The Gerontologist, 27*(4), 447–453.

Miller, B. & Cafasso, L. (1992). Gender difference in caregiving: Fact or artifact. *The Gerontologist, 32*(4), 498–507.

Pruchno, R. A. & Resch, N. L. (1989). Husbands and wives as caregivers: Antecedents of depression and burden. *The Gerontologist, 29*(2), 159–165.

Young, R. F. & Kahana, E. (1989). Specifying caregiver outcome: Gender and relationship aspects of caregiving strain. *The Gerontologist, 29*(5), 660–666.

6

Saying Goodbye

Our interviews focused more on the emotional, spiritual, and social aspects of widowhood, but we were also interested in how the men handled the practical details related to the loss of their wives. In this brief chapter, we report on those details having to do with the time immediately after the wife's death: services and the disposition of remains, going home alone, and disposing of or keeping personal items.

Supportive People at Time of Death

Adult children and their spouses were most often named as supportive people at the time of the wife's death. George called a son who came from out of state the same day and stayed for three weeks. Curly praised his daughter-in-law for arranging in which dress his wife would be buried. Frank said his son-in-law took care of all the funeral arrangements, while his daughters took care of him. Each of his daughters stayed with him for a week at a time. "That went on quite a while," he said. "I finally told them, 'You guys get out of here.'"

Jacob's mother-in-law had stayed for long visits helping when her daughter was ill. He recalled both sides of the family coming to sit Shiva. He mentioned his mother-in-law in particular. "She was so heartbroken, so her other daughter said, 'Mom, you come back [home with me]'. So they took her back."

Funerals and Memorial Services

Most of the men offered very little detail about the funeral or memorial service. In most cases, the service had been whatever was traditional for their religious denomination. A few spoke of the service as being something different or special. Craig said, "She had a beautiful service. It was on the 23rd Psalm. [The pastor] would say, 'I walk through the valley of the shadow of death,' and then he'd say something about [my wife]. Then he'd take the next line and he'd say some more about her."

Conner described the memorial Mass for his wife. His wife had said she did not want a solemn formal Mass like her sister's, so family members spoke and sang at hers. Then, Conner said, the family decided that one celebration of his wife's life was not enough, "so they all came back [in the summer] and we had another celebration!" Ned also remembered his wife's service as a joyful occasion. He said, "It was 'a joy service.'" Louis had a scrapbook from his wife's service, complete with written out eulogies. He initially said that the scrapbook would provide all the information needed to understand his wonderful marriage. "It's a very glowing thing."

Jerry seemed to feel uplifted by the large attendance at his wife's service, "We made her funeral a celebration, we really did. The church was packed, God, incredible!" Robert has the opposite experience. He was disappointed that friends stayed away. There was a funeral with casket; well-wishers were received at the funeral home. Her family all came, but Robert was upset that their friends in the retirement community stayed away. "Many of those people that I thought of as being friends didn't come to the wake. And other friends . . . didn't come to the funeral, and they excused it by saying it bothered them to come. Well, I can understand their feelings to a degree, but it wasn't an excuse. I still would have come, out of respect."

Claude said there had been no service for his wife. "She wanted, both of us decided a long time ago that we wanted our bodies to go to a medical center." His wife had no siblings, "only another lady, a niece of hers, a child by her mother's sister. But somehow they didn't get along together." So he didn't call anyone when she died. They had no children, and maybe there were not many people who would have come to a service.

Burials and Cremations

Many of the couples had preplanned their funeral and burial or cremation arrangements. For some, it was a matter of doing what many older couples do in order to save the surviving spouse and the couple's children stress and expense at the time of the loss. Henrik said, "We bought our stone I think ten years at least before she died. We both agreed that if we got this stone put up there, whichever one of us that was gone first, then our kids wouldn't have to fool around. Everything was decided. . . . I firmly recommend that. . . . When she died, there was no hassle at all."

For other couples, the arrangements were prompted by the wife's illness, not necessarily because they believed that she would die soon, but because her illness brought their mortality to the forefront. Cordell said, "Cremation was set up in advance. Her ashes are at the Catholic Cathedral. That's where I'll be, all prepaid."

In other cases, the wife's impending death or the death itself prompted the arrangements. Don recounted this story:

> So she says, "You know what I would like? I would like to be cremated. And I'd like . . . my ashes put under a tree right here . . . and I want for you to pick the tree. But I would like to the tree to be independent, self-sufficient, and good looking." (laughs) I said, "Well, just like you. Done deal. Done deal. I commit to that absolutely."

Curly's wife had gone into a nursing home, with her stay subsidized by Medicaid. Curly said, "I had to buy her a funeral before she died on account of Medicaid. And I had; that was done."

Yussef characterized his wife as extremely independent, and that quality came through even in her final arrangements. Yussef commented, "If I had passed away, my wife would have carried right on, right on through. Yes sir. Before she died, she gave me instructions. 'I don't want to be buried, I want to be cremated, I want this, this, this, this,' and that was it."

Arch made arrangements in accordance with circumstances existing at the time of his wife's death. He took his wife's body back to her hometown for burial so her ill mother would not have to travel to the service. Will said his wife's ashes were buried in a lot in the local cemetery next to their infant son's, but he had other plans for his own remains. "If there's anything in this old carcass that's usable when I kick off, well, they can have it. Maybe they can use skin and bones and blood nowadays, I don't know."

Stuart said that his son designed the family stone at the cemetery and his daughter had written what was put on the stone. When Bill's wife's ashes were given to him, the family went down to their cabin to scatter them. Then they celebrated her life at the local pizza pub, he concluded.

Snowbirds: Where Buried or Ashes Scattered?

Couples who had moved to retirement communities far from their hometowns had to decide on the location for services and for burial or scattering of ashes. In most cases, the final resting place was back home. Art and Benjamin said they had had their wives' bodies sent back to the northern cities where they had lived. Sy said, "[The funeral was] up north. After all, she did so much work in the synagogue that the rabbi wanted to give the eulogy and tell them what she did for the synagogue and all that."

Cordell said there were two services simultaneously, one in their retirement community and the other in their northern hometown. He said both he and his wife would have their cremated remains in a special garden next to the church in their retirement community. He explained:

> It made such good sense to both of us. Where those ashes are makes no difference whatsoever and there's no maintenance. . . . If you are a person of faith and you believe that you came from dust and to dust thou shall return, what difference does it make if it's quick or gradual?

Alvin also described memorial services in the two locations. He had said that he would scatter his wife's ashes in the ocean near their home, but she wanted them scattered back in their home state, so that is what Alvin did.

Second Spouses: Buried With Whom?

When either or both of the spouses had been married and widowed earlier, the question of final resting place was more complicated. We asked the men who had been married twice or more what decision was made and by what reasoning it was made. Daniel said he asked his second wife if she wanted to be buried with him or with her first husband. She said she wanted to be buried with him. So he bought another plot and would, upon his own death, be buried between his two wives. Kenneth said his first wife was buried here in their local cemetery and his second wife in the cemetery near her hometown with her first husband. People asked him if he would bury his second wife with him. He said, "No, I borrowed her from her first husband and I'm going to put her back with her first husband."

Don's first two wives died young and died accidentally; no arrangements had been made in advance and Don did not describe services or disposition of remains. His third wife was a self-assured woman who managed her own living and dying. She chose the spot for her remains, described earlier in this chapter without making plans for Don, whom she probably assumed would live for many years and would make a new life for himself.

Going Back Home Alone

Many of the men had experienced time alone at home; their wives may have been in and out of the hospital or may have moved to nursing homes. Still, going back to the house after the service was dramatically different. As Curly said, "I knew where she was [when she was in the nursing home]. I could come up [to visit her], but now she's gone and the only place I can go is up to the cemetery." Three men spoke specifically of their first night back home after the burial. Stuart said, "I can remember telling my daughter I didn't really care if I ever went back home again at that time. So it was difficult to come back here." On the other hand, Conner recalled, "I don't know that I did much thinking about it. This was home, and it was still home although [my wife] had gone to another." Carlo said that he had seen his wife in their bedroom after returning home from her funeral and burial. "If I had to take an oath, I would say I saw her. . . . I also know that it must be my desire to see her that makes me see her sometimes. Could be."

It was common for the widowed man to have a relative stay with him for a while. Frank, mentioned at the beginning of this chapter, finally told his daughters he could stay alone. George said his son had stayed three weeks. Craig's daughter came for the funeral and then took him to her home for three months. Finally though, nearly all of the men lived alone for some length of time. Boredom and loneliness were mentioned frequently, worries or fears much less frequently. Robert did feel concern about having a health problem when no one was there to help him. Alvin said he had a lifelong habit of checking the doors at night. Arch had a security system on his home; again, this concern about crime was longstanding.

Keeping Photos of Wife

Most of the men had photographs in their home. The most common situation was a display of family photographs: children, grandchildren, family groups, wedding and anniversary couples. Conner and Frank had retained their wives' collections of photographs on display on a wall or on the refrigerator. We asked each man if he had a photograph of his deceased wife; nearly all of the men said yes. For men such as Conner and Alvin, showing the interviewer a photograph was as simple as pointing to it on a nearby table. In fact, Alvin volunteered mention of the photograph without being asked. Photographs were displayed in the living room or in the sitting room where the man spent a good deal of his waking time; in apartments where the eating table and the sitting area were together, photos would be on the table or on a shelf nearby.

Jacob did not want photographs to be too much of a presence in his home. He said, "Sometimes I have a sense of her presence. I have here a picture, but I've never hung up a big picture of her. I don't want to make [her memory] a picture; it should be here" [touches his chest].

If photographs were not displayed in the room in which the interview took place, the man would usually go quickly to his bedroom and return with a photograph or an album. Clyde and Leroy returned to the interview with albums. Clyde's was neatly put together by his wife and was filled with family photos. Leroy's was not organized at all, nor were any of the pictures identified. Arnold returned with snapshots, Benjamin with a photo smaller than a postage stamp, cut from an identification card.

Benjamin was remarried. The remarried men tended not to have a photograph of the deceased wife on display, since they were at the time living with a new wife. Usually they said the photos were put away, too far away to be retrieved to show the interviewer. On a follow-up visit to Stuart, he had a couples portrait with his new wife in the living room, while his children's wedding party pictures, including his first wife, still hung on the walls. Frank had a large painting of his wife in a prominent location. His lady friend had visited in his home with it there, but he said if she would ever live there, he would have to remove the painting.

A few of the men said they had no photographs on the premises. Louis had a World War II era photograph of himself and his wife, taken before the operation that disfigured her face. When asked about a more recent photo, he replied, "Oh yeah, I have some beautiful pictures I left at my daughter's home. There's no room here for that. How do I know how long I'm gonna be here?" Malcolm was remarried; he said he had given all pictures of his first wife to his daughter.

Don commented that he had no pictures of his first wife and could not bear to see pictures of his second wife until his third wife died. Then he displayed photos of his second and third wives. He said that he had not brought those photos when he entered his fourth relationship. He said, "When I came here, I didn't come with any of those mementoes of the other women in my life because this was a new woman in my life. . . . As a matter of fact, I gave everything to my daughter. I believe that's the way to do it, the clean way to start a new life."

Wife's Possessions

We found several typical patterns. Ill wives would designate the recipients for their good jewelry, usually a daughter or granddaughter. After the wife's death, a female relative would help the man dispose of the wife's clothing; often it was given to charity. Sometimes the man kept some items by which to remember his wife. The man would allow possessions to remain until someone came to help him deal with them; if he had to dispose of them himself, it usually took some time.

Louis said that all of his wife's clothing was given to a charity. His wife had wanted her "gorgeous engagement ring and a gorgeous diamond wedding band' to go to her daughter. It was very expensive and the daughter didn't want to take it at first, Louis remarked, but he told her, "It's your mother's wish." He gave some of her other jewelry to his granddaughter. "I didn't keep anything, because that was her wish, and I abided by her wish."

Benjamin said his wife knew that she was passing away. "She made sure she gave my daughter the things she wanted her to have. Jewelry, being a mother, I suppose she wanted for her daughter rather than my daughter-in-law. It wasn't that she disliked my daughter-in-law, . . . it was just one of those things. . . . She probably did give her a couple of pieces. Most of it she gave away while she was aware. Whatever was left I gathered and gave to the kids. The clothes I took down to a charitable place." Benjamin said he had given most of the china to his children.

Alvin said his daughter took all of the clothing. "I think there might be some clothing here that my daughter needs only when she's here, like bathing stuff. I don't mess with it, I never had to concern myself with the clothing." Jacob said that his wife's family came and "they cleaned up. There was jewelry and things that, I said, you take it." Jacob said that the family left with some items that were his. He indicated that he had told them to take the items, but his way of telling the story indicated some bitterness. Further questioning did not clarify the matter, but Jacob finally said that he would have been upset only if they had taken his books.

Jerry and Yussef waited until female relatives came to sort through things. Jerry kept some personal clothing items; the rest of the clothing went to two battered women shelters. Yussef's wife's clothing was distributed among her relatives and friends. Her jewelry, computer and other "tools of the trade" went to their son. Robert sold his wife's clothing and jewelry. "It took a little while to get around to it, but eventually I did." He had kept some items, not for sentimental value, but because the consignment shop did not want them. He did have his home still decorated with his wife's very artistic and elaborate needlepoint pictures and her collection of porcelain. He was very proud of both.

Changing Things in the House

The men who had not remarried were remarkable for how much they had left things as they were when the wife had lived in the house. Clarence pointed out the decor as his wife's choices. Our contact person for Jacob described the front rooms of Jacob's house as he remembered them 15 years earlier, and the interviewer found the description a perfect match. Will said, "I did not change it at all. Well, the one change. I moved downstairs" [to the room his wife used for 6–7 years when she could no longer walk upstairs]. Frank and Conner had their wives' collections of various items still prominently on display, and identified the collections as belonging to their wives. Clyde, in his vehement statement about not ever remarrying, was very protective about his decor:

> I'm not gonna bring someone in here, throw the pictures and stuff down in the basement in a box somewhere, put up theirs, to get rid of another woman. The woman will do that because they don't like another woman. . . . They'll change everything including me and I'm not gonna put that burden on myself.

Being Held Back by Possessions

As time went on, some men found themselves burdened by possessions that had belonged to their wives. Kenneth had many reasons for not wanting to remarry, but he pointed out the difficulties it would present if he were to bring a new wife into the home that was filled with the possessions that were destined to be divided between his children and his second wife's children. Stuart's new wife had brought things to the home in which Stuart and his first wife had lived. She had been gracious about blending her items with those of his first wife, but they finally decided that they should build a house and have a place that was simply theirs. Bill and his new wife had blended their household furnishings, according to Bill, without much difficulty.

Discussion

Redfoot and Back (1988) found that older women have meanings attached to their possessions, significant meanings that help them maintain "the reality of the self, the environment, and of relationships that are most important to them" (p. 166). McCracken (1987) also found meaning attached to possessions among a group of older women who had to give up things they owned when they moved. Loss of possessions associated with deceased loved ones "contributed to a loss of continuity with life history" (p. 18). Other items symbolized certain roles in a woman's life; McCracken used the example of giving up the dining room table, conveying to the woman that she would no longer preside over family gatherings but would now be served at a table that was not her own. Household items did not have the same role-defining meaning for the men in our study, since the household domain primarily had belonged to their wives. However, clearly they held certain items as their own cherished memories of their wives. Most of the men had kept at least a few items that had been special to the wife. Some had kept many. Rubenstein (1986b) refers to unchanged decor in a widower's home as "a profound connection to the life shared with the spouse" (p. 37). Granted, the men probably had little experience in making decor decisions while their wives were alive, but in showing the interviewer around the home, many spoke of the importance of various items to the wife. Arnold pointed out his wife's recliner, Conner, her reading chair, both standing in exactly the same spot where the wife had sat. As already mentioned, Clarence was proud to point out his wife's decorating choices. The men were most attached to things that had belonged to their wives; they did not convey significant emotional attachment to other possessions, such as cars or tools or items associated with their professions. Exceptions would be Jacob and Daniel who loved their books, their active daily connection with their Jewish faith. They would have been highly distressed to lose them, as Jacob's earlier comment indicated. Clyde's statement above about not allowing another woman to come into his home demonstrated the connection he saw between changing items in the home and changing his very selfhood.

Jacob in his refusal to have a picture of his beloved wife dominate the room in which he lived, demonstrated an exception to this meaning-in-the-possession phenomenon. Redfoot and Back (1988) suggest that some individuals have "located the 'real self' entirely outside the temporal framework of the 'life world' in the eternal temporality of their religious worldviews" (p. 167). This may be too strong a statement to apply to Jacob, who did love his books, but he was a passionately religious man and he wanted to carry the memory of his wife in his heart rather than investing it in a photographic image that was not really her and would not last forever.

Don also demonstrated the powerfulness of meaning attached to possessions. The photographs of his second wife had taken on the meaning of her tragic death and her family's accusations of his culpability for the lifestyle that brought her death. He could not look at those pictures, for they defined him as a despicable and guilty person.

Such was the way he described his frame of mind after her death. While there could be no doubt of his love for and devotion to his third wife, he left behind almost all material reminders of her when he entered a new relationship. He praised her for her wisdom as she guided him to greater emotional maturity in the short time they were together. He said she had taught him to leave reminders behind, to make a fresh start to a new life. She asked him to choose a tree to stay with her ashes. When she asked for a tree that was independent and self-sufficient, he took that to mean a tree that symbolized her strong qualities. But her choice was also a statement that he need not stay and tend this tree, because it would be independent and self-sufficient. Her husband, in his mid-sixties, could start a new life free from encumbrance; in effect, he could start a new life history.

Findings

Adult children and their spouses were helpful to the husband as he dealt with the details of services, burial or cremation, and disposition of property. Final arrangements were pre-planned when the wife was ill. Sometimes arrangements for both spouses had been made, either before she was ill or a result of her illness. Burial and cremation were both common. Snowbirds were memorialized and put to rest back home.

Men who had not remarried had photographs of their wives displayed or close at hand. Remarried men did not have photos or had them put away. Usually a female relative helped the man deal with his wife's clothing. The wife herself usually designated who would receive her jewelry.

Men living alone, who still lived in the home they had shared with their wife, usually made no changes or very minimal changes to the decor of the home. Items in the home were meaningful to the man as memories of his wife.

Possessions could be an obstacle to remarriage, or at least posed problems in blending households and in dealing with reminders of the deceased spouse.

REFERENCES

McCracken, A. (1987). Emotional impact of possession loss. *Journal of Gerontological Nursing, 13*(2), 14–19.

Redfoot, D. L. & Back, K. W. (1988). The perceptual presence of the life course. *International Journal of Aging and Human Development, 27*(3), 155–170.

Rubenstein, R. L. (1986). The construction of a day by elderly widowed men. *International Journal of Aging and Human Development, 23* (3), 161–173.

7

Grief and Adjustment

This chapter deals with the emotions experienced by the men as a result of losing their wives to death. The scholarly literature refers to the various feelings that accompany loss of a spouse, charts the process of adjustment to grief, and identifies factors that aid or hinder adjustment.

Normal Grief

Shuchter and Zisook (1993) suggest that, after an initial period of numbness, the acute mourning phase takes place, lasting for a lengthy (but variable by individual) time. That period is characterized by intense emotional discomfort, somatic complaints, social withdrawal, and preoccupation with the deceased. Acute mourning is gradually replaced by a returning sense of well-being that allows one to go on with life. Lund, Caserta, and Dimond (1993) state that they could not find support for a stages model of bereavement. They find the bereavement process more accurately described as "a roller coaster of many ups and downs with gradual improvement over time" (p. 247). They have found diversity among bereaved persons negotiating the bereavement time. For example, some felt they were socially active and involved in meaningful activity while others were lonely and miserable. Still others would report being active with others and yet feeling lonely. The best predictor of bereavement adjustment, they conclude, is the amount of time that has passed since the death. McCrae and Costa (1993) state that widowhood does not appear to have permanent effects on psychosocial functioning in older men and women. Older widowed respondents reported having friends, feeling healthy, and seeing themselves as capable in their daily activities.

Nearly all of our respondents had returned to some sense of well-being. Our study was to be a study of adjustment, so we sought respondents who were past the acute mourning phase. They had memories and feelings of loneliness, but they were no longer preoccupied and bereft. Some had remarried and others were in close relationships with women companions. Most of them were living on their own; many had developed a sense of competence in taking care of themselves.

We did have interviews with two men who had been widowed less than one year. Their input was quite instructive regarding the individual variability of the bereavement process. Craig had been widowed just four months earlier and was taken out of state to his daughter's home right after the funeral. He had been back in his own home only two weeks before the interview and was sorting through things in preparation for moving. He still seemed somewhat dazed and numb. He said he guessed he did not miss his wife because he had not cried for her. Cordell had seen his wife through a decline of 20 years. Their sexual relationship had ended many years before her death. Final arrangements for both of them had been made and paid for. Within a few months of her death, he was "comforting a widow" and otherwise energetically pursuing the interests in his life. These two examples demonstrate that the grieving process is quite individualized, depending upon many factors.

Conventional wisdom and some research projects conclude that positive qualities such as good self-esteem, specific skills for daily living, and good interpersonal skills facilitate adaptation to loss (Lund, Caserta, & Dimond, 1993). However, Wortman, Silver, and Kessler (1993) suggest that those who have the highest feelings of mastery over their lives may suffer the most in the loss of a spouse. The loss shatters their perception that they have control over what happens in their lives. Scheier and Carver (1985) also suggest that the optimistic person may not know what to do with a negative reality so foreign to their positive view of life.

Janoff-Bulman (1992) explores the ways in which people come to grips with events that are contrary to their worldview. The chapter on Life Values considers the role of optimism in the lives of our respondents. Like many people who survive to an old age (Johnson & Barer, 1997), almost all of our respondents appeared to have some measure of optimism. One of our respondents, Richard, was a very competent individual and had a very positive general outlook on life, but he had suffered two devastating losses and, as a result, had fallen into a deep depression. It seems that the persistence of friends trying to help him urged him to the point where his optimism returned. He described the "black cloud over me" disappearing literally overnight. He awoke one morning and did not know why he felt better. He felt guilty at first, he said, then decided that he might as well face his loss and go on.

Lund, Caserta, and Dimond (1993) find the best predictors of long-term adjustment in bereavement to be "amount of time since the death, . . . initial or early bereavement adjustments, . . . positive self-esteem and personal competencies in managing the tasks of daily life" (p. 253). They found that social support could be positive or negative. Close relationships providing opportunities for self-expression and mutual helping had positive effects. Friends and relatives could also disappoint the bereaved person or appear inconsiderate, thereby causing more stress. Stylianos and Vachon (1993) found that lack of contact with friends was a significant stressor in early bereavement. Three of our respondents found the staying away of friends to be highly distressing. Many other respondents spoke with great appreciation of the friends who came around.

Lund, Caserta, and Dimond (1993) found age, gender, education, income, religious membership and religiosity, and factors such as perceived health status, happiness in the marriage, and pet ownership to be relatively unimportant as predictors of bereavement adjustment in older spouses. Their respondents were primarily female (74%) and averaged 67.6 years of age, almost 13 years younger than the average age of the men in our study. In the following chapters, we explore these factors in our population of men. Wortman, Silver, and Kessler (1993) state that men are vulnerable in widowhood because of their limited social relationships and their problems in assuming daily tasks around the home. They also report that men are less close to their adult children than are widowed women and they have more difficulty asking for help. They conclude that "widowhood is not the same event for the two sexes."

Pathological Grief

To this point, we have considered the normal bereavement process that leads—in its individual variations—to some resolution of the grieving. Middleton, Raphael, Martinek, and Misso (1993) explore various categories of grief experience that are outside that normal pattern. We have used their categories to consider the few respondents in our study who could be placed in these categories.

Absent Grief

Only Yussef, among all of the 51 men, claimed his life had not been much affected by his wife's death. When asked about his feelings during the first year following his wife's death, he responded, "I never missed a beat." His explanation of how he shut out the feelings is recounted near the end of this chapter in the section on men's expression of emotion.

Cordell, mentioned above as the newly widowed man so quickly going on with his life, may be considered an example of absent grief. He said that he had done his grieving in advance. Wortman and Silver (1989) suggest that absent grief may not be pathological, but simply an indication that the person was able to handle the loss in a way not defined as conventional grieving.

Delayed Grief

Malcolm had remarried seven months after his wife died, but he sobbed bitterly when asked about his first wife's death. He apologized for the loss of control and said that this was the first time he had spoken about his wife's death. He had been widowed four years at the time of the interview.

Inhibited Grief

Clarence was a friendly and open man, but he grew tense and turned aside questions relating to his wife's death.

Chronic/Unresolved Grief

John became tearful very easily during the interview. He had been widowed four years. Bapuji said his grief came back to him as if his wife had died just yesterday; she had died 23 years earlier. His nonverbal communication substantiated his statement. Curly's grief would never be resolved. It is described in the category below.

Distorted Grief

Curly's grief was distorted, chronic, and unresolved because of his poor treatment of his wife during their marriage. He suffered great guilt, wanted to talk about how badly he had treated his wife, and could not be persuaded to consider any of the positive aspects of his life.

Considering these categories of pathological grief, we were struck by the high number of our respondents who could not be described in any of these categories. Their adjustments in general were quite positive and "normal." We realized then that the men who had refused to be interviewed were the ones who tended to have inhibited, chronic, and unresolved grief. One man reluctantly agreed to be interviewed, then called and canceled because the thought of talking about his wife's death was keeping him awake at night. Two other men said they could not talk about their wives without breaking down; another said he just did not want to talk about his loss. Apparently, being willing to be interviewed was an indication of having resolved the grief.

TYPE OF DEATH AND ITS EFFECT ON GRIEF

Sudden Death

The hallmarks of sudden death were (a) shock that left emotional scars, and (b) no time to prepare for the loss, to begin grieving, or to anticipate adjusting to life alone. Typically, the men who had experienced such a loss would say that they wished there had been some warning. The men in this category would acknowledge the difficulty of watching a loved one waste away in a lingering death, but their own horrors were characterized by abruptness. One man in a support group, who was not a respondent in our study, said poignantly, "My wife said good-bye to run some errands, and an hour later I learned she had died in a car accident. I couldn't believe it." Our respondent Bert would no doubt have echoed this statement if he had been willing to talk about his own visit by the police.

Comparing sudden deaths with anticipated death, Sanders (1989) and Lundin (1984) found persons bereaved after a sudden death have more somatic symptoms. Lundin also found more psychiatric illnesses. Sanders identified anger, a feeling of loss of control and loss of trust in the world. Parkes (1975) found disbelief that leads to severe distress, social withdrawal, difficulty in performing important roles, and intense yearning for the deceased spouse.

Glick, Weiss, and Parkes (1974) found that grieving persons have not returned to full functioning after four years. Lundin (1984) concluded that after eight years had passed persons grieving after a sudden death were similar to those grieving an anticipated death. Lehman, Wortman and Williams (1987) studied grievers who had lost a spouse or child in an auto accident and found them still having severe symptoms and unresolved grief four to seven years after the event.

Doka (1996) dealt with the sudden deaths that have a degree of expectedness to them, such as Alvin's situation in which his wife had a terminal diagnosis but no clear timetable for the dying process: Alvin found her dead very unexpectedly. Because of the complexity of the situation, responses to such situations are highly individualized. Observed responses include: (a) intensified grief, as the loss cannot be prepared for and there is no chance to say good-bye or finish business,

(b) a shattering of the person's normal world, (c) series of concurrent crises and secondary losses. Typical feelings include: anger, guilt, hopelessness, a lingering sense of disorganization, and a consuming obsession with the deceased person. Alvin commented that he was glad she was out of her misery, but he sure wasn't out of his. He had just ordered a motorized cart for her, a reminder of unfinished business and of the unexpectedness of her death. He also said that his psychiatrist had told him that it was a good thing he had a sense of humor to help him through this time. It is possible that Alvin's compulsion to find a new female companion was his way of ameliorating some of the distress he felt over the sudden loss of his wife. A desperate search was action, and it was proof that there was some hope for the future.

Curly's wife was in a nursing home, but he could not allow himself to accept her failing condition. So he was surprised when the death occurred. He recalled that he was in the hospital with an injury when a doctor informed him that his wife had died. He said, "We all knew she wasn't going to get well, but it came so unexpectedly. Dr. Mitch came down about 8:30. He said, 'Abby just passed away.' Oh, Dr. Mitch! I'll never forget that!"

Lengthy Dying Process

The hallmarks of grieving for a longer-term death include various responses to impending loss. Mace and Rabins (1999) describe the process of grieving during a loved one's illness. There is grief for the loss of one's companion, for the way she used to be. Sy's wife anticipated this response in Sy as she grieved for her own loss of womanliness after a mastectomy. With dementia in particular, loss of companionship while still being a spouse is very painful. Ned spoke poignantly of his feelings of loss as his wife progressed with her dementia. Typical feelings include sadness, discouragement, and anger; crying is common. A person may have alternating feelings of sadness and hopefulness. Kenneth spoke of praying for recovery and then praying for a quick and peaceful death. As the dying person's condition changes, there is renewed grieving. The grief experienced during chronic illness is often misunderstood by friends and neighbors, who save their attentions until after the death has occurred. Persons grieving during a loved one's illness may experience depression, fatigue, apathy, listlessness, worry, feeling isolated and alone, and illness.

Pine (1996) writes that anticipatory grief serves as "a social psychological buffer to the impact of the eventual death" (p. 109). The grieving process has begun and the survivor is able to construct a new reality which includes the dying person's death. However, this hypothesis is not supported by the findings of Roach and Kitson (1989).

Relief and Sorrow

Some of the men said that the declining condition of their wife's health prepared them for the loss. They still were not "ready" for it, but at least it was no surprise. A few of the men held onto a belief that they would die before their ill wives; such was the power of the statistical stereotype of women living longer than their husbands. Sy wondered who would take care of his very ill wife when he died. Stuart joked that some younger man would be interested in his wife when he was gone because of their savings for retirement. Still, early or late, they all had come to the realization that they were to be the ones left behind. It was difficult for men to state in an interview that they were relieved when the death finally came, but for some that was clearly the case.

Jerry said, "I had a mixture of profound sorrow and relief." Kenneth had lost two wives to cancer. "When [my first wife] died it was a relief. The same way with [my second wife]. I wanted them to get better, but when I found out . . . ." Sam asked, "How can you explain it? You get the instant relief and then the other things start kicking in. You know, she's gone. You're going to miss her. She's not going to be back with you anymore. It's a great relief, but here (touching his heart) it is not a relief."

INDIVIDUAL EXPRESSIONS OF GRIEF PROCESS

We asked each man what the grieving process had been like for him. The following comments suggest the variety of ways in which our respondents navigated that difficult time. Clarence said, "To put it into words, I probably thought this is the greatest problem that I have had to face. I don't think I thought about not being able to face it, because I was facing it. One doesn't ever adjust to the loss of a mate; you develop calluses that make it easier for you to bear it." Art said, "I have to recreate my life, have to recreate my thinking."

Don had a strong feeling for his third wife as a teacher—a mentor—in life. She had helped him see his way through his earlier losses and out of his life of substance addiction. He said, "She taught me about death, too. She taught me how to die with dignity and grace, and surrender, and it's not to be that fearful. Not to be fearful at all. It's a natural process. She was so strong and wise."

Cordell's wife had many years of physical and psychological decline. Cordell was singular among our respondents with the bluntness of his comment, "My grieving was minimal. . . . I'm so blasted pragmatic. The marriage was terminated in reality, we were together, we were living together as friends for a number of years. The marriage had ceased." The few months following her death found him active and involved in social life, including a new intimate relationship, as mentioned in the opening of this chapter.

Jerry said, "I had a real tough time for about 8 months. I missed a lot of work. I couldn't even get out of bed in the morning. I was really suffering clinical depression. I went to a lot of therapy and everything. I just couldn't do anything. I was almost like paralyzed." Richard also had suffered depression that kept him in bed.

Physical Expression of Grief

The men were asked about appetite and sleep disturbances related to the death of a wife. Almost none of the men mentioned an appetite disturbance, but many recounted difficulties with sleep. Alvin identified his sleep difficulties as an anticipatory grief response that started when he knew his wife was terminally ill. At the interview, he said that he still did not sleep well. "In the middle of the night I'll ride an exercise bike. Sometimes it helps me get back to sleep. . . . If I get tired enough, then I sleep. But mostly I don't sleep." Curly suspected the doctor was giving him a sedative so he would go right to sleep. But at 3:30 or 4:00 a.m. he would awaken. He had been listening to be certain his wife was still breathing. After her death, he did not hear her breathing, so he would become "edgy" and would have to get up. Craig said that he "crawled into bed and everything was all right" the first night after his wife's death. "I slept good," he said, "but the longer it's been, the harder it is to go to sleep." Russell said he was so upset about his wife's sudden death that he couldn't sleep and did not eat much.

Michael described his typical night. After watching TV until 11:30, he would try to go to sleep. Then he would wake up sometime between 2–4 a.m. to go to the bathroom and sometimes would not get back to sleep. "You fight the pillow," he said. But he attributed the pattern to age, not to grief.

Disruption of the Retirement Plan

Some of the men spoke of plans they and their wives had for retirement. Bapuji said that he planned to retire and have a good life in

India, but then his wife died of a stroke when he was 60 years old. Stuart also was widowed at age 60. He regretted how they had always saved for retirement instead of spending their money; he was left with the savings but without his wife. Jerry, widowed at age 54, was traveling alone, wishing he could turn to his wife to comment on a beautiful sunset. It is important to note that all three of these men were widowed before retirement age. They seemed to feel this disruption more keenly because the retirement plan—for all the planning—never happened at all. Those who were widowed at an older age were living in retirement already. The older the man, the less he spoke of his widowhood in terms of disrupted plans.

On Time/Off Time

Roach and Kitson (1989) found younger widows exhibited significantly greater psychological distress than their older counterparts, regardless of forewarning about the death or length of the marriage. This would be in keeping with Neugarten's (1968) conceptualization of events being "on time" or "off time."

In our study the younger men in particular were shocked and saddened by the timing of the loss of their wives. However, men in general do not think that their wives will die first, because the statistics condition us all to think of widowhood as the province of women. Older women may expect to be widowed because they see widows everywhere and could, if they were so inclined, find statistics to support their observations. For men, there may be no "on time" loss of a wife, only degrees of "off time." As we have already stated, older widowed men are not particularly visible; they are hidden by fairly quick remarriage or by their isolated way of living after widowhood. While widowhood came as shockingly off time to the younger men in our study, it seemed to be unexpected for most of the men, whatever their age and whatever the situation with the wife's health. Sy cared for his wife through a long terminal illness, yet his greatest concern was that he would die first and leave her in desperate need of care. Other men with ill wives told us they still felt they would die first.

We do not want to minimize the painful off time feelings experienced by the younger men we interviewed. As more emphasis is put on financial arrangements for retirement, as more people in fact have a significant proportion of their lives to live after retirement, and as retirement is advertised as a golden age of worry-free pleasure, the loss of a spouse just before or just into the retirement period will be more difficult for both men and women to accommodate. If individuals expect that widowhood is likely for them, if adequate financial planning will allow them to have some choices in how they live in widowhood, if they have skills in sociability and family and friends with whom to interact, these factors will have a positive impact on their long-term adjustment to widowhood. Each of these "if's" is considerable; by no means are most older people assured of adequacy in all of these areas. From this study of widowed men, we suggest that widowed men, as a group, are less likely to think that they will be widowed and that leaves them disadvantaged in adjustment to widowhood whatever their age.

Acceptance of Being the Survivor

If a man believes, with good evidence around him, that men die first and leave a widow behind, then he may not be able to believe his wife will die first. This seemed to be the case even when the wife was in an undeniable decline. Clyde said his wife did not know she would die first, and he did not know either. "Nobody knows that," he said. He acknowledged that she was very ill, but he added, "I ain't much [either]". Among our respondents, some men did finally accept that they would outlive their wives, but that realization almost always came quite late in the wife's dying process. Henrik said:

> I've lost so many family members and death to me is a normal function of life. I would say I was probably able to take it better than the average person who has only had one death or something. I knew all these years [with wife's illness] that it was just a matter of time. There were probably eight or ten times in the seventeen years when I thought . . . she was going to go.

Yet, moments earlier in the interview, when describing how he played the harmonica for his wife as she lay dying, he said, "I don't know how I controlled my emotions but I played [her favorite songs] . . . and there wasn't a dry eye in the place." He also said his wife had been in a coma for three weeks before her death and that it "just about brings tears to my eyes to think of it every time." He indicated that he and his daughter had faced the fact that they had to "let her go" when she went into cardiac arrest.

Alvin had uneasy feelings about being left with insurance money as the result of his wife's death. He acknowledged that she would have had insurance benefits if he had died, but had trouble accepting the fact that he was benefitting financially from her death. Stuart felt bad that he and his wife had saved for retirement, and now he had all that money for his use. Earl commented that he was now doing the things that he and his first wife had planned to do, but he was doing them with a new wife.

Support Groups

Only six out of the 51 men spoke of having attended bereavement groups, with only one, Karl, continuing to attend. He was a charter member of an ongoing group of older widowed people. From his description, it was a social group that met monthly for lunch and to talk. He said that it had helped him. That is what John had hoped for, but it did not happen for him. People in the group he attended would say, "We're going to have to go eat out together," but then they never called him. "I'm sure they had good intentions but really they'd be better off if they wouldn't have said anything at all. Because in the situation that you're in, you sort of expect it and it doesn't happen. . . . They just don't realize the state that person is in. But really you are expecting that and you feel, 'That would be good for me,' but when it doesn't happen, it's not so good."

The men who did not continue attending support groups found them heavily dominated by women. They felt out of place and felt that the discussion was focused on the women's needs. John commented, "I'd say it was pretty heavy for women." Alvin said he would be interested in a men's support group. "I was the only man in the one [up north]; there were some men in the one [down here] but they were recently bereaved and I didn't like it. I might be able to get along without a support group." For Alvin, the idea of a support group was appealing, but the reality had not met his expectations. He appeared to be in the process of deciding that a support group would not be helpful. Lund, Redburn, Juretich, and Caserta (1989) had substantially fewer men than women accept the invitation to participate in their groups.

Jerry attended a couple of sessions of a support group sponsored by the local hospital. He was distressed by one woman in the group who had been grieving—apparently very vocally—for six years. Jerry regretted having felt so judgmental but he said he felt at the time, "If I'm still where that woman is in six years, somebody ought to put a gun to my head." Also, Jerry was critical of the format of the meetings, considering the size of the group. With about 15 people present, just checking in with stories took an hour and a half. Alvin and Jerry attended support group meetings right after the deaths of their wives. Joe went about 2 weeks after his wife's death. He said the meetings helped him a lot and he continued to attend for a year.

Conner continued to attend a Catholic couples group that he and his wife had been part of for decades. It was his source of friendship and support. For all that we heard and read about this being a couple's society (Lopata, 1993), and how older people themselves cut off widowed persons who do not find a new partner for socializing (van den Hoonaard, 1994), this group's continuing welcome to Conner seemed exceptional and probably reflected the closeness of the spiritual and social bonds within the group. None of the other couples had yet experienced a death, but the group would probably evolve into a small group of surviving spouses as the losses occurred.

Alternatives to Support Groups

While there seemed to be little enthusiasm for bereavement support groups, several of the men had found alternative ways to express their feelings and receive support. Alcoholics Anonymous served that purpose for Don. Three men attended church groups, two had regular "lunch bunch" engagements. One said he counseled with his minister, and two said they had seen a psychiatrist. Informal sources of social support are presented in the chapter on Adult Children and Other Social Support. For example, Bruce's daughter-in-law met with him regularly and helped him talk through his feelings, he said.

GOING ON WITH LIFE

All 51 men had, each in his own way, gone on with life after the death of a spouse. The chapter on Life Values Carried Forward considers the belief systems, values, and perspectives of the men that influenced their lives in general. Here we briefly consider how the men came to grips with their grieving and moved on in life.

Religious Meaning in Death and Suffering

Janoff-Bulman (1992) describes the religious theme of "the redemptive and strengthening role of suffering" (p. 138) which she sees operating across the major religions. The Koran, she writes, suggests that suffering forms character and helps create a faithful disposition. Judaism teaches that suffering can be made redemptive, in that it becomes the basis for better things, if not for oneself, then for others. Thus is formed the idea of sacrificial suffering, so that others may benefit. Christianity offers Christ as the example of suffering which brings redemption and consolation. That quality of consolation worked for the men who believed their wives had gone to Heaven. It also worked for Earl, whose young child died as the result of an accident. His story appears in the chapter on Life Values.

The religious beliefs and denominational affiliations of the respondents are discussed in the Life Values chapter. We saw the men in the study fitting into four categories: (a) those who professed no religious beliefs, (b) those who attended, or had attended, services but gave minimal thought or feeling to beliefs, (c) those who held religious beliefs that were simple, clear, and faith-based, (d) those who examined and reexamined spiritual issues philosophically and intellectually.

Those who seemed to gain the fastest help in their movement through grief were in the third group. They felt secure in clear, simple faith that gave structure and meaning to suffering and loss. The men in the fourth group engaged in philosophical searching and struggle, which was to them probably invigorating and which no doubt intensified the understandings that they finally derived. However, the philosophical search had its most painful questioning moments at the very times when comfort would have been welcome. As Frankl (1992) describes "the striving to find a meaning in one's life as the primary motivational force" (p. 104), the hitch is that a good deal of internal tension is required to fuel this search for meaning. Frankl writes that the tension that awakens the search for meaning is indispensable to mental well-being. Thus, a man such as Richard suffered severe depression following the loss of his wife, and yet he emerged after long suffering as an optimistic elder, still intensely interested in, and involved in, the world around him. Was Richard ultimately better off than the man who believed with certainty in God as a loving father who has taken his wife, a child of God, to be with him in eternity? Do either of these categories of men achieve a more fulfilled feeling or greater peace of mind than the men in the first two categories, who have neither the faith nor the struggle to guide them? It is beyond the scope of this study and the expertise that we bring to the project to analyze thoroughly how men in each of the categories found meaning in the death of their loved one and in their own suffering through loss. However, such questions are intriguing and worthy of investigation.

Locus of Control in Grief

In grieving, having an internal locus of control was manifested as pulling oneself together and getting on with life. John referred to another widowed man, saying, "It seems like he just hasn't dealt with [his grief]." He said that others in a support group could "say the right thing and help them build on it. . . . but they have to really do the building themselves. You can't do it for somebody else." Don, who was quoted earlier as having gotten rid of the mementos of his deceased wives when he started a new relationship, made a conscious decision to move on with his life in that way. Conner said he had a choice "to be made freely"; he could continue to live as he and his wife had always lived, or he could cry about being a lonely widower. So he decided that life was worth living and that he would live as nearly as he could the way he and his wife had lived. Lund, Caserta, and Dimond (1993) found older widowed men who had learned new skills to help them feel competent around the house also seemed to be helped with their grief.

Johnson and Barer (1997) found that the personal competencies exhibited by people who were doing well in very old age were evident in their "exercising a strong sense of control over their lives" (p. 72). Stroebe and Stroebe (1993) found that persons with a low level of belief in internal control had great difficulty adjusting to the sudden death of a spouse, suggesting that they felt this life-shattering loss was proof that they had no control over what happened to them. "They will more likely respond with resignation, make only feeble efforts to recover, and remain depressed" (p. 221). As we analyzed our data, we sought answers to these questions: How much control did a man feel that he had over his own life, especially in the short and medium term? Was his peace of mind today and tomorrow up to him? If not up to him, then to whom? Unknown and unidentifiable forces? A new woman in his life? A caring God? An indifferent God? A punishing God?

Regardless of religious beliefs, nearly all of the men we interviewed expressed that they were responsible for their attitudes toward others and for how well they could manage their lives. In most cases, a man who expressed strong religious faith did seek divine direction and assistance, but also stated that it would be up to him to do the things he needed to do to get on with life. Daniel said, "I take care of myself. I know I have to do that." John said that the grieving person must determine that he will heal. He said that he prays every day for a positive attitude. On the other hand, some of the men were notable as exceptions to the perception of being responsible for one's own well-being.

Needing a New Woman

Locus of control was the overriding factor in Alvin's adjustment to widowhood. He had relied heavily on the authority and knowledge of doctors during the illness of his wife. When he realized that they could not save her life, his lifelong tendency toward anxiety became extreme. At the time of the interview, he was still relying on doctors to manage his physical and mental health. His well-being was out of his control in another way. When asked if he could be happy on his own (having lost his wife), he replied, "I don't like that concept." As for his assessment of how well he was doing on his own, he responded, "I've muddled through. And I keep my eye open for a possible companion." He indicated that his chances for happiness were very limited without a new woman companion, but absolutely unlimited if he could find one. A follow-up call two years later found Alvin in very high spirits. "Guess what!!" he exclaimed, and the interviewer guessed, "You got married!" Of course that was the correct answer. Alvin was full of superlatives about his life and all of the activities that he and his wife were enjoying.

Alvin's situation presents an interesting consideration of locus of control. Alvin, by his own admission, was not doing well and was not likely to do well in adjusting to widowhood on his own. His prospects for happiness were given over almost entirely to a woman not yet determined at the time of the interview. Had he been located and interviewed after remarrying, he would have presented himself as a man who had been happily married once and who was happily married again. The earlier desperation to be rescued by another person would have been hidden by the fact of remarriage. The statistical reality was in Alvin's favor. There are many more widowed women than widowed men, so the widower who wants to remarry can usually find another wife. A widowed woman could be equally needy for another spouse, yet might not get the chance to remarry for lack of opportunity. Should we regard Alvin as resilient because he has recognized his needs and has taken action to see that they are met? Should we regard him as not resilient because his adjustment was so heavily dependent upon another person? Was happy, active, remarried Alvin more resilient than the lonely, unhappy woman who wished she could find another spouse, but could not?

Russell may have shown us what Alvin would have been like, if we had met Alvin after remarriage. At the time of his interview, Russell was remarried and enjoying life with his new wife. Conversely, Alvin may have shown us what Russell had been like soon after the death of his wife. Russell said he had been totally miserable after her unexpected death. The extent of his misery can be discerned to some degree by the fact that he already was in another relationship a month after his wife's death. The speediness of this development upset his adult children, but Russell's need to not be alone was greater than his need for addressing his children's grieving or for maintaining harmony with them. Russell indicated that he thought he would not have survived if he had not found the woman who is now his wife. When asked what advice he would give other men who someday might be widowed, he replied, "I'd say to meet somebody as soon as they can."

Quick remarriage was characteristic of men who seemed to feel they did not have control over their own happiness, comfort or even existence, although remarrying was an active attempt to deal with their unhappiness. Sam decided in the misery of his solitary existence that it took a woman to make a home; Sy didn't feel he would ever be emotionally all right on his own. Walter lived seemingly without emotional expression; within five months of being widowed, he was married again—to a very expressive woman. Was she a balancing element in his life, providing something he needed but did not have? He didn't know, he said.

For a widowed man, needing a woman in his life but not having one seemed to result in misery. A man could take action to find a new partner, but the process had its element of uncertainty, as the woman, once located and selected, would have to be agreeable to the relationship as well. Relationships take time to develop, and uncertainty exists throughout that process. Too much haste can result in a commitment of unknown quality. With these considerations, when the man perceives the fate of his happiness to be in the hands of a woman not yet committed to that responsibility, he may spend a long time being unhappy and feeling he cannot do much about it.

Having Strong Religious Faith

Earl was an example of a man with strong faith that could be identified as fundamentalist Christian. While he was an active and assertive person, making decisions that were based on faith considerations, he told a story that epitomizes the faithful turning over to God a humanly unmanageable problem. He spoke with subdued emotion about the accidental death of a child, saying that a Bible quote came to him and his wife as they mourned. He quoted Philippians 4:7, "And the peace of God, which transcends all understanding, will guard your hearts and your minds in Christ Jesus." He said that it was indeed beyond all understanding how the grief lifted off of their hearts and they were able to go on with life after that loss.

Conner, a deeply religious Roman Catholic, had lived with his wife a life of devoted togetherness. He had not changed things in their home since she died. Her sitting chair still faced his by the front window in their living room. He said he felt her presence as he sat and read. He knew that she was dead, but lived serenely in the assurance that he would join her at the end of his life. He went on with activities and relationships with the patience of one who was certain of the final outcome.

Adding an Element of Luck

Don knew that his sobriety was up to him with the help of his Higher Power, but he credited "a new woman in my life" for teaching him how to live. "I was learning how to listen to people, I was being directed, I was being instructed, I was being taught, I was being loved, all these things, I mean, massive doses of it." Don's locus of control was outside himself—a higher power and a woman to love him—but he felt very confident that these sources would always be there for him. Don felt that his ability to love and be loved was his key to a satisfying life. In his early days when he did not care about consequences for his negative behaviors, Don had a basic feeling that things would turn out all right no matter what he did, in other words, that he would be lucky no matter what. In his 70s and leading a much different lifestyle, he still had that basic orientation that things would somehow work out. He expected his current tight finances to be remedied somehow, and at follow-up that had happened. Scheier and Carver (1985) found that most optimistic people had an internal "locus of causality" (p. 231), thereby feeling that they could control the outcomes in their lives. Significant exceptions to that sense of control within were persons who were optimistic because of their belief in a loving and protecting provider and persons who thought of themselves as lucky. Earl and Conner with their belief in God's love and purpose, and Don with his feeling of being lucky—these men were optimists secure in an external locus of control.

Being Optimistic or Pessimistic

We found a man's general outlook on life to be salient in his adjustment to widowhood. Particularly, if he were generally optimistic, he tended to find a new balance in his life after the loss of his wife. Optimism is the tendency to regard situations and events in a favorable light, seeing positive possibilities, or as defined by Scheier and Carver (1985) as "generalized expectancies for good outcomes" (p. 243). Optimism can vary from situation to situation, but individuals seem to have a disposition toward positive or negative expectancies. Scheier and Carver suggested that optimistic persons may work harder and more persistently to reach their goals, or that they may tackle problems earlier, when there is more chance for remedy. Scheier and Carver (1993) examined the suggestion that optimistic people may tend to sit back and wait for the positive outcome they expect, but stated that they have not found that to be the case. Instead, they say that optimistic people view their own efforts as part of the process of creating the positive outcome. Calhoun and Tedeschi (1998) and Tedeschi and Calhoun (1995) reported that persons who were optimistic, hopeful, action-oriented, alert to their environment, and flexible were able to grow in the wake of a traumatic experience. Janoff-Bulman (1992) suggested that people restructure their perception of traumatic events to fit their existing world view. Finding benefit in suffering is a way that the optimistic person can maintain a positive view of life (McMillen, 1999). For the elderly, forced to pay more and more attention to their health, optimism (or lack of it) is evident in their perceptions of their health and in their ways of living with its intrusion into their functioning. Johnson and Barer (1997), in their study of the very old, found examples of optimism even in the face of chronic health conditions, increasing pain, and limitations. One woman stated, " Now all my days are bad. It's frustrating, but at least I don't have heart trouble. . . . I have a lot to be thankful for" (p. 67). A male respondent reported, "I still have shingles, but they are not as painful as last year" (p. 63). Our respondent Richard, in a follow-up phone conversation said, "My arthritis is not flaring up; I am doing well." We found some expression of optimism in nearly all of the interviews we conducted. The incidence of optimism among the very old may indicate that an optimistic attitude is a factor in survival.

Scheier and Carver (1985) speculated that in a situation that seems to have no positive outcome, the optimist may not know when to give up and may suffer greatly in a futile struggle. Another possibility would be the devastation of feeling that one's optimism had been self-delusion and that the world actually is a negative place. In that case, the optimistic men would suffer more acutely in their loss because the death of their wife was an event that did not fit into a schema of optimism. It would be hard for a grieving older man—now alone—to put a positive spin on the death of a spouse. So the basic assumption of a positive outlook on life might be shaken. The extent to which a man could come back from those depths probably depends upon a values and belief system that will help him move toward understanding this death, its meaning, and the meaning of his continuing life. Calhoun and Tedeschi (1998) suggest that "when positive outcomes are blocked, the more 'flexible' outcome of hope is necessary" (p.223), as hope allows "an open response to the distress of the trauma while revising goals, perspective, and behaviors" (p. 224). Janoff-Bulman (1992) describes ways in which people cognitively restructure traumatic events so they can keep a positive outlook.

Lehman, Wortman, and Williams (1987) suggest that persons appearing optimistic may be exaggerating personal growth, often having been encouraged by loved ones to express that they are doing well, or that they may be trying to convince themselves that they are doing well. Herein is a strength of a qualitative methodology, for our respondents' statements appear within the context of a lengthy conversation spread over two days time, along with our observations of voice tone, body language, and other revealing forms of nonverbal behavior. Many of the comments indicating optimism were initiated by the respondent, rather than being in response to a question or questionnaire item. Interviews were often interrupted by phone calls or visits, so we observed many of the men interacting with others. Self-deluding or exaggerated optimism would likely be recognized.

Richard was an example of a man whose optimistic outlook was severely shaken, and yet it finally prevailed. Richard and his wife lost their only child, a son, in an automobile accident when he was a teenager. Richard and others who knew her said that Richard's wife never recovered from that loss. Richard was a particularly optimistic person among those that we interviewed, yet his child's death gave his life a sad undercurrent in the form of a continuing sense of loss. Richard spoke of Thomas Hardy's novel, *Tess of the D'Urbervilles,* with its unrelenting naturalistic march toward a dismal end for the heroine, as a remarkable insight into the human condition. Richard admitted to being seriously depressed by the death of his wife, even contemplating suicide. One cannot help but think that the two losses—even though three decades apart–were piled upon each other. Having lost the child who might have comforted him and supported him, Richard was alone as a widower. It was a remarkable triumph of optimism that, after more than a year of bedridden depression, Richard was able to decide to pull himself out of bed and get on with life. He said he told himself, "Maybe you better try. You are gonna be around here; obviously you aren't dying. You better take the bull by the horns and do something." Religious faith had played a large role in his life and in his recovery. He spoke of faith, "It makes life more reasonable and meaningful. I don't think it necessarily makes it any easier, but it does give meaning and purpose."

At the time of a follow-up interview, Richard had experienced a broken hip that had necessitated canceling a trip to Europe. He said he intended to go the next year, explaining, "Half of my friends think that's a great idea, and half think I am crazy. I just say, 'Sure, I could die in Europe just like I could die here, but if I die in France, I would have been having more fun." He seemed to be feeling well, although he was very thin. He had broken skin on his arthritis-gnarled hands, a shallow but tender-looking vertical scrape on his right cheek and dark subcutaneous discoloring on his hands and wrists. His hands were so deformed he could hardly use them. Yet his spirit was undaunted. He remained optimistic about the future, did not know how he developed this perspective, but said he always had felt that things would turn out all right. He did not like the realities of aging, but said they could not be changed and so he would live with them and go on. In a later follow-up call, he said he had not been able to make his postponed trip to Europe, but he still hoped to go someday.

Cantor and Norem (1989), Goodhart (1986), and Showers (1992) speculate that a bit of pessimism prevents a person from becoming complacent and gives him energy to make an effort to avoid what he dreads. Our respondents who were so unhappy living alone are examples of this phenomenon at work. Their discomfort in living alone, in fact for some a refusal to try to become content living alone, energized them to seek a new companion. Then too, with the dread of loneliness still in their minds, they would be motivated to make a success of their new marriages. A few of the new couples were not particularly compatible, but the partners still expressed appreciation of each other and the marriage.

Living Alone and Loneliness

Arnold said, "I don't have any trouble doing things except, well, it gets a little lonely out here. [The dog] is the last connection between she and I." Most of the men made statements of loneliness. Jacob said, "At night I stay home, but then the loneliness begins." Michael said, "Nights are endless." Their feelings were echoed by many of the men. Ornish (1997) suggests that one's perception of loneliness becomes the reality. For most of our respondents, the reality was that a man by himself did not—and could not—deal with loneliness very well. Television was a poor substitute for human company. Even avid readers were lonely at night. For older couples, evenings together had been comfortable and companionable. Evenings with an ill wife were occupied with caregiving and preparation for bedtime. Evenings alone as a widower were never-ending. Loneliness, boredom, and dragging time prevailed. Men such as Clyde and Frank had no routine bedtime; television watching intermingled with dozing, and maybe the man ended up in bed sometime during the night.

There were a few exceptions. Daniel said he did not mind being alone. "I am good company for myself," he said. Conner kept his routine of sitting across from his wife's chair in the living room, reading after dinner just as he had read when she was sitting across from him reading her own book.

Remarriage was one remedy for loneliness at night. Steady companionship was another. Nearly every man in a new relationship said that his wife wanted him to go on with his life. Whether his memory or his construing of his wife's feelings was simply justification for what he wanted to do cannot be determined. It is possible that his wife's genuine openness to his having a new relationship did encourage him in that direction. When loneliness tugged him between loyalty to his wife and seeking companionship, knowing or feeling that his wife would understand could permit him to seek relief from loneliness through a new relationship.

Going Through It All Again

Three of the men in our study had been through widowhood twice already. Another man had been widowed three times. Eleven men had been through widowhood once and had remarried; three more remarried after the interview. All but one of the women who married our widowed respondents in later life were widows themselves. Thus we saw that many people who had personal experience with the painful loss of a spouse nevertheless committed to new relationships. Those remarried men who had endured the shock and horror of a sudden death of spouse knew that could happen again. Those who gave care during a terminal illness knew they might be called upon to do that again. Additionally, these older men had health problems of their own and knew that a new wife might face caregiving and loss in their marriage. The majority of men in our study considered these possibilities, weighed them against loneliness, and decided not to remarry. We were interested to hear the stories and the views of those men who were willing to risk going through it all again.

Garrett said, "I was mainly lonesome. Nobody to talk to. And nobody to love. It just seemed empty; it just seemed all sort of worthless, futile. And I felt like I should be doing something for somebody." He remarried in five months, which was apparently in keeping with his dying wife's expectation. After about two years of widowhood, Stuart knew he wanted to marry again. He had been diagnosed with and treated for prostate cancer, so he considered his health a factor in a decision to marry. The woman with whom he was considering marriage felt optimistic about his future, so they did marry. Health and age were related to a great extent, and we found generally that men approaching their mid-80s considered themselves too old, too ill, or both too old and too ill to remarry. So a decision to remarry was in some sense an expression of optimism about one's health. The women who became the new wives had experienced some health problems but were healthy enough to be active; healthiness and activity level were probably factors operating in the selection process. When men described their new marriages, there was a strong theme of enjoying activities together, much easier to do when both are relatively healthy and active. Remarriage is considered in greater depth in the chapter with that name.

In the Caregiving chapter, we presented content on the dying wife's predictions or expectations for her husband remarrying. Fourteen of the men reported comments, concerns, or "understandings" conveyed by the wife. It appears that these wives knew of their husband's needs for care and companionship. Five of those men had remarried by the time they were interviewed. This figure does not fully reflect the accuracy of the wives' predictions or concerns, as some men had found steady companionship, some were slow in moving toward marriage, at least one had come to need nursing home care, and a couple did not want their wives to be right in predicting another marriage.

Attitudes of Those Widowed Twice or More Toward Another Marriage

Daniel was self-sufficient between marriages and was self-sufficient after losing his second wife. He was not seeking another marriage. He deeply regretted having such a short time with his second wife. Also, while he was quite healthy, he was passing through his mid-80s, an age at which most of the men had concluded that they were too old for another marriage. Leroy was bored, but not very much motivated to do anything with his life. Much of the interview content was unclear, reflecting apparent confusion on Leroy's part about things that had happened in his life and why they had happened. He was clear in stating that being in his early 80s was too old to think about marrying again. Kenneth said he felt jinxed, having married two healthy women and having them both die of cancer. He had health problems and simply ruled out another marriage. Don had lost three wives, two to drug overdoses and one to cancer. He was in a fourth relationship and had a very positive attitude toward love and its part in his life's journey. He probably would have found another if the current one ended. Daniel and Kenneth were both in their 80s; each was involved in two situations of caregiving to very ill wives. Don, for all his losses, was just 71 years old at the time of his interview. His first two wives, dying accidentally, required no caregiving. His third wife was a positive and self-assured woman who spared him as much as she could from the pain of her decline. Don was much less conventional than the other two men. Having changed his life focus from addiction to sobriety, he celebrated life and love. A sample of three is too little basis for seeing patterns. If anything can be concluded, it is probably that each man had responded to the build-up of losses in his own way. All three seemed emotionally healthy, leading lives that were congruent with their values and reasonable for their circumstances. Kenneth had been more purposeful than the others in choosing a second wife; that may have contributed to his feeling of having more responsibility for the outcome of the marriage. He did not use this thinking to keep himself feeling bad, but he would not consider another marriage and his current lady friend apparently was not very happy about that.

MALE EXPRESSION OF EMOTION

Our 51 respondents provided us with a full range of emotional expressiveness in various combinations with differing degrees of loquacity and openness. Russell, Bill, Al, Joe, and Sy were talkative and emotionally expressive, but all in very different ways. John was not talkative, but expressed his feelings nonverbally. Clyde was talkative, but kept some feelings under guard. Yussef was moderately talkative, but kept his emotions under tight control. Walter spoke very little and seemed to feel very little. Obviously, personalities differ, and individual respondents would have differing degrees of comfort with the interview situation. We looked for ways to describe the broad concept of emotional expressiveness in men.

We observed what would bring an older widowed man to tears, and found these examples: (a) Eldon was noticeably choked up several times when he referred to "my Heavenly Father who is always with me" and when he spoke of his wife being in Heaven, (b) Malcolm sobbed, saying this interview was the first time he had talked about his wife's death, (c) John cried softly when speaking of the day his wife died suddenly. Several men were subdued, spoke with hesitation, and/or had tears come to their eyes when they first spoke of their wives or when they spoke of the wife's death. Except for Eldon's overwhelming gratitude to God for his long and "miraculous" life, all of the incidents of tearfulness or choked voices accompanied a mention of the wife. Such emotion came with mentioning (a) her suffering, or changes with her illness, (b) her death, (c) her goodness and examples of it, (d) how much her widowed husband missed her. The men usually admitted readily that they had cried over the death of the wife. Craig, mentioned at the opening of this chapter, was interviewed only a few months after his loss. He said it was all right for a man to cry, but he guessed he did not miss his wife because he had not cried over her death. A follow-up two years later found him much more adjusted to the loss of his wife, settled in his daughter's home, and much more expressive than he had been at the original interview.

Sadness was frequently observed. It was expressed in nonverbal ways through posture and facial expression, down-turned eyes and subdued voice. Verbally it was described as loneliness. We considered the men's experience of loneliness and their responses to it earlier in this chapter. Happiness and joy could be expressed by men who had adjusted to the loss of the wife. These positive emotions came two different ways: (a) through satisfying involvement as father, grandfather or uncle in an extended family, and (b) through a new intimate relationship with a woman. Satisfaction was experienced also by men who were involved in volunteer activities that in some way contributed to the well-being of others. A few men, such as Kenneth and Frank, found satisfaction in crafts work. Joe and Louis combined the pleasure of handiwork with contributing to others; they made items which were sold to benefit charity.

Health concerns were taken in stride as inevitable with age by most of the men, although some men were willing to say that they had felt—or still felt—anxiety over their health and their ability to get along on their own. Worries about health were a reason given by older men for not remarrying. Undoubtedly, many of the men felt concerns that they did not want to fully express. Karl referred glumly to heart testing that he would face in the next week. Al said he was facing prostate surgery for cancer. Conner was concerned about a severe pain that could not be diagnosed. Robert worried about becoming ill with no one else there in his home to assist him. But only Alvin was willing to discuss his high level of anxiety, for which he was receiving psychiatric help. He said that he had inherited it from his mother, and that his wife had humored him in his need to make things safe and secure.

Examples of Inexpressiveness

Two of the men, Walter and Yussef, were notable for their lack of emotional expression. Walter seemed disconnected from everyone in his life, so inexpressive that one wondered how he took part in any meaningful relationships. When asked to describe his wife, he gave no personality descriptors, but simply said she had been a nurse. He did what he needed to do when his wife became ill, expressing in the interview no emotion about what must have been difficult decisions as her situation became more grave. He did not recall what had led to his rather quick remarriage. His new wife was energetic and sociable, presenting quite the opposite exterior to his passivity and lack of expression. One can imagine her providing all the energy and inspiration for the courtship while he let her do it. Then they got married. He said he knew he was holding her back from socializing with friends, but he said this too without emotion. This emotionless disconnection seemed to be characteristic of his relationships with his son and daughter, to whom he referred as "the boy" and "the girl." He seldom saw them and talked to them on the phone quite infrequently. From talking with him, one would get the impression that he was not bothered by the lack of contact. They came for their mother's funeral, but did not stay with him. After his death, Walter's daughter said they were having very little contact at the time of her mother's final illness. She said her father seldom expressed any emotion but anger, and that they were not a close family. He also had said they did not interact much with either his family or his wife's.

Walter's emotional restrictiveness perhaps can be enlightened by the extensive literature on alexithymia, a term meaning "without words for feelings"coined by Sifneos (1972) and then explored by Sifneos and others. Nemiah, Freyberger, and Sifneos (1976) characterize the alexithymic individual as having an emotional impoverishment that leaves him unable to identify or express emotions, as lacking in imaginative ability, and as unable to distinguish feelings from bodily sensations; they suggest that alexithymia is related to brain function. Other studies explore the relationship between alexithymia and somatic complaints (Cooper and Holmstrom, 1984; Taylor, 1984). Taylor is uncertain as to whether the disorder is developmental or "a defense against primitive anxieties" (p. 730). Kilmartin (2000), in reviewing the literature on alexithymia, suggests that it may originate in a social role that discourages expression of feelings and is eventually incorporated into the personality, or at least can be exacerbated by harsh socialization. Walter's daughter said that he grew up in an inexpressive family and was "raised by a maid." She said it was unfortunate that he did not break away from his family. We were certainly not in a position to diagnose a clinical disorder, but in many ways he fit the published descriptions of the alexithymic person. Kilmartin describes the alexithymic as a person blandly 'going through the motions' in a life devoid of rich experiences" (p. 167). Here is an excerpt from the interview with Walter:

Interviewer: So what does a loner do when a loner is alone?

Walter: Well, of course I spent every afternoon at the nursing home. I was at the nursing home all but 5 days in 4 years and that took a lot of time. Of course, I still had to worry about the yard and that sort of thing. I always went to bed early. . . .

Interviewer: So you did chores in the morning and then spent the afternoon with [your wife]?
Walter: Spent the afternoon with her.
Interviewer: In the evening you came home and micro-waved something to eat and went to bed when you wanted to?
Walter: Which would be very early.
Interviewer: And you could go to sleep and sleep all night? What time did you get up?
Walter: I used to get up probably around 7:00.
Interviewer: You just got a lot of sleep, didn't you?
Walter: Uh huh, yeah, uh huh.

Taylor (1984) described several characteristics of alexithymics that fit Walter: stiff posture and inexpressive face, high degree of social conformity with almost robot-like behavior, having occasional outbursts of rage but without being able to expound upon what they were feeling, inability to recognize and articulate feelings, which includes the feelings of others as well as their own, "thinking is literal, utilitarian, and concerned with minutiae of external events" (p. 726). Walter said, "I don't know" in response to many questions during the interview. His voice was monotone, devoid of energy. He was willing to be interviewed but seemed very distant the whole time. Walter allowed life to happen to him. He was a man who spoke very little and who probably had little, if any, experience considering his own emotional dynamics, much less expressing them to an interviewer, or to someone trying to be a part of his life.

Yussef, a career military man, presented another version of male inexpressiveness and control of emotions. He explained that he had been a drill instructor in the army and in that setting:

> You got to use the top of your voice, yelling and threatening. . . . You never lose control. I mean, yell and scream and the other person thinks you're losing control but you actually, that's part of the . . . that's what, as they say, goes with the territory.

Yussef described his father:

> . . . very mellow in a sense. He was one of these workaholics, liked to see everything done, everything taken care of, everything on an even keel. And if something didn't go right, then he'd lose his temper, temporarily, yeah.

When asked about missing his deceased wife, Yussef explained his philosophy:

No, actually not. I don't miss the war I went through too. I went through World War II, all of the Korean War and I shut it out. OK, now when I was working for the school board, you had a lot of rowdy kids and you could set there and block out the noise and go down the road and don't hear a thing. And I've—what do you call it?—shut your mind down and don't reminisce about previous things.

Interviewer: So it's the same way with your marriage then? Even though it lasted for many years, you're able to say, "That's in the past."

Yussef: That's in the past, let's pick up a new line and go.

Wortman and Silver (1989) caution against making assumptions about the way a person emotionally deals with an irrevocable loss. If grieving is "required," then someone such as Yussef might be viewed as pathologically avoiding the reality of his loss. However, they suggest, such a person may have a belief system or an outlook on life that allows him to deal with his loss in an immediate way. That is exactly what Yussef claimed to be the case for him. His background presented so many complex factors—his dual cultural heritage, his dual religious heritage, his growing up in Appalachia, his military career—that contributed to his development; it would be impossible to say exactly how he had come to be the friendly and helpful but austere person that he was. He was singular among our respondents in saying that he had purposely shut out memories of his wife and marriage. On the other hand, he volunteered for the study the minute he learned about it, so he was quite willing to talk about wife and marriage.

Balswick (1971, 1988) views male inexpressiveness as a learned behavior. He explores sociological theories (role theory and a functional-conflict model) that explain its genesis, and calls for research to study inexpressiveness in a situational context. It is clear that he views male inexpressiveness as a negative quality, as he suggests ways that men may be encouraged out of it. Hunt (1993) finds expressiveness to be positively correlated with positive affect intensity, whether among males or females in her study of college students. For example, the person who is moderately sociable may feel contentment, while a more nurturing and sympathetic individual could feel elation or joy. She sees expressiveness not as a sex-role issue but as a quality reflecting adaptive personality traits in either sex. Walter, it would appear, was in a state beyond commonly seen male inexpressiveness. He gave the impression of not feeling emotion. Yussef gave the impression of having very strong controls on his emotions. Those strong controls seemed to have helped him with bereavement, but they may cost him the experience of very strong positive emotions as well.

Findings

The sudden deaths were somewhat more problematic in terms of regrets and guilt getting in the way of recovery. Particularly for the younger men, there was a sense of having lost the future with their wives. Early grief was experienced physically in sleep disturbances and sometimes in loss of appetite. The passage of time helps the process of recovery, as does religious faith. Having competence in life skills or learning new skills helps the process of recovery. So does remarriage, but remarriage brings with it the likelihood of experiencing the loss of a spouse again. Depression hinders recovery and contributes to feelings of regret. Individuals have choices to make about recovery. Some men see that; some do not. Depression blocks the ability to see and make choices. Social support helps the process of recovery, but it can also hinder.

These older men were able to express a full range of emotions, including tears relating to the death of wife. However, great variability in expressiveness was observed. Extremes in inexpressiveness may be pathological or may be a personal style that has developed as a way of handling emotions different from the norm. The men tended not to express worries about health.

REFERENCES

Balswick, J. (1971). The inexpressive male: A tragedy of American society. *The Family Coordinator, 20*(4), 331–336.

Balswick, J. (1988). *The inexpressive male.* Lexington, MA: Lexington Books.

Calhoun, L. G. & Tedeschi, R. G. (1998). Posttraumatic growth: Future directions. In R. G. Tedeschi, C. L. Park, & L. G. Calhoun (Eds.), *Posttraumatic growth: Positive changes in the aftermath of crisis* (pp. 215–238). Mahwah, NJ: Lawrence Erlbaum.

Cantor, N. & Norem, J. K. (1989). Defensive pessimism and stress and coping. *Social Cognition, 7,* 92–112.

Cooper, D. E. & Holmstrom, R. W. (1984). Relationship between alexithymia and somatic complaints in a normal sample. *Psychotherapy and Psychosomatics, 41,* 20–24.

Doka, K. J. (1996). Sudden loss: The experiences of bereavement. In K. J. Doka (Ed.), *Living with grief after sudden loss* (pp. 11–15). Bristol, PA: Taylor & Francis.

Frankl, V. E. (1992). *Man's search for meaning: An introduction to logotherapy* (4th ed.). Boston, MA: Beacon Press.

Glick, I. O., Weiss, R. S., & Parkes, C. M. (1974). *The first year of bereavement.* New York: Wiley.

Goodhart, D. E. (1986). The effects of positive and negative thinking on performance in an achievement situation. *Journal of Personality and Social Psychology, 51,* 117–124.

Hunt, M. G. (1993). Expressiveness does predict well-being. *Sex Roles, 29* (3/4), 147–169.

Janoff-Bulman, R. (1992). *Shattered assumptions: Towards a new psychology of trauma.* New York: Free Press.

Johnson, C. L. & Barer, B. M. (1997). *Life beyond 85 years: The aura of survivorship.* New York: Springer Publishing.

Kilmartin, C. T. (2000). *The masculine self* (2nd ed). Boston: McGraw Hill.

Lehman, D. R., Wortman, C. B., & Williams, A. F. (1987). Long-term effects of losing a spouse or child in a motor vehicle crash. *Journal of Personality and Social Psychology, 52,* 218–231.

Lopata, H. Z. (1993). The support systems of American urban widows. In M. S. Stroebe, W. Stroebe, & R. O. Hansson (Eds.), *Handbook of bereavement* (pp. 381–396). New York: Cambridge University Press.

Lund, D. A., Caserta, M. S., & Dimond, M. F. (1993). Spousal bereavement in later life. In M. S. Stroebe, W. Stroebe, & R. O. Hansson (Eds.), *Handbook of bereavement* (pp. 240–254). New York: Cambridge University Press.

Lund, D. A., Redburn, D. E., Juretich, M. S., & Caserta, M. S. (1989). Resolving problems implementing bereavement self-help groups. In D. A. Lund (Ed.), *Older bereaved spouses: Research with practical applications* (pp. 203–216). New York: Hemisphere Publishing.

Lundin, T. (1984). Morbidity following sudden and unexpected bereavement. *The British Journal of Psychiatry, 144,* 84–88.

Mace, N. L. & Rabins, P. V. (1999). *The 36-hour day.* Baltimore, MD: The Johns Hopkins University Press.

McCrae, R. R. & Costa, P. T., Jr. (1993). Psychological resilience among widowed men and women: A 10-year follow-up of a national sample. In M. S. Stroebe, W. Stroebe, & R. O. Hansson (Eds.), *Handbook of bereavement* (pp. 196–207). New York: Cambridge University Press.

McMillen, J. C. (1999). Better for it: How people benefit from adversity. *Social Work, 44*(5), 455–468.

Middleton, W., Raphael, B., Martinek, N., & Misso, V. (1993). Pathological grief reactions. In M. S. Stroebe, W. Stroebe, & R. O. Hansson (Eds.), *Handbook of bereavement* (pp. 44–61). New York: Cambridge University Press.

Nemiah, J. C., Freyberger, H., & Sifneos, P. E. (1976). Alexithymia: A view of the psychosomatic process. In O. Hill (Ed.), *Modern trends in psychosomatic medicine* (pp. 430– 439). London: Butterworths.

Neugarten, B. L. (1968). The awareness of middle age. In B. L. Neugarten (Ed.), *Middle age & aging; A reader in social psychology* (pp. 93–98). Chicago: University of Chicago Press.

Ornish, D. (1997). *Love and survival: The scientific basis for the healing power of intimacy.* New York: HarperCollins.

Parkes, C. M. (1975). Determinants of outcome following bereavement. *Omega, 6,* 303–323.

Pine, V. R. (1996). Social psychological aspects of disaster death. In K. J. Doka (Ed.), *Living with grief after sudden loss* (pp. 103–116). Bristol, PA: Taylor & Francis.

Roach, M. J. & Kitson, G. C. (1989). Impact of forewarning on adjustment to widowhood and divorce. In D. A. Lund (Ed.), *Older bereaved spouses: Research with practical applications* (pp. 185–202). New York: Hemisphere Publishing.

Sanders, C. M. (1989). *Grief: The mourning after.* New York: Wiley.

Scheier, M. F. & Carver, C. S. (1985). Optimism, coping, and health: Assessment and implications of generalized outcome expectancies. *Health Psychology, 4*(3), 219–247.

Scheier, M. F. & Carver, C. S. (1993). On the power of positive thinking: The benefits of being optimistic. *Current Directions in Psychological Science, 2*(1), 26–30.

Shuchter, S. R. & Zisook, S. (1993). The course of normal grief. In M. S. Stroebe, W. Stroebe, & R. O. Hansson (Eds.), *Handbook of bereavement* (pp. 23–43). New York: Cambridge University Press.

Showers, C. (1992). The motivational and emotional consequences of considering positive or negative possibilities for an upcoming event. *Journal of Personality and Social Psychology, 63,* 474–484.

Sifneos, P. E. (1972). *Short-term psychotherapy and emotional crisis.* Cambridge, MA: Harvard University Press.

Stroebe, W. & Stroebe, M. S. (1993). The impact of spousal bereavement on older widows and widowers. In M. S. Stroebe, W. Stroebe, & R. O. Hansson (Eds.), *Handbook of bereavement* (pp. 208–226). New York: Cambridge University Press.

Stylianos, S. K. & Vachon, M. L. S. (1993). The role of social support in bereavement. In M. S. Stroebe, W. Stroebe, & R. O. Hansson (Eds.), *Handbook of bereavement* (pp. 397–410). New York: Cambridge University Press.

Taylor, G. J. (1984). Alexithymia: Concept, measurement, and implications for treatment. *American Journal of Psychiatry, 141*(6), 725–732.

Tedeschi, R. G. & Calhoun, L. G. (1995). *Trauma and transformation.* Thousand Oaks, CA: Sage.

Van den Hoonaard, D. K. (1994). Paradise lost: Widowhood in a Florida retirement community. *Journal of Aging Studies, 8,* 121–132.

Wortman, C. B. & Silver, R. C. (1989). The myths of coping with loss. *Journal of Consulting and Clinical Psychology, 57*(3), 349–357.

Wortman, C. B., Silver, R. C., & Kessler, R. C. (1993). The meaning of loss and adjustment to bereavement. In M. S. Stroebe, W. Stroebe, & R. O. Hansson (Eds.), *Handbook of bereavement* (pp. 349–366). New York: Cambridge University Press.

8

Living Alone

Nearly every widowed man has some experience living alone. Even if he remarries, he spends some time alone before entering the new relationship. This chapter surveys our respondents' functioning in a number of activities related to daily living, and considers areas that are often of concern to persons living on their own: their finances and their health. Disabled persons living on their own have to manage still another layer of challenges; we take an in-depth look at the circumstances of five men in the study with severe mobility impairments.

Daily Life as a Man Living Alone

We asked each man to tell us what a typical day was like for him. Some men, such as George, whose volunteer activities are described in the generativity section, were very scheduled. But most of the men were not. The following descriptions present some variety of busyness, but they show the men to have time on their hands. Jacob described his typical weekday:

> Yeah, daily routine, I can say, it's very simple, I get up between 5:30 and 6:00. It takes me about an hour to shave, to shower, to do this. At 9 o'clock I have classes. Of course, I have a short breakfast at home. Then I leave for the campus, and I meet colleagues and so on, drink coffee and so on. Then I come home, have my meal here. I never eat out. Because I don't know, the meal, then in the afternoon, I go to my second home, that's the library, where I devote much time, because they have all the books and so on. I'm sort of accepted by the librarians; they have known me now for years and years. They have accepted me as a kind of second librarian, you see, so I can go behind [the counter], and I see what's

> going on, and I schmooze them, and they have coffee. I've made friendships over the years, and then, eventually I come home. I study a good deal. One thing I must say also that attracts me to the library, amongst other things, they have the newspapers. I'm a cosmopolitan, so I read, like other people read the Bible every day, I read The New York Times every day, because I'm much interested in what goes on in Israel, in Palestine. That's part of my alter ego, as it were.

Jacob did not eat out because he was trying to maintain a Kosher diet, but for some reason was reluctant to say so in the interview. He had minimal cooking skills. He said his mother would not permit him in the kitchen; it would have been "nonboyish." His menus were monotonous, but he said that kept him from eating too much. Craig had been inclined to stay at home before his wife died. He did go to the local senior center, but indicated that sitting at home was a problem he developed easily:

> It's just I've got to force myself [to get out of the house]. [My wife] forced me to do it, 'cause I'd sit and watch, I like cowboy shows, and she'd let me sit awhile and I'd see two or three of them and she'd turn the TV off and say, "Come on. Let's do something." And then we'd do something. But I had to force myself to not watch TV. I've got back in the habit now. I got home at 12:30 and I've been watching TV ever since.

Clyde visited his companion for weeks at a time, and he would go out with an adult child many days, but he described this routine for his days alone:

> Well, I tell you what. When you're gone, and nobody's around, I'll just drive up to the store, and they got a place I can have a cup of coffee and doughnut, and if there is anybody there that will talk to you. If they don't, I know my way back home. The mail will be running pretty soon; then I have to check the mail.

TASKS OF DAILY LIVING

Lund, Caserta, and Dimond (1993) found older men "to be deficient in a predictable set of skills, including cooking, shopping, and housecleaning" (p. 246). Those who had learned new skills during bereavement reported feeling better about themselves, more independent and better able to get along with others; being competent around the house also helped them deal with their grief. Gass (1989) advised those who would help widowers to encourage the development of new roles and skills.

As we reported in the Caregiving chapter, some men did know how to cook, clean house, and do laundry before they had to care for an ill wife. Some of them were taught these skills in childhood, some learned in the military, and some said they had always helped their wives. Arnold said neither his military training nor his caregiving duties made any difference in his current housekeeping. "I get lax," he said. "Sometimes I don't make the bed for 2 days." He said his wife was an excellent housekeeper and, in comparison, "When I look at the stuff that I'm doing around here, I'm nothin'!" Robert said he was accustomed to his wife's cleanliness standards and he liked to keep the house that way too, but he was an exception. Most of the men were haphazard about housekeeping. They did not have a standard of excellence in that regard, probably because a clean house was not important to a man's sense of himself. Earl described his housekeeping before he remarried, "I wasn't great, but I wasn't terrible." Twenty of the men had a hired cleaning person come in; a few others had help from family members. Charles said, "I don't employ anyone else to [clean the apartment]." Then he added with a laugh, "Don't look too closely at it!" It was not unusual to encounter clutter and a little dust when we interviewed a man in his home, but none of the living units was badly kept and many were quite orderly. In the Saying Goodbye chapter we addressed the matter of decor unchanged from the time when the couple lived together. Whether out of sentiment or lack of interest in decorating, men who still lived where they had lived with their wives had not redecorated.

Cooking was a topic on which every man could comment. Devoutly religious Conner exclaimed, "The Lord forbid that I even attempt it!" He ate frozen dinners and other prepared foods. Clyde said, "I can burn a few things," but he went to his favorite restaurant once or twice a day. Walter referred to himself as a "gourmet microwave cook." Soups were a favorite dish for many of the men to prepare: Earl made goulash, Harry vegetable soup, Clyde chili, Benjamin fish chowder, Michael different kinds of soup, and Claude made the gumbo his mother taught him to make.

Some of the men acted slightly offended when asked about their cooking ability. Cordell said, "It's not unusual for a man to cook. I can cook." George said, "If anybody else can do it, I can do it." Some of the men were accomplished cooks. Yussef specialized in dishes using Middle Eastern spices. Karl had owned a restaurant; Frank was in demand to cook for crowd events. Henrik owned a grocery store and said, "Anyone can [cook]." Sy owned a grocery store and said, "I don't bother half the time. I just grab something." Bruce planned meals for a week, using recipes given to him by his wife and a few more that he found on his own. In summary, the men ranged in cooking ability from those who could prepare almost nothing to those who could make delicious meals. Seven of the men learned from their mother; Arch said his father taught him. All but one of these eight men seemed very comfortable and competent with cooking. The eighth, Bill, said he had learned from his mother, but "my cooking is not that good. I like to bake." Those who had learned to cook when their wives were ill were mixed in their enthusiasm for cooking. Some seemed to have that sense of competence that Lund, Caserta, and Dimond (1993) found in their respondents, but others were just getting by. Al said he bought just what he thought he was going to need. "I can open a can. I can microwave. I can make a good chocolate milkshake."

Laundry was handled in a variety of ways. Some men said they had a regular day to do laundry. Arch, Bill, Bruce, and Kenneth had learned to wash clothes when they were young and felt quite competent doing laundry. Al said he went to the laundry room when the basket of dirty clothes was full. A few men said someone came in to do their laundry, but most of the men who had hired a cleaning person did their own laundry. Daughters did the laundry for four of the men. George said he did the washing but had someone come in to do the ironing. Yussef said he sent his laundry out.

Most of the men did not mention household paperwork such as paying the bills and writing letters. Some commented that they had been the one who always paid the bills so doing it was nothing new. Earl said he had "picked it up and enjoyed it [after my wife died]." But Claude, also new to paperwork, said that he was overwhelmed by it. Art lamented the deterioration of his signature, which at one time had been "a very fine hand, an excellent business-like signature." Now his checks were written by a hired secretary and he signed them as best he could with arthritic hands.

RESPONDENTS' CURRENT HEALTH

They had been the caregivers to ill wives, but they had health problems too. Even though many of the men were active and in relatively good health, no one was problem free. Some of the men had been ill before their wives died. Others had become ill since then. We open this section on the health of our respondents with statements made by three of the men.

Craig at age 73:

I've had six strokes. I had a stroke in, let's see, '95 was the last one. It was a full-blown one and I was in the hospital and all of them were having a fit because I wanted to get home with [my wife]; she was sick here. She was staying by herself. It took me almost a year to get back. I had to walk with a walker. Then I got a lung infection and blood infection, and I went in the hospital, and they gave me large doses of antibiotics, and it brought me back, but I've had 34 TIA attacks, which is just a ministroke.

Carlo at age 94:

After about 55, things really start to change. I would always help people. Never even had to ask me, I would just lend a hand. I cut the grass for people, and I would buy salt in the winter. . . . Until about a year or two ago, when I was still walking, I still would go out there and shovel. Now I can't anymore. I can't even walk to go with my daughter shopping. A couple of times I did fall. I didn't want to be disabled, and then she would have to take care of me totally. I don't want that to happen. I do the best I can. Every time I get up she runs to me. I can never do anything alone anymore.

Robert at age 78:

At this stage of the game, I think one of the biggest things that concerns me is health; when you have health problems at this stage, and you have no one here, you're pretty dead in the water if you need help. Just a year ago I had undergone heart surgery, open heart surgery. The stepson, he did come down and spend about three or four weeks with me when I came out of the nursing home. . . . I got over that [heart surgery] fabulously, but I've developed macular degeneration in one eye. It's no handicap yet. It's a progressive type problem, and I'm very apprehensive about if it reaches a stage where I can't drive, things like that, then what do I do? . . . If you've got somebody, if your wife was here or vice versa, it's a little bit different. With her, I was able to turn around and take care of her. Now there is nobody here to take care of me, if that happens.

These statements represent three of the themes we found in the men's stories relating to their own health: (a) concerns about ability to give care, including "What if I die first?" (b) worries and regrets about loss of vitality and independence, and (c) worries about coping with illness and disability alone. In the following section on disabilities, we look at how five of the most disabled men—Richard, Curly, Carlo, Art, and Ned—managed their daily lives. In this section, we look at the illnesses and conditions that the men as a group faced.

Our respondent, Art, insisted that the study was worth little without a thorough medical examination as part of the data picture. We explored in depth the topic of current health with each man, but did not include medical exams as part of the research design. As with all other topics, we relied on the man's own description and perspective to inform us of his health situation. The self-reports always seemed freely given. A few men delayed telling about, or minimized, their reports of serious conditions, but none appeared to try to hide a health condition from the interviewer. Art was correct in perceiving that health is a very important factor in an older person's well-being. Health affects a person's ability to perform daily life activities, exercise, socialize with others, maintain independence, and maintain optimism about the future.

Perceptions of Health

We drew from the data the adjectives used by the men to describe their health. No one used the term "excellent," but one said "extra good" and six more said "good." Two referred to their health as "OK," two as "fair," and four as "poor" or "bad." The remaining 36 men told us about health conditions without assigning a specific term for their general health condition. The ones who felt they were in good health had not had serious health events and were not taking much, if any, medication. The man who referred to his health as extra good had undergone angioplasty about six years earlier; he had a family history of heart problems, and he himself died within a year of the interview. The four who identified their health as OK or fair had experienced some medical events such as prostate problems or high blood pressure. Those identifying themselves as being in poor health were very old and disabled. The youngest in that group was 89 years old and living in a nursing home, unable to walk.

Health Conditions of the Men

High blood pressure was the condition most often reported by the men; 19 mentioned it. One man had had several strokes. Seven reported arthritis, six prostate cancer, and five diabetes. Two men had experienced heart attacks. Nine had heart trouble other than a heart attack; four had had some sort of heart procedure or heart surgery, another had a procedure soon after the interview. Other surgeries were for a carotid bypass, for a ruptured disk, for a hernia, for removal of part of a lung. Six men had cancer other than prostate cancer: leukemia, skin cancer, pancreatic cancer, cancer of the colon, and esophageal and oral cancer.

Neurological disorders included Parkinson's Disease, communicating hydrocephalus, and Charcot-Marie-Tooth Syndrome. These conditions are described briefly in the following section on disabilities. Respiratory conditions included asthma, emphysema, and "weak lungs." Digestive disorders included Crohn's disease, "dumping syndrome," hiatal hernia, and indigestion. Six men had knee problems; two had bad backs. Two had pain from flat feet.

Sensory impairment was also very common. Only degrees of impairment that had become bothersome in daily living are noted here. Seven men had significant vision problems, including low vision, cataracts, glaucoma, and macular degeneration. Six had significant hearing impairment, including deafness and near deafness.

We did not ask about weight, but made note as to whether each man appeared to be overweight, underweight, or average for height and build. Of the 51 men, 28 (55%) were within average range. Fifteen (29%) appeared overweight and eight (16%) appeared underweight.

This is not an exhaustive list of the ailments, conditions, and illnesses that these 51 men faced, but should be sufficient to create a picture of a population dealing with the health problems associated with aging. They had cared for ill wives while they themselves were not in the best of condition, they lived alone with conditions that might call for assistance, and if they remarried, they took these health problems into a new relationship.

Aging and Health Status

We developed a system of categorizing health conditions so as to place the men, given all the conditions listed above and more, along some sort of spectrum of overall healthiness. We realize that our system is not medically valid because we lacked both accurate medical data and the knowledge by which to interpret it. However, it does bring some order to much information given by the men and to our impressions.

None of the men was free from health problems, but 18 of the 51 interviewed (35%) experienced only minimal health difficulties or physical limitations. We categorized their health as "good." This group averaged 74 years of age. Half of the men in the study, numbering 25, had significant health problems or limitations, but they did not appear to be immediately life-threatening, nor did they deprive the men of independent functioning. We categorized them as being in "fair" health. Men who had had life-threatening problems in the past, but seemed healthier and stable at the time of the interview were considered to be in fair health also. Examples would be long-ago heart attacks and cancers in remission. This group averaged 81 years of age, just one year older than the average of the entire sample. We categorized as in "poor" health those men who had had significant heart trouble or strokes or cancer within the past several years. Eight men (about 15%) were in that category. They ranged in age from 73 to 104, averaging 91 years. The 73-year-old was an outlying individual in that group. Their average age with him excluded was 93 years. Old age brings debilitating health losses; these men who were as a group 10 years older than the average of the entire sample had the greatest health problems. In fact, six of the eight were rated as being in declining health as well as poor health at the time of the interview.

The Healthy Men

Even the healthy men were dealing with the physical realities of aging: high blood pressure, prostate problems, declining strength and endurance. None of the men was very athletic. Michael had played tennis but had badly injured his knee. Only a few got regular exercise such as walking or using an exercise bike. More talked about needing exercise. Age did not always correlate with degree of health problems, but the very old were more commonly sedentary and less vigorous than the younger men in our sample.

We saw some attitude patterns in the healthy men: (a) expecting to be healthy today and tomorrow, (b) tending to view their health problems as minor, or to not identify them as problems at all, (c) not wasting time or energy worrying about "what if . . . ?" (d) not limiting activities because of negative possibilities, (e) realistically accepting the current state of their aging process, (f) trying to modify lifestyle (particularly diet) to promote health.

Their attitudes of optimism and accommodation may be due to the good fortune of having good health later in life; however, those attitudes also could represent a life-long approach to living that contributed to lower stress levels and therefore healthier living. Segerstrom, Taylor, Kemeny, and Fahey (1998) suggest an association between optimism and improved immune system functioning. Ornish (1997) proposes a relationship between heart disease and connectedness with others. Our medical data is not sufficient to test his proposal, but it offers an intriguing basis for further study of the health benefits associated with comfortable personal relationships. We had some very old respondents whose hearts certainly seemed to have been nurtured by loving relationships.

Use of Tobacco and Alcohol

Tobacco

In the early interviews we did not ask about use of tobacco; we observed who was currently using tobacco and found only two men doing so: Leroy smoking cigarettes and Conner smoking a pipe. Also, Yussef had a pipe collection and said that he smoked once in a while. We might have decided that we were interviewing a basically nonsmoking population. However, one or two men recounted how they had quit smoking, and we realized that we should have been asking about smoking history. In subsequent interviews and in follow-ups when we could, we inquired about smoking history and made this discovery: it was unusual to find a man who never used tobacco. Most of them had smoked cigarettes; many started smoking while in the armed services, if not before. Only one man was identified to us as a former tobacco chewer. They quit using tobacco mainly because they had decided it was not good for them. Some mentioned the U.S. Surgeon General's report in the early 1960s, while others said they had come to that conclusion on their own. For the most part, they claimed to have stopped "cold turkey" and not to have been bothered with cravings to any great degree. Some of them had wives who smoked and apparently could not give up the habit. A couple of the wives died of conditions directly related to smoking. One man said with some agitation, "My wife smoked 'til her dying day." Another man grieved over his son's smoking cigarettes when he himself had been a cigar and pipe smoker until his sixties.

Because we were not able to obtain tobacco use history on all of the men, we cannot draw conclusions. However, some patterns are suggested. Most of the men and some of their wives started smoking at a time when smoking was not considered a health hazard and was much promoted as a relaxing and sociable activity. Smoking prevalence peaked in the 1940s and 1950s for American men, and in the 1960s for American women (American Lung Association, 2001). Most of the men decided that smoking was not good for their health and so quit on their own, some in response to publicity about the hazards of smoking. Nearly half of American people who had ever smoked were former smokers in 1995. Rates of quitting were higher for men than for women (American Lung Association). Many of our respondents had relatives who died of smoking-related illnesses; the tobacco-related toll was enumerated for the interviewer in the cases of Art, Bruce, and Karl.

One tentative conclusion is that older men who quit using tobacco products are the survivors of their generation. Their reported ease of stopping tobacco use may indicate a lower level of nicotine dependence, which may be the key to who is able to break the habit and experience the health benefits of doing so. If so, studies on individual differences in addiction potential are critically important. Discovering how to counteract the addiction potential could be the key to healthier, longer lives for many people. The *10 Leading Causes of Death* report (National Center for Injury Prevention and Control, 2001) lists heart disease, malignant neoplasms, cerebrovascular incidents, and respiratory ailments such as bronchitis, emphysema, asthma, pneumonia, and influenza as the leading causes of death for males age 45–85. The American Cancer Society (2001) lists 11 types of cancers as smoking related.

Alcohol

Light to moderate social drinking or abstaining were the most common patterns relating to alcohol use among our respondents. *Alcohol Alert* (U.S. Department of Health & Human Services, 1998) suggests that "because alcohol-related illnesses are a major cause of premature death, excess mortality among heavy drinkers may leave a surviving older population who consumes less alcohol" (p. 1). The same publication reports that some research shows high rates of alcohol abuse in older persons admitted to hospitals and notes that late-onset alcohol problems can develop in retirement communities where social drinking is the norm. In our sample, abstaining often was associated with religious denominations that frowned upon drinking. Social drinking during marriage often involved a relaxing drink with the wife according to a comfortable daily routine or drinking as part of an evening with friends. With these pleasant circumstances terminated by the death of the wife, what happens to the drinking pattern of the older widower? A study of the drinking patterns of bereaved older persons (Valanis, Yeaworth, and Mullis, 1987) found that 57% had not changed their use of alcohol, while 16% increased their use and another 16% decreased their use. The study found that males tended to increase their drinking, while females decreased theirs. Lower-income persons and depressed persons tended to increase their drinking. We obtained only self-reports, but none of the men reported drinking more after loss of the wife. In situations where we had conversations with relatives, no one mentioned alcohol consumption as a problem for their brother, father, or grandfather.

Michael offered an alcoholic beverage to the interviewer, which seemed in keeping with his gracious and sophisticated style. After widowhood, Louis decided to continue entertaining as he and his wife had done. He served cocktails and hors d'oeuvres that he had made, then took friends out to dinner. Bill described his home as the family's party house. Trying various brands and types of beer was a weekly event; he mixed drinks for everyone on special occasions. These activities were the norm for his family; no one described this drinking-oriented socializing as problematic.

To be sure, there were men in our study who used alcohol in ways that were problematic. Don was a recovering alcoholic and the only man in the study to admit also having used illegal drugs. He said he had been sober for more than a decade and loved life being sober; he credited his third wife, who was deceased, with turning his life around. Leroy said he did not drink, but a social services caseworker said that he would visit bars, where others would take his money when he had been drinking. Since he did not admit drinking, we could not determine whether he had altered his use of alcohol since his second wife's death. Sam said that he had drunk too much at one point in his life. He described drinking a six-pack of beer on a weekend, which did not seem to the interviewer to be an excess amount, but he insisted that drinking had interfered with his life, and so he had quit. Russell said that he could not have survived his bereavement if he had not met his second wife. He said, "I would have probably been a drunk or something, and I don't even like to drink. Really, I don't. . . . I probably would have done it to get [my wife's death] off my mind." He had referred to times earlier in his life when he did a bit of drinking, but said that he did not drink at the present time. He said he and his wife might share a beer in the summertime, but that was the extent of his consumption. When Cordell described his son's death, he said that the son shared many of Cordell's faults. The first fault he named for his son was heavy drinking, but Cordell did not mention heavy drinking as a problem in his own life.

Relying on self-reports, we make no presumption of having received completely accurate information about drinking behaviors. Leroy was pleased to have someone ask him about his life, but he denied smoking when there was a smell of cigarette smoke in his apartment. He denied drinking when the referral source had said the behavior did indeed occur. He smiled slyly at many questions and at times spontaneously exclaimed that everything he had said was the truth. We found no other men to be so sly, but also understand that it is common for persons to minimize reports of behaviors that might be judged negatively. While in the home environment of each man, we were observant for signs of alcohol use and did not find them displayed openly. We did not look in cabinets or the refrigerator.

We spoke with one man who was happy to spend time visiting with the two of us, but he refused to sign a consent form to be part of our study. So our conversation with him did not become part of the data for this study, and he is not counted among our respondents. However, his daily routine must be noted, as it represents a pattern that we did not see in any of our respondents. This man had been widowed for more than 20 years. His daily routine revolved around his drinking. He did what he needed to do in the mornings, prepared and ate his lunch, and then spent the afternoon drinking. He would then emerge in his front yard around 4 p.m., his drinking finished for the day. We visited with him in the morning and again when he came out in the afternoon. In the later visit, his speech was slurred and his conversation disconnected. His rigid daily schedule seemed designed to keep his drinking under some degree of control; he was matter of fact about his schedule and felt that he was functioning very well.

LIVING WITH A DISABILITY

We have dealt with the health of our respondents earlier in this chapter. Age, we have seen, brings increasing health problems. Indeed, with respondents age 58–104, we have found none of the men completely free from health problems. Many were leading very active lives anyway. At the point when a health condition begins to limit a person's daily functioning or his ability to choose his activities freely, we refer to the person as disabled. The Americans with Disabilities Act of 1990 (Public Law 101-336) defines disability in an individual as "a physical or mental impairment that substantially limits one or more of the major life activities" (Office of the Federal Register, National Archive & Records Administration, 1991, pp. 328–9). Usually, such conditions limit a person in the areas of caring for oneself, working, and mobility. Most of our respondents had retired from their occupations, but the categories of caring for oneself and ability to get around from place to place were certainly relevant to their daily lives. Also, as we saw in the consideration of generativity, volunteer work often replaces employment for an older man; disability may curtail that meaningful and enjoyable part of life.

In this section, we present five respondents with significant disabling conditions. In losing their wives, they had lost not only their life companion but also the person who could have assisted them as they dealt with their disabilities in old age. We were particularly interested in their social support systems in the absence of a spouse, their living arrangements, and their ability to hire needed services. Although we had not decided in advance that mobility impairment was a necessary component in our definition of disability, ability to walk was affected in all of the cases. All of the men used some form of mobility aid. Significant hearing or vision loss was present for four of the five men.

Descriptions of the Respondents

Richard

Losses of both wife and only son, added to health limitations, left Richard with a pervasive melancholy. Yet he had a basic entrenched optimism. He searched for meaning in life in an intelligent and philosophical way (looking for universal truths being revealed in his own life). His spirituality was active and independent, tied to his personal philosophical quest rather than to a denomination's practices. He kept as active and involved as his rheumatoid arthritis would allow, and was very skilled at creating friendly relationships. He knew that his physical abilities were and would always be extremely limited. He maintained independence but accepted help that was needed. When a book slipped to the floor from a stack of materials on his kitchen table, he jokingly told the interviewer not to pick it up, as the cleaning lady needed something to do when she came.

Curly

His lack of mobility and his residence in a nursing home gave Curly too much time to sit and think about the things that had gone wrong in his life; much of it he blamed on himself. He had many regrets about his whole life, lamenting that his father did not seem to care for him, that he had not been good enough to his wife, that he did not have a good relationship with his son. He was much more animated during family visits, but regrets and despair were the hallmarks of his late stage of life.

Carlo

An earthy and self-confident man, Carlo was frustrated with his declining abilities. He recognized that his single, live-in daughter was a godsend; her presence allowed him to live in his own home where he was able to be much more comfortable and satisfied than he would have been in a nursing home. He was emotionally expressive on all topics. He lamented having lost contact with his parents and family in Italy. He approached life with an uncomplicated Catholic faith and a sentimental devotion to love, to the memory of his wife, and to his family.

Art

Communicating hydrocephalus is a brain disorder caused by blockage of the flow of cerebrospinal fluid. Brain tissue is damaged or destroyed by the excessive fluid. In Art the condition caused a gait disturbance that necessitated a walking aid. Art was frustrated also with memory problems and with arthritic fingers which no longer allowed him to sign his name or use a computer. He saw death as a natural process much like going to sleep but lamented the short time he had to learn all there was to know. He was argumentative and opinionated, enjoyed repartee with others and maintained many phone relationships. He lived very comfortably in his own home close to a loving daughter and son-in-law who brought him gourmet meals and hired the daily help he needed. He was especially proud of his "free wheelie" walker complete with cupholder which allowed him to circulate at social gatherings in his retirement community.

Ned

Charcot-Marie-Tooth Syndrome is an inherited neurological disorder causing the loss of normal use of the extremities. Ned had a "slapping" gait and his legs could not support him without the aid of a walker. He was accepting of his limitations and felt he was doing well for his advanced age. He remained very sociable and was able to participate in lively and intelligent conversation. Cheerful and well-supported by a loving family, he had lived so long that he felt grateful and perhaps even amazed by his good fortune in such a long life. Indeed, life seemed to have gotten better as he came into centenarian celebrity status. He had a comfortable and sustaining Christian belief in an afterlife.

Patterns Emerging in Disability Examples

While age was not considered in our selections for the subsample of disabled widowers, it turned out that the men in this group were among the oldest in our study, all being over age 85. It appears that to live a long life is to face disability in some form. These men were widowed at very old ages after many decades of marriage. None of them had remarried. We consistently found the oldest men in our overall study refusing to think about remarriage for reasons of their advanced age and their perceived poor health, so we were not surprised to find these very old and disabled widowers remaining single.

On the other hand, we found these men compensating for the loss of a spouse by developing other relationships through which they could obtain needed support. For Ned the support system was a nearby large and loving family. For Richard, a childless widower, his personal graciousness and unassuming intellect drew others to him. A much younger neighbor woman cooked his breakfast and ate with him each morning. Art had a well-to-do daughter and son-in-law providing services that allowed him to remain in his own home. Carlo had the intense loyalty of his middle-aged unmarried daughter, for whom he expressed great appreciation during the interview. Curly was an exception. He was filled with regrets over his shortcomings and his losses, with good reason, his family members said, for he had been very impatient and verbally abusive to his wife. His family visited him, but he was living his final years in a nursing home. The contrasting situations of Carlo and Curly show the importance of having one very supportive person being willing and able to take on caregiving. Carlo had that person and continued to live in his own home receiving loving care. Curly did not have that person and was in a nursing home with competent, but not emotionally involved, staff attending him.

An optimistic or pessimistic outlook did not seem to relate to current health or physical ability, but seemed to have been developed so early and so naturally that its course could not be recalled or described by the respondent. Richard, for example, had suffered the accidental death of his only child and had been severely depressed for a year following the death of his wife. Yet his remarks about his present life and about the human condition in general were decidedly optimistic. When asked how he had developed this optimism, he replied, "I don't know. I have just always felt that things would turn out well." The person who appeared satisfied looking back on his life was one who seemed comfortable with himself and who had the personal qualities to attract needed support from others.

Erikson (1974) described the psychosocial crisis of old age as ego integrity vs. despair. In our small selection of disabled widowers we have textbook examples of both. Erikson would have described Richard and Ned as being in a state of ego integrity. Both men looked back on their lives with satisfaction and with self-understanding. Life had its problems, but it had been good. They were glad they had lived it as they had. They were ready to accept death as the final stage of life's journey. Curly, with similar clarity, demonstrated the negative conclusion to a life's story; he was in despair. He had been controlling, self-centered, and judgmental, according to family members. Reviewing his life filled Curly with regrets which he had no way to redress. Family members encouraged him to forget the bad and dwell on the good things that had happened, but he could not do that.

Financial circumstances varied greatly within our subsample. Having adequate finances allowed for more comforts and conveniences in disabled old age. For those needing assistance, having the means to hire help allowed them to remain more independent. Art and Richard were able to afford comfortable and independent housing. Ned's resources were modest, but the travel trailer dwelling allowed his family to have him close by and to help him financially by hooking up his utilities to their home. The government supports financially needy older people with nursing home care funded through Medicaid, but does not support them living in their own homes. Curly's own resources were completely expended on his nursing home care, and then he qualified for Medicaid assistance to stay in the nursing home. Carlo was able to live at home because his modest dwelling had been paid for long ago, because he lived a simple life requiring few purchases, and because his live-in help was an unpaid daughter.

Plans for the Future

Richard indicated he would accept whatever level of care he needed. If that eventually would be a nursing home, he would make the most of that situation. Carlo would stay at home with his daughter caring for him; she had worked in a nursing home and could provide the same level of care that he would receive in a facility. Curly would remain in the nursing home where he was residing. Ned would move into a son or daughter's home as he needed more care; help would be hired by the family as needs arose. Art would continue to be cared for at home by personnel hired by his daughter and son-in-law; they would continue their daily visits and loving attention to him.

Themes in Dealing with Disability

Several other men in the study were dealing with disabilities. In looking at all of those men, we were able to see additional patterns in the ways that men have adapted to disabling conditions. We categorized men who were handling disability or serious illness fairly well in three ways: (a) the optimists who have always had a positive outlook on life and regain it even after tremendous loss, (b) the "guys with gusto" who enjoy life to the fullest, even when that is not as full as it used to be, and (c) the survivors who faced hardships early in life and have gritty determination not to get beaten down by any difficulty. Richard and Eldon were optimists; that belief in the positive came back no matter what they faced. Carlo and Ned were adventurers. Carlo had made a new life for himself in America as a young man; Ned had traveled to remote areas of the western United States, relishing every experience that could challenge him. They both still had that impulse to get all they could from the adventure called Life, even though they were keenly aware of their present limitations. Harry and Joe were survivors. Both had experienced difficult childhoods, during which they had developed a determination to get through it. Joe said he had decided to be positive and enjoy joking because he had enough negativity as a child.

The hallmarks of handling disability well include: (a) being realistic about limitations and slowing down, (b) being optimistic, doing whatever one could do in the present, not shutting down because of negative thinking, (c) accepting approaching death while still enjoying life, (d) finding meaning in life by continuing to have something to think about and do that seems significant, and (e) being able to marshal needed resources by problem-solving.

CURRENT FINANCES

We asked each man about his sources of income in retirement. We did not ask to be told amounts, but a few of the men told us nevertheless. Many others said their pensions were small, without giving an amount. We also observed the surroundings of our respondents as we interviewed them in their homes. These observations gave us some indication of economic resources, as did many of the comments made by the respondents that did not directly relate to income.

Sources of Income

Social Security was the bedrock of retirement income for the men who were U.S. citizens and were old enough to qualify for Social Security payments. Three of the men were citizens of other countries—Canada and India—and had income from their home countries. Three other men were not yet eligible to collect Social Security.

A pension from employment was the next most common type of retirement income. However, most of the men said their pension checks were small. For some, the pension plan did not begin until they were close to retirement. Two men spoke of pension checks of less than $10 for this reason. In other cases, low salaries accrued low benefits and those amounts did not withstand years of inflation.

The most advantageous pension situation resulted from a mixed employment career where one was able to retire from one job with a pension and then take another job with a different pension system. Retirement from the military or from a public school system opened opportunities for a second career and a second substantial pension. Military pensions and/or military disability benefits were sources of income for three men. Three men were retired teachers; one had another career with another pension plan.

Some men had worked their careers with no pension plan. Some of them had been self-employed. Others said they had tried to get their employer to start a pension plan but were not successful. Frank said that his employer had told him to put something away out of every paycheck for his retirement since there was no pension. He and his wife developed a regular savings plan which had given him financial security in retirement. He also finally got a pension plan at work.

Private savings were another source of retirement income. Savings had been invested in a number of ways. Government bonds, money market accounts, IRAs, and certificates of deposit were commonly mentioned. Some men spoke knowledgeably about their investment portfolios, while others stayed strictly with one simple investment strategy or turned the investment management task over to a financial advisor. Some closely followed performance of their stocks and had strong opinions about Federal Reserve Board policy.

Real estate holdings provided income for some men and income security for others. For example, Daniel held part ownership in an income-producing property. Conner lived in his own home which had greatly appreciated in value over the years. He did not realize any income from it, but knew that he could sell it to finance nursing home care if that would be needed in the future. Having a paid-for home was a definite financial advantage, and one which many of the men had. Twenty-four lived in the homes they had shared with their deceased wives; not all were paid for but most were.

Inheritance provided income for some men. Cordell had inherited money that his wife had inherited from a relative. Don received an inheritance from his brother. Alvin was troubled by the fact that he had gained a great deal of money in the way of an insurance policy payoff when his wife died. Jerry received a payment and health insurance from his deceased wife's pension plan.

A few of the men were still receiving salaries, although usually small amounts for part- time work. Alvin still worked part-time in the company he owned. Stuart was involved in business ventures. Don and Earl were employed. Jim worked part-time and Terrence earned a very small sum as a local public office holder. Henrik had his own business.

Leroy and Al lived in government subsidized housing, although Al pointed out that he was paying a far larger share of his rent than many of his neighbors in the complex. Harry and Curly were eligible for Medicaid assistance in paying for their nursing home bills. Other men received assistance from family members, usually by living with a son or daughter. Three were living with an adult child; two others were living very close by and receiving significant family support to be able to stay in their own homes.

A new wife usually added substantially to income for the couple. She added Social Security and, in some cases, a pension and investments. Giving up a deceased husband's pension upon remarriage was an issue for couples wanting to begin a life together. Garrett and Stuart married their widowed companions in spite of giving up hundreds of dollars of monthly income; both said that living together without marriage was something they would not consider doing. Clyde and Frank and their companions had decided otherwise. As Clyde said he told his companion:

> I'm going to tell you the facts, what's the best for you. Hold on to your checks because you're not going to have nothing if you get married. . . . What if I'd die in the next year, or next few days? You're taking something away from yourself that you've earned four times. If you give it up, you won't get it back.

She was persuaded by his argument, saying a man wasn't worth $500 a month to her. Clyde was pleased that she had accepted his reasoning because he did not want another woman infringing upon his domain anyway. By not marrying, he could simply go on visiting her when it was mutually agreeable. Frank said that neither he nor his companion felt it was worth her giving up her deceased husband's substantial military pension in order to marry. They lived in different states and could not agree on where they would reside together.

Money Issues

Social Security has had a significant effect on poverty. The economic status of older people improved dramatically between 1967 and 1992. . . . with "large increases in mean Social Security benefits . . . important in the increase in the total income of the elderly" (Radner, 1995). Radner reports that the poverty rate for older people fell sharply between 1967 and 1992, while the poverty rate for younger age groups rose. A National Academy of Sciences panel recommended computing poverty rates in ways that would more accurately reflect the resources available and the expenses encountered by households with marginal income (Olsen, 1999). For example, by official methods of calculation developed in the 1960s, 10.5% of persons age 65 and older live in poverty. Under the experimental calculation, taking account in particular the medical out-of-pocket expenses of the elderly, the percentage living in poverty is 17.3% (p. 3). Older women have higher poverty rates than older men, and the oldest age groups are the poorest among adults (U.S. Bureau of the Census, 1996).

The positive effects of Social Security can be clearly seen in the situations of our respondents. Some of them had been raised in families that had very little in the way of resources. Some of them worked at jobs that had no pensions or meager pension plans; they worked at salaries that paid only enough to take care of their families at the time. Social Security, usually coupled with a small pension and perhaps some investments based on frugal saving, kept these men out of poverty in their old age. None of the men was living in poor housing at the time of the interview, although Carlo's and Eldon's houses were modest and old. None of the men was going hungry, none lacked appropriate clothing for the weather, and none was ill without health care. The older men seemed attuned to frugality, whatever their present economic circumstances. They were children or young men during the Great Depression and remembered how to manage their money. Jacob referred to his youth in Germany with its rampant inflation between the wars. He said, "We learned to live a spartan life, you know, we cannot waste money." Jacob received a reparation check from Germany each month, as well as the American benefits to which he was entitled.

Medicare was an important resource for health care; some of the men had private insurance to cover the costs that Medicare did not cover. The veterans were eligible for services through the Veterans Administration. Bert said he used the VA facilities and an HMO. As mentioned earlier, the two men in nursing homes received assistance from Medicaid.

Russell was greatly annoyed over financial dealings with one of his children. No other man expressed so much feeling about money matters. Don knew that he had to work because he and his companion had few other resources to support themselves, but he felt confident that things would always work out. Karl, who had no pension since he had been self-employed, worried about having little income in his old age; fortunately, he could live with his son, but he still worried about money. Stuart said he was glad to pay for dinner in order to have company while eating out. Al was reciprocating support with his grandchildren by giving them money in return for the attention and assistance they gave him.

The men seemed to feel that they should use their resources to provide for themselves. Some of them with significant assets had set up trusts and otherwise had made arrangements for their possessions and money to go to younger family members upon their death. However, none seemed to be thinking of providing an inheritance for their children at the expense of their own comfort or current needs. Charles had a trust set up for his daughter, but he was living as he wished in the present. Cordell had devised an elaborate plan by which he would disperse the proceeds of his inheritance from his wife's estate to his children; in return, they were each to agree to send him a letter and a small check each month. His goal, he said, was to "distribute, so I have nothing." Jerry said his goal was to "die broke," referring to a book he had read on the topic of financial planning. He said he did not feel any obligation to leave his children a substantial amount of money.

Findings

Older men vary greatly in their ability to handle life skills such as cooking and taking care of a home. Those who can do these things well feel a sense of competence. Learning skills in childhood facilitates using them in older adulthood.

Older men face health problems that increase as they age. Being able to care for an ill wife, being able to manage independently, and being able to secure help when needed are concerns related to health problems and diminishing physical abilities. Persons with severe disabilities must find ways to accommodate them. Having adequate finances and a good support system are significant factors in living as independently as possible.

Social Security forms a base for retirement income. Pensions and savings put into investments are also common sources of retirement income. The pensions of our respondents were small in most cases. Some men worked all through their careers without earning a pension. Having another job with retirement benefits after having retired early with benefits appears to maximize pension income. Inheritance and paid-for homes are valuable factors for the financial well-being of a retired person. A new wife brings income to a household. However, she may lose a substantial amount of monthly income (her deceased husband's pension) if she remarries. A widowed woman who co-habits does not lose that benefit. Such policy is a disincentive to marriage.

Older men are focused on taking care of themselves financially. We did not hear men say they felt obligated to leave a substantial inheritance to their children. Families provide assistance to older relatives when formal sources of support (such as Social Security and pensions) are not adequate. Some families receive assistance from their older relatives. Frugality seems to have been learned in the Great Depression, even though not every family experienced hard times then, and continues to influence attitudes and habits regarding money.

REFERENCES

American Cancer Society. (2001, January). Tobacco and cancer [on-line]. Available: wysiwyg://291http://www.cancer.org/tobacco/.

American Lung Association. (2001, January). Prevalence based on revised national health interview survey [on-line]. Available: http://www.lungusa.org/data/data_102000.html.

Erikson, E. H. (1974). *Dimensions of a new identity.* New York: Norton.

Gass, K. A. (1989). Health of older widowers: Role of appraisal, coping, resources, and types of spouses's death. In D. A. Lund (Ed.), *Older bereaved spouses: Research with practical applications* (pp. 95–110). New York: Hemisphere Publishing.

Lund, D. A., Caserta, M. S., & Dimond, M. F. (1993). Spousal bereavement in later life. In M. S. Stroebe, W. Stroebe, & R. O. Hansson (Eds.) *Handbook of bereavement* (pp. 240–254). New York: Cambridge University Press.

National Center for Injury Prevention and Control. (2001, January). 10 leading causes of death, United States: 1998, all races, males [on-line]. Available: http://webapp.cdc.gov/cgi- bin/broker.exe?...age2=85%2B&Submit+Request&_debug=0.

Office of the Federal Register, National Archive and Records Administration (1991). *United States statutes at large, 104,* (part1), 328–329.

Olsen, K. A. (1999). Application of experimental poverty measures to the aged. *Social Security Bulletin, 62*(3), 3–19.

Ornish, D. (1997). *Love and survival: The scientific basis for the healing power of intimacy.* New York: HarperCollins.

Radner, D. B. (1995, Winter). Incomes of the elderly and nonelderly, 1967–92. *Social Security Bulletin, 58*(4), 82–97.

Segerstrom, S. C., Taylor, S. E., Kemeny, M. E., & Fahey, J. L. (1998). Optimism associated with mood, coping, and immune change in response to stress. *Journal of Personality and Social Psychology, 74,* 1646–1655.

U.S. Bureau of the Census. (1996). *65+ in the United States.* Current Population Reports, Special Studies, (Publication No. P23-190). Washington, DC: U.S. Government Printing Office.

U.S. Department of Health and Human Services. (1998, April). *Alcohol alert: Alcohol and aging.* (NIAAA Publication No. HE 20.8322:40). Rockville, MD: Author.

Valanis, B., Yeaworth, R. C., & Mullis, M. R. (1987). Alcohol use among bereaved and nonbereaved older persons. *Journal of Gerontological Nursing, 13*(5), 26–32.

9

Remarriage

When we tell someone that our research is on older widowed men, that person almost always says something like, "Oh, they just get married again right away, don't they?" The common belief is that older men remarry quickly; the presumption is that remarriage resolves their grief. Older men do have a statistical advantage in the remarriage market; 13 million men over age 65 in 1992 had approximately 19 million female partners or potential partners in that age category (U. S. Bureau of the Census, 1993). Kuhn, Morhardt, and Monbrod-Framburg (1993) reported the overall marriage rate for older men as six times higher than the marriage rate for older women, reflecting the higher numbers of women and the tendency for men over 65 to marry women under 65. Cleveland & Gianturco (1976) reported that only one-fourth of widowers over age 65 remarry; however, those who remarry do so more quickly than women who remarry. Our remarried respondents all had married women who had been alone longer than they. We found that a few of the men in our study did remarry quickly, but only 17 of the 51 men were remarried.

While being able to remarry quickly may seem to be an advantage for men, there is therefore no "society of widowers" (as there is a society of widows) for the widowed men who do not remarry (Vinick, 1978, p. 360). Berardo (1970) considered aged widowers on their own and painted a dismal picture of their isolation and failures to adapt. Vinick (1978) found widowed men to be more limited than widowed women in relationships with family and friends, less experienced with household management, and having retired, no longer in a familiar setting for being with people. Vinick (1983) found widowers who were still unmarried three years after the death of their wives were ambivalent about marriage. They viewed marriage as inappropriate because of their age, they feared needing care or needing to give care, and they liked their freedom. Over half of these unmarried widowers relieved loneliness with a dating relationship or a nonromantic relationship with a woman.

Loneliness was a feeling that our respondents freely acknowledged. We found most of the men interested in companionship, but they expressed divergent views regarding remarriage. The couples arrangements we documented include: (a) remarriage—17, including three who remarried after the interview, (b) living together without legal marriage—1, (c) sexual relationship but living separately—5, (d) nonsexual companionship, living separately—7, and (e) unstable companionship situation—1.

The men in our study varied in length of widowhood, so we expected there would be changes in interest toward remarriage as the time spent in widowhood lengthened. Actually we found stability in the men's positions on remarriage. Our population had been selected from men who (except for three) had been widowed at least two years. The studies cited earlier show that many widowed men "hook up" rapidly with a woman companion; our study showed that it happens whether or not marriage was the outcome. Thus, the 48 respondents who were two years or more past their loss were in an adjustment stage for the most part beyond acute grieving and had spent time thinking about their futures and getting a sense of their feelings. However, even the three men who were more recently widowed at the time of the interview were able to make clear a position that had not changed at follow-up.

Likewise demonstrating stability, only three of the 40 unmarried men remarried after the interview. One was planning his new marriage at the time of the interview, and it took place a few months later. Another was very anxiously seeking a new spouse; he found her about a year later. The last expressed interest in dating at the time of the interview and married a little more than a year later.

Only a few of the men demonstrated a shift in interest regarding remarriage. Daniel became interested in another marriage when he met a particularly compatible woman. John became interested in companionship and perhaps remarriage after his acute grieving, but he shifted away from that interest as he worried about various negative possibilities. The result was a more cautious man who would probably continue to find reasons not to remarry.

Constructing a Continuum

We constructed a continuum of interest in remarriage representing the positions taken by men in the study. We then extended our construct to illuminate interest in a couples type of arrangement whether or not it involved marriage. The continuum is as follows: (a) desperately needing a new marriage, (b) actively looking for a new marriage, (c) tending toward interest in a new marriage, (d) no inclination either way, (e) tending away from a new marriage, and (f) definitely not interested in a new marriage.

Desperately Needing a New Marriage

The four men who wanted to remarry quickly conveyed a sense of not being whole or all right by themselves. Alvin, perhaps because of a degree of anxiety that might have bothered potential mates, took the longest to remarry: three years. Sy married in one year, Sam in seven and a half months. Russell moved in with his long-ago girlfriend about a month after he was widowed; they married two months later.

Actively Looking for a New Marriage

Seven men were in this category. They were characterized by fairly early recognition that life would be more pleasant and fulfilling if they were not alone. Jim was dating someone from his church at the time of the interview, but that relationship did not last. At follow-up he said he had decided he wanted to remarry and was planning to seek a new wife. Terrence wanted to be married to solve the sadness and loneliness of widowhood. He waited two years, a time span he thought appropriate, and then married. Garrett felt alone and useless so he took a trip that included a visit to his deceased wife's best friend; they married five months after he was widowed.

Tending Toward Interest in a New Marriage

Early in their bereavement, some of the men thought they would not consider remarriage but then became interested in being married again after experiencing the loneliness of life on their own. Eight men were in this category. Two months after his wife's death, Bill told his family that he was going to look for a companion; he ended up with a wife a year later. Malcolm began providing transportation for a widowed neighbor lady, and it turned into a dating relationship that led to marriage about nine months after he was widowed. Stuart, Earl, and Kenneth were more purposeful in their wife-seeking. After considering various factors of importance to them, each developed a plan that finally resulted in finding a new wife. Don was inspired by the sight of a beautiful woman and reminded himself, "I never said after Marty went away it was all over."

No Inclination Either Way

Only four men out of the 51 seemed to have no inclination toward or against remarriage. After being widowed the first time, Daniel was self-sufficient and not particularly thinking of remarrying, but met someone who caused him to start thinking about it. Robert was depressed and had not sorted out any future for himself. Arnold still felt the loss of his wife's presence in their home, but he was giving a woman rides to activities at the senior center. Two years later, he reported being involved with a woman who lived in another city; he said he had no idea if it would lead to marriage; for now, he said, "It's just lovely." Leroy was lonely and bored and said he would like someone to talk to. However, 81 was too old to remarry, he said. If an interested woman had come his way, he might have been interested.

Tending Away From a New Marriage

Reasons varied among the seven men who might have decided to remarry but had come to a firm or fairly firm decision not to do so. Ned and Al were in their 90s when widowed; age and health conditions figured prominently in their considerations. Health conditions affected Craig and Richard; also Craig had a comfortable living arrangement with his daughter, and Richard was very self-sufficient. Charles spoke of many reasons for not remarrying, but his pleasant independence in very old age, along with female companionship available on his terms, made marriage seem like "asking for trouble." Will was close to his daughter and had a steady friendship with a younger woman. (We saw a pattern of men with much younger companions not marrying, which will be discussed later in the chapter.) Michael's early dating attempts were not satisfying; he was highly involved with family. At follow-up he was dating a woman and was very happy about that but said there was no reason to marry at their age.

Definitely Not Interested in a New Marriage

Fourteen out of the 51 respondents were in this category. Age, health, independent spirit, and devotion to the deceased spouse formed the disparate reasons for this very firm position on the subject of remarriage.

The Age Factor

Age alone may be a pivotal factor in consideration of remarriage. The men who said they would not consider remarriage tended to be the older men. While there were individual reasons given for considering or not considering remarriage at any age, we found in general that around age 83, the men began describing themselves as too old or too unhealthy to think about getting married again. Ned at age 100 said, "What would I have to offer a woman—two years of taking care of me, and then I would die?" Claude in a follow-up interview said with a laugh, "At 96? Who wants an old man?!" Then he said if the right opportunity would come along, yes, he would enjoy that. Bapuji equated marriage with financial responsibility and said he was too old to take care of a family. Michael said it was "kind of silly" for older people to remarry because of the tax laws. It appears from the comments made by respondents in their mid-80s or older that they felt advanced age made remarriage a foolish consideration.

Among the 16 men who were widowed before age 70, nine had remarried, including one who married after the interview. Four had been widowed again. One of those four was in a committed common-law relationship and another had a steady companion; the other two lived single and had no woman companion. Of the seven who had not remarried, two were dating, three had steady companions, and one had an unstable companionship situation. The last man in that group had not remarried quickly because of inconsolable grief; he had grown old and frail by the time he was interviewed and was no longer living in a situation in which he would meet eligible women.

The Health Factor

Vinick (1983) found dating to be higher among unmarried widowers who were healthy and mobile, regardless of their age. Health is closely related to age since debilitating illnesses and conditions increase with age, but some of the men in our study particularly referred to their health as a factor ruling out possible remarriage. Curly, confined to a wheelchair, said he was in no shape to consider marriage. Carlo said that his age and his physical problems ruled out marriage. Another man, who had been married twice and had a steady lady friend at the time, said that he would not consider another marriage because of his physical problems, not the least of which was his inability to perform sexually. One man in his mid-90s said that his recently diagnosed prostate cancer and pending operation would close the door to remarriage.

We might expect then that men in their mid-80s and older, and men who are in poorer health would be the least likely to consider remarriage, while younger men and men in good health would be more likely to be interested in a new marriage. Men in good health might be interested in remarriage at a later age, while men who are in poorer health might rule out marriage at a younger age. Old men in poor health would be the least likely to remarry, while younger men in good health would be the most like to remarry. Finally, beyond these factors of age and health, what other factors operate as a man takes his position on the continuum of interest in remarriage?

Findings Relating to Age and Health

In the chapter on Living Alone, we describe our categorization of the men's health as "good," "fair," or "poor." We found that 35% of the men had only minimal health problems, perhaps watching cholesterol or taking blood pressure medication, 50% had significant but not immediately life-threatening problems, such as hernia or diabetes, and 15% had problems that were very serious and potentially could cause death in the near future, such as active cancer and weak hearts.

None of the men who were in poor health at the time of the interview had remarried. Their widowhood experiences ranged from four months to 23 years. Most had been widowed within the preceding ten years. While common sense knowledge of physical decline in late old age would indicate that the men had been in better health when they were widowed than when they were being interviewed, we did not have access to much information to substantiate health at the time of widowhood. All but two of the men were over age 85 when widowed and had health problems predating widowhood. Their health might have been categorized as "fair" at the time, but probably not "good." The 73-year-old who was also the most recently widowed had had a series of heart attacks and strokes. The 82-year-old had been widowed at age 60 when his health was much stronger; his reluctance to consider remarriage was more emotional and cultural than health related. In general it does appear that being in poor health makes remarriage an unlikely choice. The practicality of remarriage and opportunities to do it were in the past for these eight men.

At the time of interview, six of the remarried men were in good health, as was the one man in a common-law relationship. They were in good health also when they were widowed. Seven of the remarried men were in fair health when interviewed. They reported that their health was substantially the same when they were widowed. One exception might be the man who had been widowed 16 years earlier; his health most likely would have been characterized as good when he was widowed and remarried a year later. Having some health problems does not seem to limit a man from remarrying. Some men will choose not to marry because of their limitations, but as Vinick (1978) pointed out, needing care could be an incentive to seek a new wife.

Reasons for Remarriage

Fourteen of the 51 men in our study had remarried after age 50, three of them marrying after our interview with them. One more told us at a follow-up contact that he had decided to seek a new wife.

Some of the remarried men said they were not OK or not complete on their own. Alvin saw a dismal future for himself alone but expressed great optimism if he could be given another chance at marriage. Russell told the interviewer that if she could have seen him that month when he was alone, she would have understood that he could not go on that way. Sam said that he was adrift in the months after widowhood; he concluded that "It takes a woman to make a home."

The companionship of marriage may be viewed in three component parts: (a) the "cuddle" part which includes physical and emotional closeness, (b) the intellectual part of having someone to talk to about things that matter, and (c) the helpmate part which involves taking care of persons and household. Even when a marriage had not been the happiest, even when it had been reconfigured by lengthy and stressful caregiving, most of the men found much to miss.

The remarried men did not say so directly, but some of them needed help with their household chores. A widowed woman commented to us that the home is a woman's domain; if she is widowed, she will be sad but at least she is in her familiar environment. The widowed man is both saddened and alone in a domain that he has lived in but has not controlled. Complementarity of roles in the helpmate realm usually characterizes a marriage, especially a long-term marriage (Brubaker & Kinsel, 1985). In a traditional marriage, the division of chores would have the husband caring for the yard, the car, and outdoor maintenance on the house while the wife took care of cooking, laundry, and housecleaning. The men's perspectives on their competence in taking care of themselves is discussed more fully in the chapter on Living Alone.

Many of the men, remarried and not, told us that the social scene for adults is a couples society. The single older person is left out. Van den Hoonaard (1994) described the pattern of sympathy followed by ostracizing that occurred when a widowed person in a retirement community did not find a new partner in a timely fashion. There were many activities that Stuart wanted to enjoy, but felt he could not do with a male friend or alone. Remarried, he was able to attend concerts, go out to dinner, and travel. Travel was mentioned by several of the men as something difficult or not enjoyable to do alone. Jerry became an avid traveler as a widower, but he said sadly that he wanted to share the beautiful scenery with someone. Garrett was delighted that his new wife liked to travel the same way he did. Traveling with a companion rather than a wife had many pitfalls, according to the men. Michael advertised for a travel companion for a cruise; among the many letters he received was one with an overt sexual offer, which he did not want. He asked a different woman to go with him, but she was always late to meals and so he was basically alone anyway. Other men would not ask a woman to take a trip because they felt they would be asking for or obligating themselves to a sexual relationship if they invited her on an overnight trip. Henrik traveled with the woman he would later marry, but commented that he might go to hell for having done so.

Problems to Overcome

Russell, Earl, and Stuart learned that at least one of their children had significant objections to their remarriage. Russell's solution was to keep his marriage a secret, while Earl and Stuart were trying to give their children time and space to accept the new relationship. There can be a major mismatch in perspectives when a parent remarries. The parent is filling the familiar and companionable role of spouse with a new person who will erase that daily-presence void, whereas the adult child is left with a sentimental and affectional bond that can never be replaced. This mismatch is discussed more fully in the Adult Children chapter.

Finances were sometimes a source of stress. Some couples chose not to marry because of dollar benefits that would have been lost in pensions that terminate with remarriage. Some other couples chose to marry and give up the benefits. Garrett said that his second wife lost her husband's military income when they married. They laughed about perhaps living together without marrying, but that was "not a viable option." Stuart and his second wife lost income with their marriage, but they would not live together without being married, he said. Inheritance concerns were handled with trusts more than with prenuptial agreements. Benjamin joked that since he and his new wife were equal in financial resources, they did not have to worry that one was marrying the other for money. Sam and his wife had three bank accounts—his, hers and theirs—to handle their finances on a 50/50 basis. Home sales, with their accompanying complicated and changing tax exemption regulations, were of concern to a few of the couples.

Reasons for Not Thinking of Remarriage

The same problems encountered by the men who had remarried were anticipated by many men who decided not to remarry. Charles at age

91 said he had a pleasant companionship with a 96-year-old woman, but added that they were too old to think of marriage. At 94 he had a different and much younger lady friend, but then he said he valued his independence and his personal space, would not want to complicate his finances, and would not want his daughter's disapproval. John and Kenneth both worried about needing to give care to an ill spouse or needing to receive care, thereby possibly putting the caregiving burden on a new wife. John in his 70s might have been a likely candidate for remarriage, but during the interview and in a follow-up conversation more than 2 years later, he continued to come up with reasons to be very cautious about marrying again. Stuart had just had surgery for prostate cancer when he discussed marriage with the woman who became his second wife. He too was concerned that she might face caregiving and another widowhood, but when she expressed optimism about their future, he was willing to marry. Cordell said he did not have enough money to pay for a high level of care for a long time if that should be his fate; he said his companion should not have to be responsible for him.

Some of the men were not interested in remarriage because they were very independent. They tended to be quite self-sufficient. Yussef's description of his marriage was of two friendly competitors who were there to back each other up when needed. He said he could cook as well as any woman and had moved to an apartment complex so he would be around other people. With that, he had no need to remarry. Joe could take care of himself in his small apartment. He had a girlfriend to go dancing with him, but he said a marriage would not have worked out well for either of them because they were very different. Jerry, a younger widower, said he thought his wife was the "love of his life" but he allowed that he would like to date to deal with his loneliness, and that remarriage would not be out of the question if the right woman came along. At the time of the interview, he found it doubtful that such a situation would develop. A few years later he was more open to the possibility, although he was enjoying his independent schedule very much. He said he guessed that he would be willing to give up his independence if the right woman came along.

Claude had limited opportunities to meet eligible women. He was a light-skinned African-American man living in a white retirement community. He felt other residents expressed subtle disapproval when he walked into the dining hall with a woman. Two and a half years later he seemed to have developed some good female friends, but still felt that a romantic relationship was not likely to develop. Age was a limiting factor also; at follow-up he was 96 years old.

Honoring the Woman/Honoring the Role

There was another reason for several of the men not to remarry. They were still bonded to their deceased wife and would not consider marrying again. They are the male counterparts to the women described by Erikson, Erikson, and Kivnick (1986) as "remaining married to the husband." Their feelings, examined in contrast with those of the other men who valued the marriage relationship and wanted that situation in their lives again, became an interesting arena of analysis in our study. Here we focus on the men who had definite feelings about remarriage. They fell into two groups: (a) the ones who would never consider remarrying and (b) those who decided that they wanted another marriage (or marriage-like arrangement). In comparing the interview content for these two groups, there is a distinct priority given by the first group to honoring the individual person herself, of honoring the woman. The second group, while it represents a variety of approaches to the idea of remarriage, clearly gives priority to honoring the role of wife. These men did not speak negatively of their first wives; in fact, in many of the cases a good first marriage had brought them to the place of honoring the role of the wife and left them wanting all that was embodied in that role in their lives again.

Al's situation illustrates the effects of a long marriage on the man's perceptions. He said, "I had a good woman. I had one of the best in the world, and I knew it before I married her." A young man marries a young woman and they grow old together. He grows accustomed to her and her way of doing things. She is his standard for "wife." He also grows accustomed to the partnership arrangement, giving and receiving intimacy, doing certain things for another, having certain things done for him. There is a lot to miss when that is gone. In other words, a long and happy marriage could bring a man to feel that there could never be someone else as dear and compatible as his wife had been, as was the case for Al. Or, it could bring him to feel that he is left with an impoverished existence when that wonderful companion is gone and that, to live out his remaining years with any meaning and comfort, he must find someone to fill that vacant role. That was the case for Alvin.

Age alone may be a pivotal factor in this attitude. The men who honored the woman averaged about 90 years of age at the time of interview, whereas the sample as a whole averaged 80 years. While there were individual reasons given for considering or not considering remarriage at any age, we found in general that in their early 80s, the men began describing themselves as too old or too unhealthy to think about getting married again. Still, all of these men said they could have remarried if they wanted to. Also, they are not the only men in the study who have not remarried. They are the ones who conveyed the strongest messages about honoring the woman to whom they were married. Self-assurance and a feeling of being complete in oneself, coupled with advanced age, which leads one to think perhaps there is not the time left nor the energy for a new relationship—these may be the hallmarks for men who honor the woman who was their wife to the exclusion of considering another relationship.

Two categories of men in our continuum of interest in remarriage honored the role of wife. The men in the first category of our continuum—desperately seeking a new marriage—honored the role of wife in a way that made it exceedingly important to their well-being to have that role filled again. Alvin stated it most succinctly: "We had a wonderful marriage. I was a good husband, and someone should give me the chance to do it again." Sy said, "I just wasn't any good that year I was alone." Russell said, "Until I met Betty, I was so down. . . . I really didn't know what I was doing. . . . I couldn't sleep. I just . . . Well, I don't know what would have happened if I hadn't met Betty."

Men in the second category—actively seeking a new marriage—approached interest in a new marriage from a point other than desperation. Stuart said simply, "I have a lot of love left to give." Garrett explained his visit to his recently-deceased wife's best friend in another state (now his second wife) by saying, "I didn't know it then, but I guess I had marriage in the back of my mind." Jim said, "I have come to the point where I want to find someone to marry." After several months of widowhood, Kenneth decided that he wanted to marry again, but did not want to marry someone who would have seemed like a replacement for his first wife. So he considered possible candidates very carefully, making certain that his second wife would be different from his first. When Earl realized how alone he felt, he decided to place a personal ad in a newspaper. He and one of his children screened the responses, he invited a few women on dinner dates, and finally married one.

The Importance of Sex

This topic was not particularly comfortable for the men to discuss with a younger female interviewer, although the question was posed late in the interviewing process when rapport had been firmly established and was asked obliquely: "Would you comment on the importance of a sexual relationship to an older man?" One very old man responded gently, "I wouldn't have anything to say about that." A few others responded, "Yes, it is important," and changed the subject. One expressed his embarrassment with a somewhat lengthy and oblique analogy about various types of waning appetites. One remarried man blurted out a joking little story about "bouncing the springs."

Typically, however, the response was brief and affirmed that a sexual relationship was viewed positively. One man said, "Things speed up and things slow down, and this sort of thing, you hope for and generally you end up with a mutually acceptable situation." The men also usually conveyed that companionship and the absence of loneliness were the main benefits of a new relationship; sex was nice but not the most important factor. A man in his 80s said that "neither the man nor the woman is still capable," but that other things such as companionship and sharing similar interests are more important. A younger man said, "At this point in my life, that sexual relationship is a pleasant and good bonding experience. There's no urgency about it. It's something that we both enjoy." One man said of course he did not remarry for sex; he could buy that!

For men of advanced age and experiencing health decline, remarriage or any sexual relationship did not seem to be a practical possibility. Several had prostate difficulties, including cancer. Others had heart disease or significant mobility problems. Their comments during the interview were some version of "not interested" or "cannot do." Erikson, Erikson, and Kivnick (1986) refers to unchosen celibacy. That was the case for the men in our study who were not in a sexual relationship. Some of the older men probably said they had no interest in sex anymore because their bodies and health had failed them in that regard. Those who honored the woman over the role of wife accepted and kept the unchosen celibacy. Those who honored the role of wife sought another woman for an intimate relationship (including but not limited to sex).

Finding a New Spouse

Lopata's (1979) research on widowed women showed that they tended to marry someone they already knew. It was likewise for the men in our study. Whom the men married fell into distinct categories, with the most common being a widowed woman they knew before they were widowed. The categories are as follows:

Someone Already Known

Sam married his deceased wife's widowed sister, Sy and Malcolm each married a widowed neighbor, Garrett married his wife's best friend who was a widow, Benjamin a very distant widowed relative whom he met at a reunion, Russell an old sweetheart widowed after a marriage to someone else, Bill married a long-widowed cousin of his first wife. Henrik married the nurse who took care of his wife during her long illness; she had been widowed twice.

Someone Met on His Own After Wife Died

Walter at his new retirement community, Terrence and Kenneth at work, Daniel at synagogue, Alvin through social activities. All of these new wives had been widowed.

Someone Met Through Connections

Stuart's sister referred him to a widowed woman with whom she worked.

Someone Met Through Advertising

Earl placed an ad in the local newspaper and from many responses eventually married a divorced woman.

Stuart's wife was ten years younger than he, the rest of the new wives were not more than about five years younger than the men they married. Stuart and his second wife had been widowed at approximately the same time; in all other cases, the woman had been widowed longer.

The Senior Dating Scene

Jerry described the senior dating scene as "akin to an hour on the rack" and "my worst nightmare." Stuart asked the interviewer how one could reenter the dating scene after many, many years of being out of it. Earl found advertising successful, but Michael's ad for a travel companion was not successful. When women called him, Michael would ask each to dinner once but had a policy of not asking again, until at follow-up he had found a very compatible steady companion. Other men were reluctant to ask a woman out for the first time because they didn't want to create a situation that would obligate them to continue with it and they didn't want to hurt a woman's feelings by not inviting her again. George said he would take someone out, but then he would get phone calls asking, "Well, how come you didn't call me?" He was too polite to say so, but he said he thought, "I only took you out one time, lady. You know what I mean?" Most recalled the customs and expectations from their long-ago courtships and were nervous about the new expectations they might encounter now. Terrence commented, "I was offered sex before I even dated them." He added, "I didn't want to have sex with any of these ladies and then see them later (around town)." Hence it could be concluded that the men who married someone they already knew were the lucky ones; they had been able to avoid the anxiety-producing seniors dating scene of the late twentieth century.

The "casserole ladies" are a retirement community urban legend. Supposedly legions of them descend upon the doorstep of every newly widowed man. So we asked our widower respondents about this phenomenon. One man laughed and said no, they had not come, but he wished they had. Yussef said that old men who thought they were being pursued were "fantasizing." However, most respondents acknowledged that widowed women had been attentive to them. Richard said he asked them to stop bringing food. He could go out to eat if he wanted to and actually preferred his solitary activities at home.

Two men in a predominantly Jewish retirement community had experienced the phenomenon rather fully. Their responses to it were illuminating on the subject of male initiative. Benjamin said that he received a "very strange letter" from a former neighbor, in which she had enclosed her photo; he said he never responded. He said he had "some fear of females who are more aggressive than others in that respect," but could "appreciate that when they lost their spouse, they felt that part of their life was gone." Sy said that he found several women attentive, one in particular was offering to help him deal with his loneliness, but the woman who caught his attention and became his second wife was a nearby neighbor who did not try to get his attention. "I took a liking to her," he said.

Several men who had not remarried spoke modestly of women, particularly at church, having been attentive and of knowing that they could have remarried if they had wanted to. One man residing in a nursing home commented, "Yeh, I have two or three here who I could move in with anytime, but I'm not interested." Ned found, even as he approached his 100th birthday, a woman at church regularly lingering around him after the service. It would not be overstating the situation to say that all of the men in our study could have remarried if they had wished to. (Claude might have had to go somewhere where racial prejudice would not limit him.) They could all recall women who would have been willing if they had been willing. This is a major difference between widows and widowers created by the imbalance in gender longevity and the social custom of men marrying younger women—older widowed men have the opportunity to remarry if they care to, whereas most older widowed women do not.

In two of the marriages, the wife had already been widowed twice before. The interviewers met these women and had the opportunity to observe the interaction of the spouses briefly, but the women were not actually interviewed. When an older woman undertakes her third marriage after two widowhoods, one might conclude that she feels a strong need or desire to be married. Walter's second wife was very talkative and energetic in contrast to his inexpressiveness. He said he knew he was holding her back from activities with her friends, but she spoke in glowing terms of his positive qualities, his first marriage, and their marriage together. Benjamin's wife was pleasant and energetic; she chided him in front of the interviewer for his slow driving. It seemed that she was the more dominant personality in the relationship. In both cases the wives appeared to be more energetic and active. Walter's wife put a glow on the marriage and everything else in life. Benjamin's wife seemed to tease as a mild way of attempting to change him. Neither marriage was negative; it just appeared upon brief observation that the couples were having to work through some differences in personal style. This could be the result of individuals marrying out of a need to be married, and then working through the adjustments that were needed to sustain the relationship.

Divorce Experience

Six men in the study had been divorced prior to the marriage that ended in widowhood. For four of them, it was a "mistake of youth" although one had gotten together again with his ex-wife from the 1940s after his long and happy second marriage ended in his wife's death. His ex-wife had been widowed a few years earlier. Two of the men had divorced and then remarried the women who eventually left them widowed. One man, who made it clear that he needed female companionship, had divorced and remarried, then divorced the second wife and remarried the first, lost her to death and then married again.

Men Widowed Twice or More

Four men in the study had been through the widowhood experience twice or more. Daniel's first wife was diagnosed with cancer at a young age and local doctors had written her off, he recounted. Unwilling to settle for a terminal diagnosis, he took her to a specialist in New York. She recovered for two more decades of life before succumbing to a recurrence of cancer. Daniel felt that these years together were a gift, but they heightened his grief at the loss of his second wife. He had felt self-sufficient and comfortable on his own, but after five years of widowhood met a woman who was so personable and compatible that he wanted to marry her. Their happy marriage was cut short by cancer. His greatest regret was that their time together was so short. Daniel was the only respondent in the study who had apparently made a good adjustment to life on his own, then developed an interest in remarrying as a result of meeting a particular woman. This circumstance is quite different from those of the men who clearly were interested in filling the position of wife and set out to find a woman for that position.

Kenneth was very purposeful in seeking a second wife. He wanted to make certain that she was very different from his first wife so he would value her for herself, not compare her to his first wife. He married seven and a half months after having been widowed. Each marriage had lasted more than 20 years, each of them ended by cancer. Kenneth said both women had been healthy and without family histories of cancer; he said he felt jinxed and would not marry again for fear of bringing cancer to another healthy woman.

Don had lost three wives, two to drug overdoses and one to cancer. He was widowed at ages 43, 60, and 63. At the time of the interview he was living in a committed common-law relationship. When asked about having experienced so many losses, he said he felt blessed to have such a great capacity to love. He had first seen his most recent love in a coffee bar line and knew if he did not speak to her then, he would never see her again. So he said to her, "I'm sorry! I apologize. Forgive me for staring. I can't help staring at you. You are absolutely gorgeous." She was flustered. They exchanged phone numbers and later got together.

Leroy was a "character" who appeared to have some cognitive deficits. His stories had many gaps, and his timelines did not match. He brought out from the bedroom an unkempt photo album with many photos loose and none with any information written on them or beside them. He identified someone who appeared to be the same woman as his first wife and then as his second wife. As accurately as could be ascertained, Leroy's first wife died of diabetes in the mid-1950s; his second relationship, which probably was not a legal marriage although the woman used his last name, began in the late 1960s. She died of heart trouble in 1995. When asked about the possibility of marrying again, Leroy said that 81 was too old.

Comparing or Not

A new wife can fill the void left by the death of previous wife in all important roles. That is not to say how the quality of the two relationships would compare. Indeed, most of the men seemed not inclined to compare the two women. The wife that they had lost was the one with whom they had made a home and a family, the one with whom they had matured and aged, the one whose loss they had grieved. The new wife was their loving companion now.

Men would indicate their reluctance or refusal to compare by speaking of the pleasures or the realities of the two relationships independently. However, sometimes comparisons would slip into their comments. One man spoke of his current wife's love of traveling and about the similarities in the kinds of trips that they enjoyed. "My first wife did not like to travel like that," he said, "so we are really having a good time now." Another man spoke of his first wife, who had lost interest in sex during a long period of declining health, in a kind and understanding way, but then literally sparkled when he exclaimed about how much his new wife enjoyed sex. "[My first wife] would complain if I woke her up when I was getting into bed, but [my second wife] doesn't care when I wake her up. We're having a great time!" On the other hand, comparisons sometimes ran in the other direction. "This marriage is good for both of us," one man commented, "but nothing could be like the first time." Another said likewise, but gave indications that his second marriage was not really very good. Stuart had been married to a nurse and then married another nurse. He said that nurses are "caring people." Having a healthy second wife, he said he now realized how much his first wife's health problems had burdened her through the years.

Deceased Wife's Presence

Papernow (1989) refers to the memory of a departed person as a presence in a stepfamily; a similar phenomenon operated for some of the men in their new marriages. Sam, who married his wife's sister, said they were both grieving for the same person and that helped bring the two of them together. He said that sometimes when they were traveling by car they would talk about both of the deceased first spouses and how they might have enjoyed the trip. Stuart and his new wife were building a new house because Stuart's house still held so much memory and memorabilia of his first wife. He said his second wife was very good about fitting in around the things in the house, but they both felt that they needed a place that was just theirs. Another man in the study lived with his new wife in her home, but kept the house he and his first wife had built—complete with its furnishings.

Erikson, Erikson, and Kivnick (1986) identified a mismatch of recollections about the marriage in the process of "smoothing over." Nearly all of the men spoke of good marriages; we had to poke around to get some details that shed light on disagreements and discord. Russell was very open about disagreements because he was an expressive person and because some of those disagreements were still having an effect on his relationships with his children. Some men who had relatively peaceful marriages were free in talking about how they handled disagreements. Richard said, "We might have a knock-down, drag-out after he was in bed," but he and his wife had agreed not to argue about a child-rearing matter in front of the child. Most of the men had to be encouraged to talk about handling disagreements. Clyde, for example, apparently had a verbally stormy marriage, but admitted it only in oblique ways with a lot of encouragement from the interviewer:

Interviewer: How did you and she settle differences when you didn't agree about something?

Clyde: I'll tell you what. We never did fight but a very little. We got along good. We weren't perfect, but we got along good. And she'd give and I'd give. It wasn't no problem.

Interviewer: So if you and Mary Ellen didn't agree about something, would you talk about it? Would either of you give each other the silent treatment, or how did a disagreement go?

Clyde: I'll tell you, we got along pretty darn good. On the average, we were better than average. Yeah.

Interviewer: But when there was a disagreement, how did you handle it? Now, you can't tell me you lived all those years and never disagreed about anything.

Clyde: Well, I didn't say that either.

Interviewer: Okay. I just wondered, how did you handle a disagreement?

Clyde: We did. Well, she'd usually let me manage that part of it and we'd figure it out and go from there. Like buying a house, or renting and moving and something like that. There's always things come up that you have to get along with, and so, lot of times I'd go ahead and do things when I saw that it was interesting, she didn't know nothing about it until later. . . . She was always so scared to even do anything, that in other words, in one way she was a hinder to you when it comes to success because she was so afraid that she'd lose.

Interviewer: Okay, so you were more willing to take a risk?

Clyde: Yes, I was.

Interviewer: Okay. And so the way you dealt with that is sometimes you would just do something and tell her later?

Clyde: Yeah. We used to buy a house and fix it and resell it and just kept on doing that until we got on our feet. And I'd do anything I'd wanted to and that way, that's the way we managed.

To summarize, our respondents tended at first to present their marriages as relatively conflict free, but upon encouragement to give more detail, presented a variety of ways in which conflict was handled, from healthy exchanges to heated verbal arguments to tacitly agreed-to subterfuge.

Most of the men reported no conversation with their ill wives about the future, but the remarried men usually said their first wife would have wanted them to go on with their lives. A few reported their wives had told them they should remarry. Terrence's wife had said, "You have to have somebody," and even tried to fix him up, he said. The wives' comments and predictions about remarriage appear in the Caregiving chapter in the section where communication is discussed.

Remarriage Alternatives: Living Together, Living-Separate Companionship

The respondents tended to have strong opinions regarding the types of intimate relationships they thought appropriate. The variety in these opinions reflects the trend in society away from the importance of a legally sanctioned marriage. However, as in society as a whole, there were many who still felt that being married was the only acceptable circumstance for an intimate relationship. Stuart, for example, said he and his second wife did not sleep together until they were married. That to him signified the respect that they both had for the new relationship. He acknowledged that they had given up quite a lot financially to enter the new marriage, but that nothing mattered more than doing the whole thing right.

Others were persuaded by dollars and cents that a new legal marriage was too costly. Frank's lady friend would have had to give up her deceased husband's military pension. Clyde's love interest would have lost more than $500 a month from her deceased husband's black lung benefits. "She was wanting to marry me," he said, "but I told her I didn't think I was worth that much to her. What if I would die in the next year, or the next few days. Then she wouldn't have nothing." "How accepting was she of that statement?" the interviewer inquired. Clyde laughed, "Yeah, she seconded it and said a man wasn't worth $500 a month to her."

Vinick (1983) found more than 75% of unmarried widower respondents disapproving of living together without remarriage. Most of the men in our study had internalized the propriety of being married to one's sexual intimate. Those who held most strongly to it at the time of the interview did so for religious reasons, although they spoke more of "rightness" than of the need to follow the rules of their denomination. For them there was not a decision to be made about whether to marry the woman with whom they wanted an intimate relationship; that was simply the way it would be done.

Some of the men with a decision-making process less faith-based considered the change in social mores and then came to their own conclusions. In most of these situations, the practical consideration of finances won out, although the presumed opinions of others, especially their own adult children, would sway them in the direction of marriage. It is important to note that only small numbers are involved here. Only one man out of the 51 interviewed was living with a woman without being married to her. One more had lived with his second wife before they were married. Six others told the interviewer they had a current sexual relationship; one was preparing to move in with his companion. We presume a few more presented their "current woman" relationships as nonsexual when they were not because the men might not have felt comfortable enough with the situation to share it with a younger woman interviewer (whom they might have perceived as daughterly). Seven stated that their relationships were not sexual.

Enjoying the independence of living alone while having the companionship of a pleasant person when that was mutually agreeable was an ideal situation for many of the "coupled" men and their companions. Rubenstein (1986) describes the intimate companion as a same-cohort confidante with whom the widowed man has a special bond, without giving up his independent lifestyle and the haven of his home. Charles and his lady friend ate together in the retirement community dining hall and watched TV together, but they joked about not inviting each other over to eat at their own apartments because they did not want to get an obligatory pattern started. Extended visits to a companion in another state worked well for Clyde; he could maintain his own home space, which he swore no woman would come in and change around on him. Arch undertook many activities with a neighbor woman. Joe and his long-time lady friend went dancing together and would "play house when we want to." Will and his much younger companion attended cultural events together.

Not in all cases was the situation mutually agreeable. Kenneth enjoyed going out to dinner regularly, but his companion was more interested in marriage than he. George and his long-time companion had agreed not to marry when they began their dating; he later proposed to her, but she said she wanted to keep their independent arrangements. He agreed to that.

A few of the men seemed to have no discomfort in admitting their acceptance of a non-marital sexual relationship. These men either did not have a religious base for their decision-making, or felt that the rules of their denomination did not affect their choices.

As mentioned earlier in this chapter, the men who remarried tended to marry someone close to them in age. Conversely, we found that the relationships that involved greater age differences tended not to result in marriage. When the woman was older by more than just a few years, the couple did not marry. In three out of the four situations where the widowed man was younger than his companion, the relationship included sex. One man who lived by values expressing great tolerance said nevertheless that his lady friend's older age was of concern to him in thinking about marriage. The stereotype growing out of the social custom of men marrying women a little younger than they seemed to affect men's thinking about marrying an older woman. When the widowed man was much older than his companion, friend, or steady helper, there was not a marriage, nor was a sexual relationship likely. Berardo, Appel, and Berardo (1993) found that age disparities in marriage increase with ages of the persons marrying and are greater in remarriages, but also found that extreme age disparities are rare in any case. Their findings are in keeping with ours; matchups close in age were much more likely to marry than companionable arrangements where parties were far apart in age.

Findings

Older widowed men value companionship and couples activities; age and health play important roles in whether or not they consider marrying again. Older men who want companionship tend to seek and enter a new relationship within months of the death of their spouse. Sex is viewed positively but is only part of a good relationship. Older men seem not to appreciate forwardness in women who are interested in dating. All are lonely but some accommodate themselves to loneliness rather than remarrying because of age, health condition, or devotion to deceased wife, or to avoid what they view as very likely problems. Those who decide to marry tend to marry a widow close to them in age and someone they already have known. First wives are not replaced, but the role of wife is filled with another person. Because older men are so greatly outnumbered by women in their cohort, and because it is social custom for men to marry younger women, almost all older men are able to remarry if they want to.

REFERENCES

Berardo, F. M. (1970). Survivorship and social isolation: The case of the aged widower. *The Family Coordinator, 19*(1), 11–25.

Berardo, F. M., Appel, J., & Berardo, D. H. (1993). Age dissimilar marriages: Review and assessment. *Journal of Aging Studies, 7*(1), 93–106.

Brubaker, T. H. & Kinsel, B. I. (1985). Who is responsible for household tasks in long-term marriages of the "young-old" elderly? *Lifestyles, 7*(4), 238–247.

Cleveland, W. P. & Gianturco, D. T. (1976). Remarriage probability after widowhood: A retrospective method. *Journal of Gerontology, 31,* 99–103.

Erikson, E. H., Erikson, J. M., & Kivnick, H. Q. (1986) *Vital involvement in old age.* New York: Norton.

Kuhn, D. R., Morhardt, D. J., & Monbrod-Framburg, G. (1993). Late-life marriages, older stepfamilies, and Alzheimer's disease. *Families in Society, 74*(3), 154–162.

Lopata, H. Z. (1979). *Women as widows: Support systems.* New York: Elsevier.

Papernow, P. L. (1989) Stages of becoming a stepfamily. In M. Burt (Ed.), *Stepfamilies stepping ahead* (pp. 27–48). Baltimore: Stepfamilies Press.

Rubenstein, R. L. (1986). *Singular paths: Old men living alone.* Guildford, NY: Columbia University Press.

U.S. Bureau of the Census. (1993). *Statistical abstracts of the United States, 1992.* Washington, DC: Government Printing Office.

Van den Hoonaard, D. K. (1994). Paradise lost: Widowhood in a Florida retirement community. *Journal of Aging Studies, 8,* 121–132.

Vinick, B. H. (1978). Remarriage in old age. *The Family Coordinator, 27*(4), 359–363.

Vinick, B. H. (1983). Three years after bereavement: Life-styles of elderly widowers. *Interdisciplinary Topics in Gerontology, 17,* 50–57.

10

Life Values Carried Forward

The 51 men in the study came from a variety of backgrounds, including several with immigrant parents and two who themselves had immigrated to the United States as adults. In spite of cultural and religious variety, all of the men reported having been brought up with basic traditional values; most notable in their memories were honesty and hard work. We found the generative impulse—the desire to give something to the future—to be broadly experienced, giving structure and meaning to later life, and connecting an older man to family, the wider community, and to the future. Volunteer work seemed to be a natural extension of men's work and provider roles from earlier stages of life. In this chapter we examine the values and perspectives that guided the men's lives before widowhood and that had an impact on the way they adjusted to widowhood.

VALUES REGARDING EDUCATION

The educational achievements of the respondents are listed in Appendix C. Public opinion regarding the value of formal education has changed during their lifetimes. In the early twentieth century, parents guided sons toward work roles. The jobs for which many of them were destined did not require a great deal of education. Some parents told their sons directly that going to work at a young age was more important than getting more education. With formal education having become more important as the century went on, it is not surprising that many of the men we interviewed regretted not having gotten more education. They acknowledged the importance of education and, no doubt, many of them would have reached higher achievement levels if they had been born later.

The men expressed their feelings about education in a number of ways. Leroy said that he wished he had been smarter, so he would not have had to work in a factory all his life. Carlo was proud that he could read, even though he had almost no schooling. Russell said he always had to work and could not finish school. Claude attended night school to get the education he missed as a youngster. Al said he did not regret having left high school because he got educated as he prepared for different jobs; he highly respected his wife for being educated. Bill was disappointed that his correspondence courses in engineering did not qualify him to become a licensed engineer. Clyde felt inferior for not having an education; he thought his wife was smarter ("oversmart"), and he was very proud of his educated children and grandchildren. Art, who had left school early to support his family when his father died, was an avid reader and well-informed on many subjects; he said:

> I tried to get young people to read, especially those who are not going to school and trying to educate themselves. I try to explain it this way, "You sit in a dark room . It has thousands and thousands of pictures and windows, but the shades are drawn on those windows. Once you enter that area, every shade you succeed in raising gives you additional outlook and greater understanding of what this world is like." One or two of them have said, "Yes, that has helped me read." Most, they think it's a bunch of bunk.

The respondents who were young men during the Great Depression and of age to serve in the armed forces during World War II experienced a dip in the otherwise rising educational achievements of the twentieth century, notwithstanding the G.I. Bill. That phenomenon is explored in the final chapter where cohort effects are considered.

VALUING WORK

The Appalachian men were some of the least educated men in the study. We found in them a remarkable level of occupational achievement considering the level of education. They had been enterprising enough to take advantage of out-of-school educational opportunities that helped them gain skills for their work. For example, Clyde learned how to do electrical work for the coal mines, then left the coal mines to make use of his electrician skills in a less hazardous and better paying setting. This finding held true for nearly all of the men in the study. They sought opportunities to learn skills; they worked hard and were dependable. They achieved good positions considering their education because they were good workers. The occupations of our respondents are listed in Appendix C.

Hard work was the most common theme initiated by the men during the interviews. Most of them prided themselves on being good workers. Russell stated simply that he always liked to work and still liked to work. One daughter attributed her father's long life to the fact that he always worked so hard. A son who found little to praise about his father nevertheless said, "He worked hard to provide for his family." Always being a smart and reliable worker was the theme of Harry's 100 years of life; he struggled to complete eighth grade because he already was working so much he could not complete his lessons. As an African American, Claude found himself working extremely hard for long hours just to maintain himself; he was bone weary from his life of hard work. Nearly every man in this study had worked steadily and diligently to support his family. Some of the men stayed with one job; others made changes. Of all the 51 men, only Don had an irregular work history. Much of his life had been occupied with drugs and alcohol; he said he usually worked at jobs that he likened to hustling although they were legal; in his early 70s and sober, he still worked to support himself and to some extent relied on charm and good fortune to create opportunities for him.

Another way in which men expressed the value of work was in the lack of a definitive time of retirement. Some of the men moved to part time in the same job, or they were asked to continue in some other capacity, or they took a different job after retiring from one job, or they began to do volunteer work. This indefinite retirement pattern is considered more fully later in this chapter in the section on generativity. Then, when finally and completely retired from an occupation, hardworking men such as Russell continued to work very hard. At the time of the interview, he was busy landscaping the property around his new home. Arch had worked long arduous shifts as an emergency room physician; in retirement he kept his yard meticulously manicured. Earl was thinking of retirement from his paying job so he could help build churches.

RELIGIOUS BELIEFS AND SPIRITUALITY

In the chapter on grief, we considered ways in which a man might process the meaning of his loss and suffering in the terms of his religious faith. Among our respondents, we found men (a) who professed no religious faith, (b) who attended services without much consideration of beliefs, (c) who had secure and uncomplicated faith, and (d) who searched for spiritual and intellectual understanding. In this section we consider the religious background of the men, including the beliefs that they brought to the widowhood experience.

Having Faith

Almost all of the men mentioned religious beliefs and practices as something important they had learned from their parents. Some were deeply philosophical in their consideration of religious faith. Conner was completely immersed in Catholic beliefs and practices; Jacob and Daniel were equally immersed in Jewish scholarship. They went to a great deal of trouble to maintain Kashrut for the sake of keeping the Commandments. Earl's life choices were based upon the values of his Christian faith. He said that his father had not seen those values modeled by his parents, but decided to seek beliefs and values for himself after observing the way his parents lived; that faith was his father's gift to his children. Richard was a philosopher to the core; he reasoned through his beliefs to a point that might be termed philosophical spirituality; he had concluded that faith was essential to humans, but not to God. He referred to twentieth century Presbyterian theologian George Buttrick saying that God does not need our prayers but he wants them. Bapuji's daily schedule of Hindu worship and study were all that sustained his nonphysical being in the alien culture of the United States. Bapuji explained the journey of the spirit to Heaven where a lifetime of good or bad deeds, noted by the god Yama, would be rewarded or punished. Bapuji said that he personally believed in an afterlife. "No one has experienced it to come and tell us about it. . . . however, I believe it."

Eldon's faith was simple and very strong, as was Craig's; they believed in God's goodness as revealed in the Bible and in their own lives, and they looked forward to Heaven. Garrett said of his denomination (Church of Christ), "There isn't any [hierarchy]. It's a real simple Biblical concept and that is, if the Lord saw fit to cause the Bible to be written and give directions to the people, why should the people have a convention every few years to decide what they'll teach and believe?" Stuart used faith to help him process the loss of his wife:

> I guess I just believe the Lord decided it was time. As a human being there are certain things that I just leave to faith, that we don't understand because we aren't God and that's why he is the Omnipotent, and so who am I to continue to ask questions why?

Alvin had moved toward more involvement and deeper faith than his parents. He said, "My mother felt it was unfashionable to be too religious and I went along with that. . . . As I got older though, I went into it a little deeper, and I think I'm more devout than my parents were." He had been raised as a Reform Jew, but said he would join a Conservative congregation if he ever moved away from the combined-denomination Jewish congregation in which he was active at the time of the interview.

Yussef said that his father had dropped his Muslim religion as soon as he came to the United States. The family attended the Baptist Church, which was the mother's denomination. He explained, "It wasn't a southern Baptist. It's that Baptist they got around here; it's different than a southern Baptist. Southern Baptists, understand, are hard-shell Baptists and here it's just a mediocre Baptist. . . . mainstream more or less." When he married, they attended his wife's Presbyterian church. Yussef professed an interest in all religions, and he had certainly encountered many—in his own family and in his military travels around the world. However, when the interview dealt with values to live by, Yussef spoke of the influence of the Muslim faith in his life, "I have the same feeling that Muslims have, 'Insha Allah,' it's God's will, it happens here. . . . By that [philosophy], you don't have any stress whatsoever. You're not getting angry or nothing."

Attendance at Services

While some were more philosophical than others, most of the men professed belief in God and said they were—or had been—faithful in church, synagogue or temple attendance. Some have remained involved in the denominations of their upbringing, although for some men a change of denominations occurred while they were children. Kenneth's explanation was memorable:

> As far as a religion was concerned, it was kind of a mixed ball because Mother was a Methodist, Dad was a Lutheran, I was baptized a Lutheran. . . . But Dad was with his religion like I am with chicken. Dad got a lot of it when he was younger, and he got tired of it. I got a lot of chicken when I was younger (laughs) and I don't eat chicken much anymore.

In adulthood, movement between Protestant denominations was common; young husbands and wives, like Kenneth's parents in the example above, had to sort out which church they would attend. Earl said:

> I have learned that [denomination] is not the significant thing about our beliefs. But by mentioning denomination, it usually locks people in some

> thoughts about where you're at. I was raised as a Baptist. I've been in other churches. Right now my wife is a member of the Free Methodist church, and we've been going there. I consider them to be brothers and sisters in Christ, as I do many denominations.

There was also movement between Jewish denominations, especially as American-born Jewish persons left the Orthodoxy of their immigrant parents. Daniel, for example, changed to Conservative so that he could sit with the womenfolk in his family at services. He attended services regularly; so did George.

Some men—both Christians and Jews—who had moved to retirement communities were attending services less frequently than they did back home. Church services on the radio sometimes were an alternative to church attendance for Christian men. Eldon was housebound at the time of the interview, but he listened to services on his chair-side radio. Yussef was listening to a Presbyterian service on radio the morning of his interview.

Sy talked about the rituals and obligations of Orthodox and Conservative Judaism, but said that he attended the synagogue now just for the holidays and to pray for the dead. "I'll usually go for my parents every year," he said. He also said he and his wife stopped keeping a kosher kitchen because of the expense of the foods. Benjamin thought that being Jewish had influenced him to be charitable and respectful. He thought he would attend synagogue more frequently after he retired, but found that he had tapered off rather than increased his attendance, which was currently limited to holidays. He and his present wife did not keep a kosher kitchen although he said he still had no taste for pork or shellfish, a remnant of his upbringing.

A few of the men expressed anger or irritation toward their congregations. Malcolm faulted church members for not being more attentive to his ill wife after she had been so attentive to church members in need all through the years. He emphasized that he faulted the people, not the church. Curly complained that no one from the church that he had attended for 60 years came to visit him for eight months after his wife's death. Michael seldom attended services any more because of his disapproval of changes in practices within his Reform congregation. However, most of the men found the church, synagogue, or temple of their choice to be a place where their values and beliefs were sustained, where congenial fellowship could be found, and where they could take part in meaningful and fulfilling activities.

A few other men felt that they had religious faith, but that was something separate from church attendance. Bill explained:

> I am a firm believer in God, and I don't think that anybody who is a scientist or anything like that, I don't see how that they can possibly not believe in God. I believe God is an intelligence basically. . . . I have never been baptized, never actually been a member of a church. I'm not anti-religion, it isn't that at all, I just am not motivated that way, I guess.

Richard, mentioned earlier, also spoke philosophically of faith and said that he had concluded that faith did not have to be expressed within the form of structured worship. He had been criticized by religious friends for not attending church regularly, but said that each person had to come to terms with the expression of his faith. "I would say if [being religious means] a strong faith in God and a true faith and belief that Christ's message was real and meant for all of us . . . then I am a religious person," he said.

Russell and Walter were examples of men who had attended services but made little connection between that activity and religious beliefs. Russell said of his childhood, "[My parents taught me] all of the good things, really. Going to church. They tried to teach me to go to church (laughing) which I did when I was a kid, most of the time." When asked if he and his second wife currently attended church, he said, "No, we haven't so far. We've been thinking about it, and the preacher did stop in here." Walter did not know what had attracted him to his denomination, but said what he enjoyed most was keeping the financial books for his group.

Conceptions of an Afterlife—Protestant Christian

The Protestant men usually said that they believed in Heaven. Some had fairly well-developed ideas about what Heaven would be. Garrett said he had just about decided that people would not recognize each other there, because the perfect bliss of Heaven would not be realized if one could look around for a loved one from earth, and never find him or her there. "Would you be thoroughly happy if grandpa wasn't there, or if your mother wasn't there?" he asked. Then he added, "I can imagine and understand a thorough, blissful existence without knowing anybody." Earl said scripture tells us we don't know what Heaven will be like, but:

> . . . we can kind of speculate because at the Mount of Transfiguration Moses and Elijah were both recognized by the disciples as who they were. If they would recognize them and they had come from death back to that experience, then certainly there is a good possibility that we are going to recognize our loved ones when we meet again.

Clyde was less a student of scripture than Earl, but he had strong ideas about Heaven. He said that people would be "all of one." Any ideas of recognizing others in Heaven came from what some people "dream up in themselves. . . . I am not an educated man, but I do know that. . . . We can't control it. Somebody else controls it, we're just in it."

Uncertainty about what to expect was common. Craig said he was torn between believing that people went directly to Heaven and believing that Jesus would gather the dead "back to life" when he came the second time. Kenneth was uncertain about Heaven itself. He said, "I was nothing when I came in, when I was born. And when I die, I'm gone. . . . There may be life hereafter. I won't say there isn't. But I think I'm a little skeptical."

Conceptions of an Afterlife—Catholic Christian

Conner explained, "Believing there is a God, I believe there is life hereafter. So I don't consider [my wife] dead. I consider her as in Heaven and if God permits, I'll be able to join her." Jerry, also, was sure of Heaven and that his wife had gone directly there. Mack, a convert to Catholicism, said, "I don't know what form it takes, and I don't think you go to sleep and never wake up, no. There is something out there. . . . That's about all I know. I expect to see [wife] again." Robert's statement expressed similar uncertainty about the form that Heaven would take; he described his uncertainty as stressful for him. Cordell was skeptical, not believing in a heaven because he could not accept the existence of a hell.

Catholic Sensing Presence of Deceased Wife

The Catholic men had a strong sense of the deceased wife's presence, ranging from Mack feeling as if she were watching him on occasion to Carlo's very vivid experience of seeing his wife in their home the day of her funeral. He said, "The night I came home after we buried her, I saw her walking by the dresser. I said, 'Rose! What are you doing!' but she disappeared that quick. If I had to take an oath today, I would say I saw her." Jerry felt his wife's presence strongly when he found a letter she had written to him during their courtship. He said, "I feel very close to her at times, I really do. I talk to her. I just believe in that spiritual part of life." Conner kept the same daily routine that he and his wife had kept; he said he knew she was not far away. Robert said, "There are times when I can almost feel that perhaps she's trying to tell me something, or comfort me in some way." Feeling a presence with this intensity was characteristic of the Catholic men. Cordell expressed his memory of his deceased wife as a presence, "She hasn't really left me. Her spirit or her being or whoever will always be with me as a part of my life." Non-Catholic men would speak of missing their wives and remembering them, but not of experiencing a presence so strongly.

Conceptions of an Afterlife—Jewish

Remembrance of deceased loved ones was mentioned often by the Jewish men, but not the hope or plan of meeting them again in another existence. Daniel said, "We believe God will take care of our souls, but that's about it." Both George and Jacob said that they never gave the existence of an afterlife any thought. Of course, Jacob said, he would like to meet his parents again. He said he knew that Christians felt very certain of an afterlife, and "to a degree, I am jealous because they know; because it is believed, that makes it work." Benjamin said, "I'd like to think there was, but I've never heard of anybody come back and relate to you that there was. . . . Like the field maybe that does exist, but I've never seen it. It's just something that you like to think." Sy said that some people would feel that there is an afterlife, but he does not believe in it. Alvin said emphatically and succinctly, "There ain't any." Sy mentioned how vividly he dreamed of his parents and his deceased wife. Jacob said passionately that his wife was in his heart, and Alvin said his wife was in the memories of those who had loved her. For Jews, remembrance was a strong theme and was a way in which their loved ones continued to exist.

Religion and the Oldest Respondents

The most elderly cannot be categorized by any generalizations with regard to religious beliefs or practices. But the ones who had been deeply involved in a family and community religious experience displayed their faith in oldest age in the way that they had come to peace with the closing of their lives. They did not talk so much of beliefs and practices; Louis glowed with the satisfaction of a life well lived; Ned had processed his beliefs over a lifetime and at age 100 he seemed to be completely sustained. He said:

> You have the possibility of . . . things that seem to die in one form and appear again in an advanced form. . . . Maybe that's what happens to us too, I don't know. But certainly not physically. Skeletons don't graduate into butterflies! But I do feel that Providence is divine and benign, and it's going to be all right, whatever happens."

No Religious Faith

Only a few of the men said that they did not have religious faith. Joe called himself a heathen and referred to some of his neighbors in the sectarian retirement community in which he lived as hypocrites. Art said he was "largely a nonbeliever" and that he had turned against religion because of the evil he had seen done in its name. Still, his current reason for not attending Orthodox services, which he said he always enjoyed and found beautiful, was that he did not have transportation. He sprinkled his comments in the interview with Yiddish terms because he found that language to be so expressive. Obviously, he was still immersed in his Jewish identity. In his very old age and infirmity, he said that he viewed death as a natural process. "Nature finally gives you that relief," he explained. Bert and Don were Jewish, but not religious. Bert had been born into a Jewish family but said he had no interest in religious observance. Don said when people ask him what denomination he is, he says he is Jewish and does not know what God is. He had adopted the Alcoholics Anonymous concept of a "higher power," using that belief to help him feel that he did not need to manage the difficulties of life on his own. Beyond that practical application, he did not articulate much in the way of religious beliefs. As a recovering alcoholic who had seen more than his share of "bottoming out" and tragedies, he was understandably focused on managing his own life of sobriety and with helping other alcoholics. When asked if he thought there was an existence after life, he replied:

> I hope so. I don't know. I'd like to be in a place where all my friends are, and all the people I've loved and that loved me are playing, with a big restaurant that I can pick up the check. A big restaurant in the sky or something like that. But I have no fear. You know, it might be another journey.

Religion, Meaning and Peace of Mind

To return to the four categories of religious orientation named at the beginning of this section, it appeared that those men with religious faith—whether derived from strong and unexamined beliefs or from a philosophical quest—were the most at peace in their late life. At least they could articulate their peace of mind. The men with philosophical leanings seemed to have suffered more along the way, but may have come to more satisfying understandings. This would be in keeping with the expectations of Frankl (1992) who concludes that the inner tensions and the resultant search for meaning are necessary for mental well-being. Our interviews did not explore deeply the belief systems that sustained the men who were not religiously inclined. However, given the variations in human qualities, beliefs, and behaviors that we found among our respondents, we should expect as much variety in meaning and sources of peace at the end of life. As Frankl states, the "will to meaning" is unique in each individual and "must and can be fulfilled by him alone" (p. 105). Erikson's (1950) stage of Integrity versus Despair intersects with the conceptualization of search for meaning. This final accounting of the worth and rightness of one's life might well be formulated in terms other than religious, although we most commonly find religion dealing with and attempting to answer those meaning of life questions, and we most commonly find individuals turning to religion for those answers.

BEING GENERATIVE/BEING PRODUCTIVE

We found among our respondents a very strong theme of working on behalf of others, as well as a strong theme of family involvement. We started with Erikson's concept of generativity to explore the tendency for an older man to be involved in activity that is meaningful and beneficial to the recipients of his efforts. We discovered that such activities were also meaningful and beneficial to the man.

The term "generativity" (Erikson, 1974) represents the developmental stage of mature adulthood in which the psychosocial task is to create something that is given to the future. For most people, having children and rearing them is a way to express the generative task. However, generativity can extend beyond parenthood and is associated with ongoing interest in other people, a feeling of responsibility for the well-being of others, and a sense of the continuity of life even after one's own life has ended. Snarey (1993) defined societal generativity as caring for younger adults, mentoring, leading, and contributing to the strength and continuity of subsequent generations. For the men in our study, generativity generally took two forms: caring attention to the younger generations of their families (parental generativity) and volunteer work in the community (societal generativity). This pattern also was noted by Whitbourne (2001) in her review of the literature on generativity and older adults. We found generativity to be widespread among the men in our study, and to be particularly strong in the subset of Jewish respondents. In this section, we will look broadly at generativity as it was expressed by older widowed men.

For the purposes of our analysis, we defined parental generativity as focusing on one's children or grandchildren. Only in cases of a very close and special relationship did we categorize nonfamily helping efforts as parental generativity. Societal generativity became a broad category, including such diverse activities as tutoring school children, raising funds for medical research and helping the elderly with their tax returns. The following statements taken from transcripts of the interviews provide examples of the generative impulse in the three categories. Arch demonstrated biological generativity, saying "I would love to be a grandfather." Michael made this statement of parental generativity:

> I wrote one letter which I xeroxed and sent to [all the children]. Now I increased it to nieces and nephews because of the same thing I said to you, that families become separated. . . . If I stay in touch with those people, because that's information about them that goes into the letter . . . they will know each other. That's my whole purpose.

George expressed societal generativity with his activist concern for heart surgery patients, the elderly people in his local Jewish community, and older people in general. In a follow-up phone call he explained his latest new program:

> I saw old people carried out of those senior high rises into ambulances every day, and I knew precious time was lost because the EMS crews did not have medical data right at hand. So I started a program to get that information collected in advance and put in an envelope just inside each person's apartment door.

Our study found nearly all of the respondents involved in some activity that has an "other focus," as would be expected from the very premise of a developmental theorist such as Erikson: that this motivation to care for another is a stage that every normally developing person will encounter and deal with. Many of our respondents were active in organizations that serve others; volunteer work was a particularly popular way for these men to structure their caring efforts. We found little if any differences in the altruistic impulse of those men who focused on youth and those who assisted the aged. One might posit a difference in the sense of leaving a legacy, but that seemed not to be the case for men in our study. Our respondents who helped the aged conveyed to us a sense of being part of an effort that strengthened community in the present, that laid groundwork for programs that would remain a part of the community in the future, and that demonstrated respect and caring for all persons, in effect modeling for younger people how to regard and treat older people. In some cases, these men were helping to develop or sustain a supportive service that might one day in the future serve them, just as parental generativity tends to be repaid when a parent or grandparent comes to a time of needing assistance.

A "Normal" Way for Men to Express Caring

One of the defining characteristics of traditional masculinity is the agentic orientation (Bakan, 1966), the highly individual need for self-assertion and mastery which manifests itself in action and accomplishment. It is oversimplifying to state that men are valued for what they do, but there is a strong tendency among many people to evaluate a man by his accomplishments or by the status of his occupation. Having internalized these perceptions, many men do not want to give up the activity that defined them and gave them value and meaning. Retirement research examines men's feelings about work and retirement to analyze the adjustments that are made during that transition. Maddox (1968) saw retirement as differentiated by a number of factors that make`adjustment very individualized. Reichard, Livson, and Peterson (1968) identified variable responses to retirement. In our study volunteer work allowed many of the retired men to not "call it quits." As mentioned earlier, it was interesting to note how many men could not give a simple answer to a question about when they retired. Some, like Richard, were asked by their employers to do part time what they had previously done full time. Others, like Ned, found another job requiring similar skills, but for fewer hours. Still others went directly from paid employment to volunteer work. When asked about his retirement, Yussef's story led smoothly from military retirement through a second career occupation and into his volunteer work at a V.A. hospital. In his mind, retirement occurred when he no longer did the volunteer work. For those men who might have a "no longer productive" crisis upon retirement, part-time employment and volunteer work clearly extend that period of feeling useful and occupied. Such an extension may eliminate the crisis altogether, as Kilmartin (1994) suggests that older men "find new roles that grow out of the opportunities created by retirement, disability, and widowerhood" (p. 120).

Relationship Between Generativity and Health

Health and sensory decline can put actual physical limitations on a person' ability to do things. Health problems also can draw a person's attention inward because it takes an increasing proportion of one's energy to take care of one's own needs. The research of Hammel and

Walens (1999) suggests that self-absorption represents the marshaling of limited energies to the roles of self-care. As one's health diminishes, one has to devote a greater percentage of current resources—including energy, which is itself diminishing also—to taking care of personal needs. Roles involving others, which used to be very important, must be put aside in order to take care of one's health and maintain a daily routine. Arranging medical appointments and getting to them may take the energy and focus that a widowed man had been able to give to friendly mutual support with his neighbors or to teaching his great-grandson to fish.

However, poor health does not necessarily negate generativity. Richard was disabled, but he continued to be very other-focused. Joe had prostate cancer, but his cancer and the treatments were just another topic of conversation as he went about his busy life which included philanthropy and service to others, as well as Big Band dancing on the weekends. George's serious illness could have limited his activity, but actually seemed to intensify his need to do good, perhaps because he saw ahead the end of his ability to work and be helpful.

Continuity of Generativity

Generativity seemed stable in older adulthood. Those who were low in generativity tended not to under-take new activities. Leroy was bored and unhappy, but he did not consider getting out and being active either in socializing or in service-oriented ways. Those who were high in generativity tended to remain active. An exception would be when health decline became a factor; still, most generative men continued activities as long as they could. Yussef moved from work to volunteer work without pause and quit only when his feet hurt so bad that he could not continue. Harry, at age 100, brought back candy to the nursing home staff when he went on an outing and regretted that he could no longer exercise his caring, helpful nature to the extent that he used to do it. Ned, always caring and positive, said in a follow-up interview when he was 101 and recovering from a heart attack, "You know, sometimes I think I ought to be doing something, but I don't know what." When asked if he hadn't done enough in all his years of living, he responded brightly, "Evidently not!" He knew that his long life had been a blessing to his adoring family. That continuing parental generativity seemed to buoy him up even as he thought he might have to end his generative activities (tutoring second graders) in the community.

Louis had made a very positive adjustment to his declining mobility and general health. His entrepreneurial inclinations found a new outlet when he designed a reversible expansion bracelet made of safety pins, plastic beads and elastic cord. He rode the retirement home van to the shopping mall for his supplies and sat in his chair to make the bracelets. He carried the bracelets in a canvas bag on his walker and sold them to whomever passed his way, giving the proceeds to the American Cancer Society. Becoming unable to contribute was a painful experience for Curly. His occupation and his work through service organizations were important parts of his self-concept and perhaps in his mind had made up for some of the deficits in his family relationships. Once no longer productive, he said that he was useless. He lived in a world of woe in which there was no longer enough energy to sustain himself, much less give to others.

Relationship Between Marriage and Generative Activity

Most of the men were more involved in parental generativity when their children were living at home. For many, there was an increase in societal generativity after the children left home and perhaps another increase when their wives died. Szinovacz (1992) found married retired men socializing with friends less than their wives did. Many of the men in our study said that their wives had been the social director of their partnership. They had a desire to be out doing something, but were unfamiliar with making social arrangements as their wives had done. So for a man, doing volunteer work could be viewed as a new avenue to meeting a need that was previously taken care of by the wife.

Some illustrations emerged from our study. John, a quiet man who had been married to a sociable woman, waited for people who promised at the funeral to call him to go out for lunch; when they did not call he was disappointed. Did he ever call any of them? No. The question left him nonplused. He did however volunteer for various projects at church, a familiar environment for him. The projects gave him an opportunity to be with others. Garrett, on the other hand, was always more outgoing than his wife. When she died, he felt very lonely and adrift, but within a few months he found a new wife who enjoyed traveling and other activities that his first wife had not enjoyed. He brought his second wife into his large family circle and his church activities.

Generative activity sometimes dropped when a widowed man remarried. A new marriage at any age requires an investment of time and emotional energy, thus leaving less time for activities such as volunteer work. Benjamin had worked as a hospital volunteer for a very long time. He increased his volunteer work when his wife died, because it helped him fill the lonely days. However, many of the men said that the evenings alone at home were times of crushing loneliness. A new woman filling those hours would be a benefit surpassing the benefits of volunteer work. Remarried, Ben and his new wife enjoyed cruises and playing cards with other couples. He was still active and proud of his volunteer work, but he did less of it than he did while living alone.

Occupation, Education, Socioeconomic Status, and the Generative Impulse

Maddox (1968) noted that "prestige, money, and education are . . . important social resources known to be positively correlated with participation in voluntary organizations, general involvement in community activity, and access to power structures" (p. 362). Respondents in the current study were identified by education level and type of occupation and placed in broadly defined socioeconomic categories, then rated for degree of generative behaviors. The ratings took into account the types of activities the men undertook, the significance of such activities in daily and weekly schedules, and the emotional investment in such activities expressed by each respondent.

Seven of the 51 men in our study had occupations that are identified with generativity, such as teaching and medicine. In looking for patterns among this group of men, we found them all to be at least moderately high in parental generativity. Four of the seven were high in societal generativity beyond the activities of their teaching or helping career; for the three who did not rate as highly, health and environmental constraints were factors.

The men who rated highest in societal generative activity had been involved in these occupations: owner of a prosperous wholesale business, middle-level manager in a large company, chemical engineer, two college professors, teacher, and executive in a national humanitarian organization. The commonalities here would appear to be a sense of professional competence and the ability to take a leadership role.

Keyes and Ryff (1998) found that generativity tended to increase with age and education in their sample of over 3,000 adults age 25–74. Our study included respondents older than the oldest respondents of Keyes and Ryff. We saw generative behavior negatively affected by very old age, although men who were strongly generative managed to stay active in some way. We did find that increasing education levels tended to coincide with increased generative activity. Education appeared to be more of a factor in societal generativity than it was in parental generativity. Among those who were high in societal generativity, 86% were college-educated while 45% of those who were high in parental generativity were college educated.

The current economic status of the respondents has been leveled somewhat by Social Security, thus masking to some extent the socioeconomic background that influenced their values and their activities in earlier years. Through the sharing of stories from early life, the men did convey a description of that status, which we could then bring forward to consider in relation to their current or recent past generative activity. To a great extent, as would be expected, we found educational level and occupation to align with socioeconomic status. Thus, we found higher levels of generative behavior in the men who had come from families that were middle class or above. The lower level of generative activity persisted even when Social Security brought some measure of economic security to the poorer men. We found socioeconomic status to be more strongly linked with societal generativity than with parental generativity.

Some interesting patterns emerged in this analysis. The six Appalachian men in our sample were from low-income families, some extremely poor. Only two were high-school graduates. All seemed to value education and spoke with pride of children who were better educated than they. At the time of the interviews, none was well off, yet none was in serious financial want. Only the one man who had left Appalachia for a career in the military described any societal generativity in his life; he was moderate in parental generativity, in regular contact with one child, and somewhat alienated from the other. Some of the other men had ambivalent relationships with their children. Carlo and Clyde complained that their children did not want their advice, yet they interacted very regularly. Russell was greatly annoyed by one daughter who often demanded money of him, yet he gave it to her every time she asked.

Farm families tended to be poor, but the family ties stayed strong between the generations. Jewish families tended to be more prosperous than the average in our study; those who maintained their Jewish identity seemed to have strong family ties. Several of our Jewish respondents lived in retirement communities, but they had frequent contact with their children and grandchildren who lived elsewhere. However, the Jewish subgroup also produced the two most serious cases of parent-child alienation described in the study.

Men of all socioeconomic levels become fathers. In expressing biological generativity, they are given the opportunity to express parental generativity. Thus we find the opportunity and expression of strong family connections regardless of family income or social status. Societal generativity appears to be more of a learned perspective, the taking of a broader view of the human condition in ways that may be made possible by relative freedom from want and the opportunity to be educated.

Religious Affiliation and the Generative Impulse

Generativity was evident in men of both Jewish and Christian faith traditions and in some who had rejected any religious involvement. However, the Jewish men stood out for their almost universal devotion to community service and to their families. The good works of the Jewish men in this study may reflect the traditional Jewish religious expectations expressed in the Pirkei Avos for "kind deeds" (p. 9). Applebaum (1959) writes that one of the requirements for a good Jew is "to be charitable and ethical and socially just" (p. 81). Tzedakah involves the giving of one's money to those in need, Gemilut Chasadim the acts of loving kindness that may require one's body, time or money, and are not meant only for the poor but can be directed toward everyone (Cohen, 1949; Robinson, 2000). Rabbi Telushkin's *Book of Jewish Values, A Day-to-Day Guide to Ethical Living* (2000) is filled with practical advice for meeting these expectations. Our respondents seemed to have internalized them so completely that they did not even think about the origins of their desire to care for others. Only Benjamin stated directly that he thought being reared as a Jew made him more charitable and more sensitive to the plight of those less fortunate.

The teachings of other religious groups, such as the Christian concept of loving one's neighbor, and an individual's own role models could strongly influence the generative impulse. Christian men ranged from low to high in both forms of generativity with no appreciable patterns emerging.

Benefits of Generativity for Older Men

Expressions of generativity benefit both the receiver and the giver, as Erikson, Erikson and Kivnick (1986) noted. Whitbourne's (2001) review of literature on generativity suggests "generativity is an important route toward positive adaptation in the middle years and beyond" (p. 420). In a study of hospital volunteers, Fisher, Day, and Collier (1998) identified the following intangible rewards: praise, appreciation from persons who were helped, enhanced perspective on one's life or situation, opportunities for personal growth, and positive self-concept brought about by seeing that one has had a positive impact on the well-being of others. In a meta-analysis of 37 studies of generativity, Wheeler, Gorey, and Greenblatt (1998) found beneficial effects for eight out of ten volunteers. The most beneficial effects were noted for active volunteers working with clients in face-to-face helping. It is clear that others receive tremendous benefit from the loving attention of a grandfather or from the diligent work of a volunteer. Bradley (1999–2000) identified three ways in which volunteer workers benefit from the work that they do: (a) they have an enhanced sense of purpose, (b) they have enhanced identity, and (c) they have structure to their daily routine.

Our analysis expands upon Bradley's categories of benefits to the person who expresses generativity. The giving of care pays immediate dividends to the giver in the following ways: (a) meaningful activity in store for a given day, (b) a chance to pursue one's personal interests, (c) the mental stimulation of problem-solving, (d) a chance to interact with others, (e) association with younger people and vitality, (f) an opportunity perhaps to be appreciated, (g) a feeling of connectedness to humanity in a tangible way, and (h) a framework for placing oneself in a universal or spiritual scheme. Volunteer work is a logical way for a man to express generativity. He worked all his adult life being a provider for his family and drew meaning from his work for his personal identity. With his children grown and his career ended through retirement, he continues to work, now as a "volunteer." He continues to be active, useful, involved, and appreciated. Our respondents made many comments indicating the benefit they received from their volunteer service. Jacob said that looking at young faces made him feel young. George said he knew that his program's continuation was up to him; he had to stay involved. Ned said of the students and the staff where he tutored, "I've had a wonderful experience with them. . . . They are the nicest people. . . . They're some of my special friends." Clyde pointed out his importance in helping a son, "You see what a lift he got. And that was all because of me. . . . Dad, yes, Dad put him right!"

Generativity and Life Satisfaction

The voluntary nature of generativity in later life may explain its important contribution to life satisfaction. Mouser, Powers, Keith, and Goudy (1985) found voluntary association memberships to be a factor promoting subjective well-being in older widowed men. Men in our study demonstrated their positive feelings about the volunteer work choices they had made. Joe looked forward to the weekday morning when he worked in the retirement community's furniture repair shop; a visit to the shop revealed Joe feeling relaxed, competent, purposeful, and content. He spoke with great enthusiasm about what a good service it was for the many elderly people there who did not have carpentry skills. If someone in the retirement community office had said, "Joe, we are assigning you to the furniture shop so you can help people by repairing their furniture," he probably would not have been very excited about it. But Joe found out about the furniture shop, remembered that he had enjoyed woodworking earlier in his life, and decided to volunteer.

For most people, their occupation—even if they had chosen it freely and pursued it enthusiastically (and that was a big "if" in this population that often found limited options for work)—had many elements that were not voluntary. Examples would be: having specific work hours, lack of choice about vacation time and schedules, boss and co-worker difficulties, and paperwork and other uninteresting and unrewarding activities. On the other hand, a volunteer worker could choose what he wanted to become involved in. If elements of the work were not pleasing to him, he could move along to something else. It was a good feeling after years of not being able to make such choices.

Findings

Life values in older men are influenced by the basic beliefs and values of their parents. Education is valued more highly now by most people than it was in the early twentieth century. Older men may not have received much education, but they want their children and grandchildren to be educated. Educational achievement appears to have been negatively affected by the Great Depression and World War II, notwithstanding the G.I. Bill's intent to help returning servicemen gain an education.

Most of the men in the study used religion to answer meaning-of-life questions. Most felt they had at least some control over their lives, and that is valuable for adjustment.

Older men express the generative impulse by being involved with their families and by engaging in volunteer work that benefits others. These activities also benefit the men by giving structure and meaning to their lives as well as broadened contact with other people. Parental generativity is expressed across the spectrum of educational achievement, occupational choice, and socioeconomic status. Societal generativity is much more strongly linked to higher educational, occupational, and income levels.

REFERENCES

Bakan, D. (1966). *The duality of human existence.* Chicago: Rand-McNally.

Bradley, D. B. (1999-2000, Winter). A reason to rise each morning: The meaning of volunteering in the lives of older adults. *Generations, XXIII*(4), 45–50.

Erikson, E. H. (1950). *Childhood and society.* New York: Norton.

Erikson, E. H. (1974). *Dimensions of a new identity.* New York: Norton.

Erikson, E. H., Erikson, J. M., & Kivnick, H. Q. (1986). *Vital involvement in old age.* New York: W. W. Norton.

Fisher, B. J., Day, M., & Collier, C. E. (1998). Successful aging: Volunteerism and generativity in later life. In D. E. Redburn & R. P. McNamara (Eds.), *Social gerontology* (pp. 43–54). Westport, CN: Auburn House.

Frankl, V. E. (1992). *Man's search for meaning: An introduction to logotherapy* (4th ed.). Boston: Beacon Press.

Hammel, J. & Walens, D. (1999, December). Testing a model for examining how older adults develop a self-care manager role following acute and long-term disability experiences. Paper presented at The International Meeting of the Rehabilitation Engineering Research Center on Aging, National Learning Center of the American Society on Aging and the Rehabilitation Engineering and Assistive Technology Society of America, Arlington, VA.

Keyes, C. M. & Ryff, C. D. (1998). Generativity in adult lives: Social structural contours and quality of life consequences. In D. P. McAdams & E. de St. Aubin (Eds.), *Generativity and adult development: How and why we care for the next generation* (pp. 227–264). Washington, DC: American Psychological Association.

Kilmartin, C. T. (1994). *The masculine self.* New York: Macmillan.

Maddox, G. L. (1968). Retirement as a social event in the United States. In B. L. Neugarten (Ed.), *Middle age and aging* (pp. 357–365). Chicago, IL: University of Chicago Press.

Mouser, N. F., Powers, E. A., Keith, P. M., & Goudy, W. J. (1985). Marital status and life satisfaction: A study of older men. In W. A. Peterson & J. Quadagno (Eds.), *Social bonds in later life: Aging and interdependence* (pp. 71–90). Beverly Hills, CA: Sage.

Reichard, S., Livson, F., & Peterson, P. G. (1968). Adjustment to retirement. In B. L. Neugarten (Ed.), *Middle age and aging* (pp. 178–180). Chicago, IL: University of Chicago Press.

Snarey, J. (1993). *How fathers care for the next generation: A four-decade study.* Cambridge, MA: Harvard University Press.

Szinovacz, M. (1992). Social activities and retirement adaptation. In M. Szinovacz, D. J. Ekertdt, & B. H. Vinick (Eds.), *Families and retirement.* Newbury Park, CA: Sage.

Telushkin, J. (2000). *The book of Jewish values: A day-to-day guide to ethical living.* New York: Bell Tower.

Wheeler, J. A., Gorey, K. M., & Greenblatt, B. (1998). The beneficial effects of volunteering for older volunteers and the people they serve: A meta-analysis. *International Journal of Aging and Human Development, 47*(1), 69–79.

Whitbourne, S. K. (2001). Generativity. In G. L. Maddox (Ed.) *The encyclopedia of aging* (pp. 418–420). New York: Springer Publishing.

11

Adult Children and Other Social Support

Forty-two of the men reared biological children. Five men and their wives adopted very young children and reared them. These figures include some overlap, since two couples had both biological and adopted children. Five men reared both stepchildren and biological children. Beyond these situations, stating who was a father was not so simple. Seven of the men reared stepchildren brought into their lives at various ages; in some cases the stepchildren were adopted, in other cases not. Additionally, 12 men had acquired stepchildren in later life as the result of remarriage; these children were not reared in the man's home, and the relationships resembled extended family or friendships more than parent/child.

Family size ranged from one child to 11. Ten of the men reared five or more children, including two stepfamilies. One man had more than ten children, all biological. In most cases of adoption, the men spoke of being as connected with their children as they would have been with biological children. Yussef and his wife had one biological child and one adopted child. Yussef got along better with the biological child, although he did not attribute lack of closeness with the other child to his being adopted. Relationships with stepchildren were generally good. Michael and Carlo proudly told the interviewer that they had raised those children as their own. John spoke with great concern about the health problems of his deceased wife's children. However, Bert indicated he had never gotten along with his stepdaughter.

Almost all of the fathers had frequent contact with their children. We identified adult children as the overall major source of social support for widowed men. We also sought to identify how childless men compensated for the lack of a natural support system.

Three men had no biological, adopted, or stepchildren. Three others had particular situations which, for purposes of considering social support in widowhood, led us to designate them also as childless. Richard and his wife reared a biological child, but the child died in his late teens. Robert's wife had a son adopted out before her marriage to Robert. The man was in contact with Robert, but Robert could not accept the man as "family." Bert's wife brought an adolescent daughter to the marriage; apparently they were never on friendly terms and he had had no contact with her since her mother died.

Men Who Have Had a Child Die

The death of a child is considered by some as the most difficult loss, as it is not in keeping with normal expectations for the natural order of events (Rubin, 1993). Six men in our study had faced that loss. Two men lost children in childhood, four in adulthood.

Earl and his wife experienced the accidental death of a young daughter, as recounted in the Grief and Adjustment chapter. He quoted Philippians 4:7 to describe the relief and release that they experienced in the "the peace of God, which transcends all understanding." He said it was an amazing but not unexpected confirmation of faith; their grieving time was shortened and they were able to go on with their lives. Unlike Earl and his wife, Richard and his wife suffered prolonged grief over the loss of their only child, a son, in an automobile accident when he was a teenager. Earl and his wife had other children to fill their lives, whereas Richard and his wife did not. Earl's spirituality was faith based; he could welcome the comfort of faith-based reassurance. Richard's spirituality was an intellectual, philosophical quest that accepted no simple answers. Earl and Richard were a generation apart in age. Earl was relatively healthy and remarried. Richard had crippling arthritis and lived alone, although he was in contact with many friends. Both had come to an acceptance in their own minds regarding the losses of child and wife.

Cordell had a large family. One of his sons was killed in an automobile accident when he was in his mid-30s. He said the tragedy was very difficult for him because "he [the son] had most of my faults without having my saving graces." He said that his son was obese, was a heavy drinker, and was unhappy in financial matters. "I'm sure he missed the curve because he was drunk." Cordell said his wife was planning to seek her son in Heaven, but Cordell did not have that comfort because he was not able to believe in a hereafter.

Al was living with his son and daughter-in-law after his wife died. Apparently both Al and his wife considered the daughter-in-law to be difficult to deal with. So it was not working out particularly well for Al to live there; then when his son died suddenly, he simply had to move. He lived first with a grandson and the grandson's very large young family, then with a granddaughter and her smaller but still young family. Although there seemed to be much affection, the stresses of the intergenerational households were too great. Al moved into a seniors apartment complex; according to both Al and his granddaughter's husband, that move had given Al "a new lease on life."

Bapuji had lived with his oldest son in India. But the son became ill with emphysema and was no longer able to care for his father. Bapuji came to the United States to live with a younger son; his son in India died soon thereafter. Bapuji was isolated from his culture and from potential friends. There were older people from India in other communities but none were close enough for regular visiting. Also, his daughter-in-law explained, the others were in more vigorous health than Bapuji; his frailty kept him from being able to visit and be active with the other older immigrants from India.

Harry, at age 100, had outlived three of his six children. When asked if his oldest son were still alive, he said, "Oh, heavens no! He died at 73 of a heart attack!" This man who had a very caring nature must have suffered greatly with the sudden losses of three sons—one to a heart attack, one to a traffic accident, and one to a suicide—but he told of their deaths with the tone of a storyteller recounting tragic tales that are part of the local folklore. Indeed his whole life was interwoven with the history of the area; he saw himself as the survivor who was left to tell the stories.

Adult Children's Roles in Father's Life

In our study, adult children were part of their fathers' lives in the following ways: (a) they provided emotional support, (b) they participated in social activities with their fathers, (c) they provided specific help with laundry, cooking, and shopping (d) they were a local or long distance telephone contact, (e) they gave care when it was needed, and (f) they received things from their fathers, such as advice, money, and companionship.

Hoffman, McManus, and Brackbill (1987) found that the majority of elderly parents had frequent contact with their children, even when they lived far apart. Mothers were more likely than fathers to be in contact; daughters were more likely than sons. In our study, we found great variety in the amount of interaction between the fathers and their children. Men such as Carlo, Karl, Bapuji, and Ned, who lived with adult children, had the most constant contact. Art, who lived alone, had a daily visit by his daughter and her husband. Other men had daily contact with an adult child by phone. Most common for men with children living close were visits and phone calls several times per week. It was not unusual to have our interviews interrupted by a phone call from a family member. Bill's home was a gathering place for whoever felt like showing up on Sunday afternoon; attendance ranged from nobody to 20 family members. Children living farther from the widowed man had fewer face-to-face visits, but called frequently. Louis and Will had frequent phone conversations with daughters who lived in another state. Bruce and his four children had a timetable for rotating calls and visits. Michael phoned all of his children on Sundays. Children usually called less frequently after their father remarried, apparently because they knew they were no longer his main source of companionship. However, in most cases friendly contacts continued.

Infrequent contact between fathers and children usually signaled tensions in the relationship. George and Yussef, for example, had much more frequent phone contact with the children with whom they got along than with those from whom they felt estranged. Some men would tell us how often a child called or visited, obviously equating that frequency with attentiveness and concern. For example, Sy reported on frequency of phone calls and visits in both directions as evidence of his family's closeness. Don knew that increased contact with his daughter meant an improvement in their relationship. Significant estrangement would result in very infrequent contact. George and Walter had very little contact with their estranged children; even interaction around the time of the death of the wife/mother was minimal and very strained.

Preston and Grimes (1987) found that 58% of unmarried elders found ongoing socioemotional support from family members. In our study, adult children were usually named by the widowed man as his mainstay of emotional support through the loss of his wife. They grieved with him and comforted him, they took care of funeral details, they helped him dispose of their mother's possessions, they helped him adjust to life alone. They invited their widowed father to family activities, they participated with him in activities he would enjoy (eating out, going to a movie). Sometimes they provided instrumental help. Frank was quite capable of taking care of himself, but his daughter still did his laundry each week. Stuart mentioned that his daughter would send leftovers home with him after a family meal. Clyde said his son went with him to lunch at a restaurant where older men congregated.

Adult children sometimes acted as caregivers to their fathers, especially when the father was very old. Carlo's daughter had work experience as a nursing assistant. She was prepared to care for her father at home as long as he lived. Ned's family provided whatever assistance was needed to their beloved centenarian patriarch. Art's family delivered a home-cooked gourmet meal for his evening meal each day; they hired and managed additional help to make certain he was comfortable and safe in his own home.

While this chapter focuses on fathers and children, it is important to note that the man's grandchildren and siblings sometimes fulfilled the roles mentioned above. Langer (1990) found that the majority of grandparents and their adult grandchildren did not have relationships with reciprocal support, but a sizable minority of grandparents did feel such reciprocity existed. They felt they received more emotional support than they gave and about the same amount of instrumental support as they gave. For example in our study, Al's only living child was in a religious order, so her daughter (Al's granddaughter) checked in with him daily by phone; she took him shopping and to medical appointments. It appears that grandchildren will step into the caregiving void if a parent is not available to give care and emotional support, and as Langer reports, they "bolster the sense of self-worth of the grandparent" (p. 107).

Fathers Giving to Children

Even through very old age, the father's relationship to his children had a strong element of reciprocity. In other words, the father had not become a needy recipient of services and attention; he was still giving something to the relationship. The men wanted to continue to be independent, productive, and capable of providing something for their loved ones.

Advice

The theme of fathers giving advice to their adult children came up in many of the interviews. Some of the men indicated that they refrained from giving advice as they felt that would be interfering. Conner, for example, had thoughts about the way his daughter was dealing with her adolescent son, but indicated that he would be "out of bounds" if he made suggestions to her. Louis said that he and his wife had long been grieved about their son's smoking, but he had ceased to express his worries. He said that he and his wife had expressed themselves fully and had decided to say no more.

Our interviews also revealed some examples of advice still being given. It was a way for the men to share the knowledge and wisdom that they felt they had gained through a lifetime of experience. They told the interviewer of advice given to their children and grandchildren; they frequently offered advice to the interviewer. The Appalachian men were prolific advice givers. Carlo and Clyde were disappointed that their wisdom was not better received and used by younger family members, but they seemed to know that each generation must learn hard lessons for themselves. Yussef joked that his advice wasn't worth much, but he was noticeably pleased that his son sought his opinion on important matters. The men's penchant for giving advice was clearly seen in the advice they gave to the interviewer: where to eat, how to get somewhere, how to raise children, how to have a successful marriage, how to conduct research. Sam was restless during a follow-up interview, but when the interviewer's car wouldn't start, he was focused and full of recommendations for dealing with the problem.

Money

Hoffman, McManus, and Brackbill (1987) found some children giving financial assistance to elderly parents, but even more were receiving financial benefit from their parents. Our respondents, accustomed to being family providers, continued providing in many ways. Stuart and Karl would take their families out to dinner and pick up the tab. "Helping out" with major purchases was common. Again, the Appalachian men provided our examples. Al commented that one of the reasons his granddaughter was so good to him was because he had given her a large sum of money to build onto their house. Langer (1990) wonders, "To what extent is giving financial gifts 'with a warm hand' an expression of 'deposit' to the adult grandchild with a silent hope for future 'withdrawals' in the form of expressive or tangible support" (p. 108)? Yussef gave a small home outright to his son. Russell gave money to his daughter on several occasions and was making payments she missed on a land contract. This situation, explained more fully later in this chapter, caused Russell great stress. In general however, it seemed that the respondents in this study gave their money freely as a way to give something to the relationship with their children.

Companionship

Many of the men knew that their presence was a welcome part of family relationships. Hodgson (1992) found adult grandchildren to have strong emotional bonds with at least one of their grandparents and that face-to-face contact was common. At younger ages, the men joined in family gatherings as father and grandfather. In older age, they were elevated to a place of special honor and care. Eldon's family knew that he, at age 104, would not be with them much longer; they rotated their visits to his little home so that someone was always looking in on him. They listened to his stories and enjoyed bantering conversation. Louis proudly said that his son had a good time visiting him, that it was not just a matter of duty. Art and Ned also had children who were grateful for their father's long life. They were providing care, but the respect they accorded him and the enjoyment they obviously felt in his company were the most noticeable features of their relationship with him.

Tensions Over Father's New Relationship

Tensions with adult children involved both sons and daughters. The strongest factor in stressful relationships seemed to be the interplay of personalities. Some of those situations will be discussed later in this chapter. The most common situational tension arose when the father wanted to date, or started to date, or chose another wife. Since the younger men were more likely to enter a new intimate relationship, this tense situation developed most often between our younger respondents and their adult children. Lund, Caserta, and Dimond (1993) found that new intimate relationships for the bereaved could violate the expectations of others and caused tension. For some of the men, at some point in a new relationship, the adult child seemed to feel that he was betraying the mother's memory by becoming interested in another woman. This was the case for both sons and daughters. In Earl's case, his daughter encouraged him to place an ad in the local paper to meet compatible women, and she helped him sort through the replies. But then she felt resentful when he chose to marry a woman he had met through the ad. He felt torn between wanting a good relationship with her and not wanting her to be overly involved in decisions that were his to make.

Two of the men found their sons to be upset when they allowed a new woman into their lives. Stuart's son was much less accepting of his father's remarriage than was Stuart's daughter. At follow-up Jerry said his son was instantly indignant to hear his father had become friends with a much younger woman. However, at the first interview, Jerry had reported that his daughter was worried about the fact that he was sitting at home too much. All of Russell's children—sons and daughters—were upset with his new relationship that developed very soon after their mother's death. Lester and Lester (1980) discuss how adult sons and daughters sometimes perceive it as infidelity when their surviving parent is involved sexually with another person. Cordell went quickly into a new relationship; he reported a daughter asking him if he ever thought about Mom any more.

A new relationship too soon brought the most intense feelings, but for some of the men's children, a new relationship at any time brought up negative feelings. For the widowed man, new companionship may have been the answer to many of his problems. He would always remember his deceased wife, but he would invest himself in a new intimate relationship that would provide his present life with the comfort and enjoyment he had experienced in his earlier marriage. Kenneth, for example, said that his first wife had been the mother of his children, for which he would always cherish her. He said he felt he had "borrowed" his second wife from her deceased first husband. For children, the affectional tie cannot be transferred so easily. One cannot replace the mother or father of one's childhood memories. So no matter how nice a woman their father had found, she was not mother. It seems that some of the children were hurt by the father's ability to make that transfer seemingly so easily when they could not make it at all.

PARENTING PRACTICES BROUGHT FORWARD

Three of our oldest respondents—Louis, Art, Ned—had such respectful and loving families that one could imagine only the most genuine and appropriate parenting practices having been the norm all during family life. Most of our respondents seemed to have basically positive relationships with their adult children, but not all did.

Parenting Issues in Alienation

We cannot draw conclusions about "poor parenting" because we have insufficient data to figure out how and why relationships turned out badly for some of the men in our study. However, our observations and our data suggest that problematic circumstances in the parenting relationship led some of our respondents to have less than satisfactory relationships with their adult children. Family members were open about the controlling behaviors that had led to alienation for some of the men. Curly's family members spoke of his self-centeredness, his perfectionism that never was pleased with anything, and the verbal abuse toward his wife. To their credit, they did visit him and encouraged him to think of the good things in the past rather than lamenting all his wrongdoings. But in late life, Curly was reaping the pain of his own guilt and the disaffection of family members. Karl tried to hide the nature of his family relationships, but he signaled the interviewer that he was less than forthcoming by turning aside every question that had to do with expression of emotion. A relative said that he had been very controlling of both his wife and his son, and that he would usually express only displeasure. Karl's son was a good-hearted and patient man whose wife said she "loved him all the more for truly turning the other cheek." He had made a home for his widowed father and treated him with respect.

Some of the men conveyed negative information about themselves nonverbally. Walter, for example, demonstrated emotional barrenness and evident detachment in his relationships. After his death, his daughter told the interviewer that her father was always inexpressive, except when he expressed anger. She had felt quite alienated from him, saying that they had not been a close family and that it was too bad her father had not broken away from his own family. She seemed to feel that she had some of the traits and tendencies carried down through this family line, and that made it more difficult for her to carry on a satisfying life. Curly, Karl, and Walter gave us our most substantiated examples of harsh parenting, in that family members were available to comment.

George and Alvin initiated comments about getting along poorly with one of their children. We heard only one side of the story, the side presenting the father as reasonable and the child as not. Parenting could have been a factor in these adult child/parent tensions, but we had only indirect evidence of parenting styles. George felt close to his younger son, but was quite critical of and bitter about the older son. He spoke with great emotion about the older son's laziness and callousness in taking advantage of people, especially expecting his parents to continue to provide for him. George blamed his wife for coddling him as a young adult when he was being irresponsible; he expressed anger that his son had "messed up" good opportunities. He described a dramatic scene in which he threw the son out of the house and told him he would have to support himself. The son lived in another state at the time of the interview; George said bitterly that his son would make time to have lunch with him (if he went there for a visit) "if there were something in it for him." George had just been diagnosed with a potentially terminal illness. In many areas of his life he was trying reach some closure, but that attitude did not seem to extend to reconciliation with his older son. George was a highly acclaimed volunteer in his community, known for his compassion and dedication. But his enterprising and dynamic nature in the community may not have been conducive to harmony in his family. He made several forceful statements during the interview about disliking pretentious and know-it-all kinds of people. Similar attitudes within the family could account for discord. As stated earlier, we heard only one side of the story.

Alvin was an example of a man who did not like someone who had married into the family. He was very clear about disliking his daughter-in-law. He was quite unflattering about her, blaming her for the 26-year-long estrangement between Alvin's son and the parents. He said the son got back in contact when he heard his mother was terminally ill. Alvin said that his son and daughter-in-law were nice to him since his wife died, but he resented all the years of estrangement. Alvin's bitterness was sharply expressed in the interview; it could be imagined in a conversation with his son.

Other Reasons for Alienation

Alienation sometimes resulted from tensions that developed with the man's widowed status, as mentioned earlier in this chapter. Earl and Stuart had children who could not accept their father's remarriage. These situations seemed to have occurred in basically good relationships, but the matter did not resolve quickly or easily. Earl was subdued when he spoke of the alienation, but said that he hoped his daughter would come to understand why he married again. In other words, Earl was sorry about the rift, but he felt he had done what was best for himself, and his daughter was the one who had to adjust. Stuart's son had difficulty with his remarriage. Stuart said his new wife was being patient and gracious; he thought that the son's feelings would finally be resolved through the grandchildren, who were enjoying the attention of their new grandmother. Like Earl, Stuart was happy in his new marriage and looked for his child to understand.

Both Earl and Russell were alienated from daughters, but the circumstances were very different. Earl knew that his daughter was dealing with natural feelings of loyalty to her deceased mother. He was firm in letting her know that he must go on with his life, but also let her know that he wanted to have a good relationship with her. Russell, on the other hand, unhappily went on playing his part in what appeared to be a manipulation game orchestrated by his daughter. His complaint about the situation was a recurring topic as he spoke to the interviewer; one wonders what he actually said to his daughter as he handed her money again and again. He never indicated a direct conversation with her, but the following quotation expressed his feelings, his ambivalence, and his supposition about the cause:

> It's my own fault for letting her. I mean, I could throw her out of the house right now for not paying them taxes, and she's late on every payment. But I just can't do my kids that a way. . . . It's hard, really. . . . She wasn't raised that way. But her mother always babied her. I gotta say that.

Yussef expressed disapproval of the younger of his two sons and did not have much contact with him. He considered the younger man (30 years old at the time of the interview) immature, trying to live the same irresponsible lifestyle that he lived through his 20s. Like George, he blamed his deceased wife for coddling that son. Like Russell, he had given things (even a house) to the young man at the same time as he had bitter feelings about the adult child not managing on his own. Yussef seemed to be more able than Russell to minimize for himself the emotional stress of the relationship. However, in every way Yussef was a less expressive man than Russell, so their feelings might not have been so different as the expression of them might have suggested. George seemed intensely bitter toward his son in a way that seemed to be very stressful for him; Yussef seemed to have detached himself from his son without so much internal wear and tear.

Malcolm gave several examples of being irritated with different people about different things. In family life, he found reasons to favor and disfavor certain people. He kept in touch with both of his children, but he was geographically more distant from his son and the son's family than from his daughter and her family. That itself made a considerable difference in the amount of interaction.

Robert could not acknowledge his wife's son as family. He said early in the interview that he had no one now that his wife was dead. Then it turned out that his wife as a very young woman had a son whom she placed for adoption. The young man found her many years later, after she was long married to Robert. She and Robert decided to have contact with him and his family, but not to acknowledge him as her son. With that decision they lived a life of deception that had lasted past the death of Robert's wife. Even with a move to a retirement community, they could not bring themselves to tell new acquaintances that they had a son. The story was sad for the stress that it brought to Robert and his wife, but was even sadder when one saw snapshots from visits by the son and his family. They appeared to be trying to be a family for Robert, and yet he could not acknowledge them or let them buffer his feelings of aloneness.

Leroy had an adopted son whom he raised alone after his first wife died; the son was not giving Leroy the attention that he felt he deserved for having raised him. Leroy said that the son's family invited him to dinner about once a month, but the son was always working and so did not interact with him much when he was there. Whatever his son's feelings might have been, feeling slighted was Leroy's reality in his relationship with the younger man. Klingelhoffer (1989) commented that being neglected by an adult child is very painful for an older parent who is alone. Leroy's later years were filled with boredom that led to ruminating on regrets, and this regret was a major one.

Analysis of the Alienation

Thomas (1994) reported that fatherhood in later life has not been subject to much research attention. He found that fathers and their adult children have to restructure their relationship as life events occur if they are going to continue to get along well. Some of our respondents had difficulties with children in the "launching stage" of early adulthood (Thomas, 1994), while other cases of alienation came about after the father was widowed, whatever the child's age. Six patterns emerged in our assessment of alienation between the widowed fathers in our study and their adult children: (a) a child was viewed as immature or irresponsible and the mother was blamed for having coddled the child, (b) the father disliked the person whom a child had married, (c) the father had strong opinions and expressed little tolerance for someone who did not live up to expectations, (d) an adult child had negative feelings about the widowed father's new intimate relationship, (e) the father was not actively trying to resolve the alienation, and (f) all children were not equally alienated from the father. We did not have the opportunity to investigate fully family life for these men, so are not suggesting that we know who was responsible for bitter feelings in any given situation. We observed alienation from both sons and daughters, and from older as well as younger children.

Nydegger and Mitteness (1991) found that men feel different about sons and daughters. Sons are easier for them to understand, but men also tend to be more critical of their sons. Yussef and George were each alienated from a son, and each blamed the mother for having coddled that son, thereby encouraging him to be irresponsible. Russell was very upset about his younger daughter taking advantage of him financially. Thomas (1988) and Greenberg (1991) found that providing help for adult children may be stressful. Thomas found that older fathers are more satisfied with the relationship when a balanced exchange exists. Russell certainly was not satisfied with his relationship with his daughter; he struggled to understand her behavior and could identify only that her mother "always babied her." He said that he and his wife argued only about money; now he was in conflict with a daughter over money. Neither Yussef nor George reported extraordinary conflict in their marriages, but indicated disagreement over dealing with the problem child. George said, ". . . we never had a disagreement in all the years we were married, except twice. Never raised our voices . . . but twice when he [the problem son] had done something that was beyond plain stupidity, and she talked me out of doing anything drastic to really get him put back in his place." George said that his wife had not protested when he told their son to leave the home. However, Klingelhofer (1989) suggests that throwing an adult child out of the home affects the feelings and relationships of everyone involved and may bring more difficulty than it solves. Both Yussef and George were firm in their beliefs and feelings about how things should be, which probably extended to their ideas about how a young man should develop as he grew up. Klingelhofer writes that fathers "believe each generation ought to surpass in its accomplishments those of the preceding generation" (p. 108). A son perceived as lazy is not doing that. Russell was less decisive an actor than Yussef and George; he tended to complain rather than take action in a situation he did not like.

Dislike of a daughter-in-law surfaced as a reason leading to alienation for Alvin, Curly, and Malcolm. Still, it appeared that a tendency toward making judgments existed before the child's marriage. Even for the parties involved, the original reason for discord was difficult to determine; the discord simply existed and was powerful in distancing family members from each other.

Harshness in parenting and in treatment of the wife has been discussed as reason for alienation for Walter and Curly and their adult children. The attitude of caring and forgiving taken by Karl's son, a Christian minister, saved Karl from alienation based on his parenting and treatment of his wife.

Most of the men were not happy or satisfied with the conflicted relationships but they were not making attempts to improve them. Alienation built upon decades of poor relating or lifetimes of negative personal styles would not encourage hope of resolution. Only Earl and Stuart expressed hope of resolving the alienation. Their alienation was a new feature in what had been good relationships; such alienation could be expected to mend, given its recent development and the positive history preceding it. However, they were both mainly counting on time to heal their children's wounded feelings.

In families with more than one child, the alienation was not equally strong. George and Yussef felt more positive feelings toward one son than the other. Alvin got along with his daughter, but had been estranged from his son. Both Earl and Stuart had other children who were more accepting of their remarriage. None of Russell's children had been happy about his new relationship a month after their mother's death, but only one daughter was in continuing discord with him over money. Both of Walter's children experienced alienation, but the daughter seemed to feel it more keenly.

Some of the cases of alienation were outside any observed pattern because of their special circumstances. Robert's alienation from his stepson resulted from the shame and secrecy with which Robert and his wife handled the fact of the young man's birth. Robert seemed to have nothing against the younger man, acknowledging that he (the stepson) "tries to be family," but Robert was unable to acknowledge the connection. Because of this circumstance, we will consider Robert also as a childless widower in the following section. Leroy's sense of alienation came from feeling that the caring attention that he had given in earlier years was not being reciprocated. These cases of father/child alienation were intriguing. Alienation from an adult child is a relationship problem that either brings continuing stress to the widowed man or that he claims to have put out of his mind until the subject is brought up and inflames his emotions.

CHILDLESS WIDOWERS

Six men in the study did not have children or grandchildren to call upon. We were especially interested in how these childless men built a support system when the natural system of younger generations did not exist for them. We found very differing personalities and personal styles among these childless men. Jacob and Richard had attractive personalities and good social skills that drew people to them. Arnold was pleasant and active in the community, where he had many opportunities for interaction. Claude and Robert were less outgoing; they spent much time alone but did not enjoy it. Bert was a loner who seemed to eschew genuine relationships.

No Children at All

Three of the men were childless; their wives had not borne children, and they did not adopt. Jacob lived alone and enjoyed his private domain. He had kept the house just as it was when his wife was alive and had a set routine of daily tasks and religious studies. He still worked part time and found his social contacts in that context. He was a regular at the university library, where he had coffee with the librarians every weekday. Also, he had made friends with a much younger woman in the local Jewish temple congregation. She offered him a ride to services, had invited him to dinner, and was eager to learn Hebrew from him. He also had contact with nieces and sisters, and knew that he could live closer to relatives when he no longer could live alone.

Arnold lived alone in the home where he and his wife had lived. He described his old dog as his last tie to his wife. He was active in the local Jewish center. He often visited his brother's family in another state. At follow-up he had found a lady companion in his brother's hometown so his trips there were more frequent.

Claude lived in an apartment in a retirement community. He was a contemplative and kindly man who felt sad about not having children and grandchildren. He felt his nephew visited him only because he wanted to inherit for his own children a parcel of land owned by Claude. At the interview Claude seemed lonely and isolated; at follow-up he was more relaxed and more actively socializing within his retirement home.

Lost Relationships

Three other men were childless in their old age by virtue of having lost or foregone a connection with someone who could have functioned as an adult child.

Bert said he had never gotten along with his wife's daughter, who was an adolescent when her mother and Bert married. He had no contact with her after her mother's death. Bert lived in an apartment and drove to the local senior center for lunch nearly every day. He talked to many people at the senior center, but he joked sarcastically and then made comments about not liking the people once they were gone. He had no other regular involvement in the community.

Robert was mentioned earlier in this chapter as having a "secret" stepson, whom he could not acknowledge as "family." Robert seemed lonely and depressed; he said he felt he had a sour attitude toward others that discouraged them from wanting to be involved with him. He volunteered for a local organization that assisted older people, but he felt that his volunteer work was furthering his depression.

Richard was an intellectual but also very warm and personable man. His only child was killed in an automobile accident, as previously mentioned. When his wife died, he was deeply depressed. He contended with debilitating rheumatoid arthritis, which had limited his ability to perform activities of daily living. Instead of being crushed by the hardships of his life, Richard viewed them philosophically, seeing what lessons were to be learned from his experiences and what meaning they might have had. He lived in a one-level condominium arrangement. He had developed a friendship with a divorced neighbor in her 50s. She came to his apartment each morning, fixed breakfast, and ate with him. He sometimes accompanied her on outings, such as having lunch with her and her mother. He took an active interest in young people and education.

Berardo (1970) concluded that older widowers in general are alone and isolated. Giranda, Luk, and Atchison (1999) found childless widowed persons to have less family contact and fewer confidants. Johnson and Catalano (1981) described childless unmarried persons as being more resourceful than childless married couples in finding support for their needs; knowing they have no spouse to rely upon, they plan for increasing support in the future. With widowhood, our respondents had a change in status from married to unmarried, a circumstance that may have sent them looking in a wider circle for support. Our data suggest that some childless persons use their social skills to create relationships and support systems that function in ways similar to the natural system of younger generations within a family. However, Johnson and Catalano suggest that the quality of caring in sibling, niece, nephew, or friend contexts may not be the same as in a spousal or parent/child context. We examine those sources of support for all of the men in the following section.

OTHER SOURCES OF SOCIAL SUPPORT

Most research on sibling relationships in old age find these relationships to be positive. Avioli (1989) and Connidis (1989) found that a majority of older adults consider a sibling to be a close friend. Cicirelli (1982) described the sibling relationship as unique in its shared biological and cultural heritage and its long history with so many shared memories. According to Connidis, declining sibling rivalry contributes to increased closeness in old age. Gold (1987, 1990) found feelings toward siblings to be "strong and positive in old age" (p. 741) and stated that awareness of a sibling still being alive contributes to positive feelings in an older person.

Gold (1989) found brother dyads to be less close, while Cicirelli (1977) found sisters to be emotionally supportive to their brothers. Curly's sister regularly visited him in the nursing home. Stuart's sister was supportive of him through his widowhood and introduced him to his new wife. Our respondents spoke of close relationships with brothers as well as sisters. Arnold regularly traveled several hundred miles to visit his brother and family. Art had weekly phone conversations with his only living sibling, a younger brother. Terrence was involved with siblings also, and Yussef said he visited with his siblings more than with his children. Clyde told of making a visit to his brother's children as a way of strengthening family ties. He said:

> You never get away from your family. Some people have said, "I don't want any family." That's wrong. Somewhere along the lines you're gonna need that family. . . .You're gonna need their feelings and what they think. . . . I don't write them off. They're welcome. I went down to my brother's children's house and I said, "[Nephew], I never knew you boys; I would like to get to know you." He said, "I would like to get to know you too." "Well," I said, "then I'm glad to see you and glad to know you and glad to talk to you." You know, that seemed like it did him more good than anything I ever said to him, because I talked to him like that.

Fitzpatrick (1998) reviewed the literature on older men's experience of bereavement and found support for viewing many kinds of losses as significant to that population. Losing a sibling is the end of a lifelong relationship and a reminder of one's own mortality. We inquired about siblings but did not ask the men to talk at length about the loss of a sibling unless a respondent wanted to do so. Craig said he hoped to see his brother before his brother died of cancer. Some of the men commented with chagrin that their siblings had died of smoking. Art, Bruce, and Karl had lost siblings to smoking-related cancers.

Religious Organization Involvement

Garrett, Earl, Daniel, George, and Arch were all busy with church activities. Garrett had remarried just months after his first wife died; he brought his new wife into the church activities at his home church. Earl had started attending the church of his new wife; he was comfortable with her denomination, and became very active in supporting the church's projects. Arch said that church had always been part of his life. He had cut back on activities while giving care to his wife, but the church had again become the focal point of his activities. He said that the church members took good care of him and that the pastor was very thoughtful too. Malcolm, on the other hand, while still attending his church, had hurt feelings about how congregation members neglected his wife when she was ill. Those feelings limited his participation in church activities. Lund, Caserta, and Dimond (1993) found that religious activity had a positive association with adjustment in bereavement, but they conclude that it was the general favorable influence of social interaction that led to positive outcomes, not necessarily the religious nature of the activity. For many of our respondents, the church or synagogue had been a place for social interaction while they were married, and it remained so for them in widowhood.

Social Groups/Support Groups

Caserta, Van Pelt, and Lund (1989) reported that bereaved persons perceived themselves to be able to cope better with their loss by keeping busy and socially active. In a study of Catholic widows, Gass (1987) found that 10% of the women participated in social groups, such as senior citizens groups and church groups. Often they continued to do what they and their spouses had done together. Some of our respondents were active in religion-identified groups. Arch and John increased their involvement in their churches after they were widowed. Arnold continued his activities at the local Jewish center, staying in the activities that he and his wife had done together. Bruce, on the other hand, said clubhouse activities at his retirement community were dominated by women; he did not want to sit around talking about children and shopping. The single men in the community had not developed any ongoing group activities. Gass found that 5% of her female respondents used support groups to help them cope with grief. We found lower participation rates among our male respondents. The few who had attended a self-help group session found it to be dominated by women and their particular concerns; they felt uncomfortable, did not find the group useful, and usually did not return. Clearly, many men are not attracted to bereavement support groups and are therefore missing group support that could be helpful to them. In the final chapter we will discuss ways that support groups might be made more appealing and appropriate for bereaved men.

Volunteer Work

Volunteer work provided opportunities for men to be with others. The work was rewarding from an altruistic perspective; in many cases its structure and the abilities required were comfortably similar to familiar work settings for retired men who liked the idea of still being productive (Wheeler, Gorey, & Greenblatt, 1998; Bradley, 1999–2000). Having a purposeful reason to get out and be with other people was much easier than trying to arrange a social get-together for most of the men. Having to be somewhere to do something kept the men from sitting at home in the "social isolation" described by Berardo (1970) as the fate of older men who had lost both their spouse and their work role (p. 17). The benefits of doing volunteer work and the examples given by our respondents are considered in depth in the Life Values chapter; a section of that chapter is devoted to generative activities and their benefits to the older man.

FRIENDSHIPS

Popular stereotyping says that men have more difficulty creating and maintaining friendships than do women. This viewpoint has probably been a bias in research on gender differences in friendships and social support. Indeed, we held that opinion as we designed our study to explore the realities of life for the older widowed man. However, Wright (1982) concluded that there are many more similarities than differences in the friendship patterns of older men and women. According to Blau (1961), if widowhood and retirement populations are plentiful in the area, there will be less detrimental effects on friendships; the widowed are "in the same boat." Johnson and Troll (1994) found that nearly half of persons over age 85 said they were still making new friends. Our respondent Ned exclaimed that the children and the school staff where he volunteered were his good friends; at age 100 he had outlived everyone in his cohort. Johnson and Troll found that older people expand friendship possibilities by redefining who is a friend to include acquaintances and by accepting the idea of friendship as existing without the opportunity for face-to-face interaction.

Ferraro, Mutran, and Barresi (1984) proposed a compensation model, wherein persons who had faced a stressful loss would find alternative means of meeting needs and gaining social support. The ability to relate as a friend or to form new friendships may be low during acute grieving, but after three or four years, the person may have more friends than before, having compensated for the loss of companionship by reaching out to others. Our respondent George's volunteer work put him in contact with literally hundreds of people; he referred to himself as a man with many friends.

Preston and Grimes (1987) found that married men rely heavily on their spouses for emotional support. In widowhood, elderly persons receive the most social and emotional support from family, with friends ranking next. Crohan and Antonucci (1989) reported, "Both family and friends had a positive impact on the older person's well-being" (p. 142), both positively related to life satisfaction. However, family can also relate negatively to life satisfaction, whereas friends seem not to.

Friendships often have the benefit of being within the same generation, for the comforts and congeniality of shared values, interests, and historical perspectives. Then, too, friendships are a matter of choice; having a friend means someone has chosen to be a friend.

Friendships With Men

What we were able to learn about men's friendships in older age is that they are not very plentiful. As noted earlier, Vinick (1978) wrote that there is not a society of widowers, groups of men who would engage in social activities together as widowed women do. Married men socialize with their wives, so who is there to be the widower's man friend? Sy, one of our remarried respondents, said he ate lunch with a group of three men about once a week, but he did that only if his wife were not free to have lunch with him that day. Bruce said he played golf and cards with his buddies. Al wanted a man to play pool with, but there were only three men in the apartment building and all of them were disabled. In Al's age group of 85+, women outnumber men by two to one, and half of the men are living with and spending their time with spouses (U.S. Bureau of the Census, 1999). The numbers available for men's friendships are low to begin with; then disability and death take their tolls. The older man who loses a friend will not find him easy to replace.

Seidler (1992) characterizes men's friendships as based on shared activities and lacking in shared emotions. He accounts for the lack of intimacy as a feature of the underlying competitiveness in male relationships. He writes that men admire their own self-control and feel superior to those men who do not have the same ability to control their emotions. However, Swain (1992) argues that shared activities and mutual problem-solving ventures, typical of masculine style interaction, can be an avenue to intimacy. He does acknowledge that men typically have fewer friendships as they grow older. We found a few disparaging comments made about male acquaintances, usually in the context of incompatible values or ways of doing things, but no evidence of competitiveness with male friends. It appears that the survivorship aspect of older men's lives led them to value whatever friendships they could create. Robert was in a group of four men, but he said sadly that the other three had since paired up with women.

Friendships With Women

Friendships with women that did not have sexual activity, overtones, or potential were not very common either. Swain (1992) refers "to ambiguous sexual boundaries," stating that "women and men questioned the reality of the 'platonic' friendship" (p. 164), feeling the sexual dynamic of the relationship could change. John had a woman friend from church, and then another. He liked the companionship, but he was very wary of anything that might lead to the possibility of marriage. Men who wanted companionship for dinner in a nice restaurant sometimes were reluctant to ask a woman out, for fear of creating expectations. George pointed out that women developed those expectations far too easily. Michael would have women call him; he would take them out to dinner one time, but not again, he said. Alvin told of friendships with several women, but Alvin clearly wanted another wife and the women with whom he interacted certainly would have been aware of that. Arch's relationship with his older neighbor was hard to define; they traveled together, they apparently irritated each other over differences on various issues, and apparently were not sexually involved. Perhaps it was a friendship. Richard said that he had told some women not to continue bringing him food when he was widowed. He felt he had correctly read their intentions and wanted only to discourage them. Richard, however, was the only man who described a friendship with a woman that appeared to be purely friendship. His neighbor was about 30 years younger and divorced. She would come to his condo every morning and fix breakfast for the two of them and eat with him. She also took him on outings, such as to lunch with her mother who lived in a nursing home. Will had a much younger companion with whom he frequently went to dinner and to cultural events; they offered each other support and intellectual stimulation. The townsfolk in their small town were speculating on the nature of the relationship. Cross-sex friendships are often interpreted as romances or sexual relationships, and claims of just being friends are regarded as withholding information about the sexual or romantic nature of the relationship (Swain, 1992).

The Current Woman

Nearly all of the men in our study had a significant "sustaining" relationship with a woman at the time of our interview. For some, it was another wife. For many others, it was an adult daughter. Some men had relied on an adult daughter during bereavement and later found a new wife or companion. Female companions were "the current woman" for several men, ranging from live-in committed relationships to women neighbors or church members with whom the men regularly engaged in some type of social activity (typically, eating out or watching videos at one home or the other). Companionship arrangements ran the spectrum of intimacy; most that were sexual also included a significant component of emotional closeness. Some were steady dating, but with an understanding that sex was not part of the relationship. Typical reasons for a nonsexual steady relationship were: (a) not believing in sex without marriage, (b) not feeling sexual attraction, usually tied in with feelings toward deceased wife, (c) being impotent, or (d) just feeling too old to get involved. A few companionship arrangements seemed to be somewhat conflicted in tone, but were convenient in terms of "having someone to do something with."

Once having identified these more common categories of "current woman," we found that some men had, by reason of necessity, convenience, or creative social maneuvering, fashioned another type of relationship. Some had reestablished a close relationship with a sister or had developed close ties with a granddaughter or niece. It was interesting to note situations of closeness with daughters-in-law; while most sons seemed quite interested in the welfare of their widowed fathers, the utilitarian relationship and usually some emotional closeness developed with the daughter-in-law. Ned's daughter-in-law fondly called him "Dad." Bapuji lived with his son and daughter-in-law; it was she who spent mornings with him before going to work. Bruce described his daughter-in-law as a confidante and the person who would probably take care of him if he needed help.

Childless widowers demonstrated social adeptness at establishing a relationship with a woman. Friendliness with a neighbor, a work colleague, or a service provider sometimes led to a supportive personal relationship.

A few of the men we interviewed had no one woman that could be identified as "sustaining" in his current life. These men, for the main part fairly independent persons, interacted with both men and women, obviously seeing that their socializing needs were met, but not depending upon any one person on a regular basis.

Why a "Current Woman"?

Being paired with a woman may seem to be doing what comes naturally; it may represent a special attraction and affinity between genders, a combination of comfort, complementarity, and the familiar tension of natural and socialized differences. A widowed man may be seeking someone to fulfill long-accustomed roles of daily task performance, an emotional foil for someone who learned not to express his emotions fully, someone to go out with in a decidedly couples society, someone who likes to go places and do things that men are not supposed to like to do on their own, such as dining in nice restaurants, or going to the theater or on a cruise. A woman may be someone to talk to in an accustomed way.

There was a current woman in the life of almost every man, not just the sociable ones who were active in the community. Even the most introverted men had such a connection; in fact, the more introverted men seemed quicker to find that one person to be close to, perhaps in that way eliminating the need to interact with many others or to undertake a prolonged search for companionship. One such man said he was not sure how he met and courted his current wife, it just happened and he found himself married five months after his first wife had died. The flip side of such a connection is the woman who is socialized to care for loved ones. With her husband dead and her children grown and gone, she is attracted to a man who needs to be cared for. We found second wives who were superlative "kin-keepers" (Hagestad, 1986). They knew more about their new husband's children than the husbands did. Garrett's second wife was a good friend of his first wife. He called out to her in a far room of the house several times when the interviewer asked about his children and their families; finally we agreed that she would join us in the last minutes of the interview to provide this information.

Minimal Social Support

Bert had minimal social support because, judging by his interactions at the senior center where he ate lunch, he did not act as if he wanted to be friends with anyone. Claude was a racial minority in his retirement community and was finding other residents not particularly cordial to him; in time, some people became friendly. He was a kind and friendly man, in need of company, so he was surely receptive to any pleasant overtures. Robert, mentioned earlier as losing his men friends to couples relationships, seemed depressed and said that he had a feeling that he was turning friendly people away. He had not figured out how to behave differently. He was very appreciative of the interview situation that gave him the opportunity to talk about his feelings, but told the interviewer later that he had not followed up on the idea of seeking professional bereavement counseling.

Findings

Our respondents identified adult children as a major source of social support. Men who experienced the death of a child handled the loss in very individualized ways. Contact between the widowed men and their adult children varied from daily to almost never. When a man remarried, there was less contact with children than there had been while he lived alone. Tensions between father and child resulted in less frequent contact. The very old widowed fathers received caregiving assistance from their children.

The fathers valued reciprocity in relationships with their children. They appreciated the companionship and support of their children; they also wanted to give something to their children. They gave advice, money, and companionship. While adult children were concerned about their father's loneliness, they were sometimes unhappy when he found a new female partner. This was particularly true when a new relationship developed soon after their mother's death.

Parenting styles appear to be reflected in parent/adult child relationships. Several cases of alienation seem rooted, at least in part, in the father's approach to life and relationships. However, in most cases the interviewer did not talk with the alienated child for his/her perspective; neither was the mother's role in the situation available for study. Alienation usually involved only one adult child. Fathers dealt with alienation by putting it out of mind rather than trying to resolve it.

Childless widowers include those who never had children and those who had lost children or gave up a relationship with stepchildren. Some childless widowers are skilled in forming relationships with others to gain the social support that other men receive from their children.

Older men often have positive relationships with siblings. They also participate in church activities, social groups, and volunteer work; they gain social support in these settings. Friendships with other men are valued but are not plentiful. Such friendships may be lost through death or when a man friend finds a new woman companion. Friendships with women could have some tension because neither party knows when one might redefine the friendship as a relationship with sexual interest.

Almost every man had a "current woman" in his life. Sometimes the woman was a new wife, daughter, daughter-in-law, granddaughter, sister, or niece. In other cases the woman would be a neighbor, a woman from the man's religious congregation, or a dating companion. The "current woman" functioned in at least some of the roles that were left vacant by the deceased wife. The prevalence of the "current woman" in the lives of widowed men indicates the importance of gender complementarity in older men's lives. For example, second wives functioned as "kin-keepers" for their husbands, keeping track of birth dates and other details of his family.

A few men had very little social support. Each situation was different, but life satisfaction seemed diminished for these men when compared with the men who had close connections with family, friends, and social groups.

REFERENCES

Avioli, P. S. (1989). The social support functions of siblings in later life. *American Behavioral Scientist, 33,* 45–57.

Berardo, F. M. (1970). Survivorship and social isolation. The case of the aged widower. *The Family Coordinator, 19,* 11–25.

Blau, Z. S. (1961). Structural constraints on friendships in old age. *American Sociological Review, 26,* 429-439.

Bradley, D. B. (1999-2000, Winter). A reason to rise each morning: The meaning of volunteering in the lives of older adults. *Generations, XXIII*(4), 45–50.

Caserta, M. S., Van Pelt, J., & Lund, D. A. (1989). Advice on the adjustment to loss from bereaved older adults: An examination of resources & outcomes. In D. A. Lund (Ed.), *Older bereaved spouses: Research with practical applications* (pp. 123–133). New York: Taylor & Francis/Hemisphere.

Cicirelli, V. G. (1977). Relationship of siblings to the elderly person's feelings and concerns. *Journal of Gerontology, 32*(3), 317–322.

Cicirelli, V. G. (1982). Sibling influence throughout the life span. In M. E. Lamb & B. Sutton-Smith (Eds.), *Sibling relationships: Their nature and significance across the lifespan* (pp. 267–284). Hillsdale, NJ: Erlbaum.

Connidis, I. A. (1989). Siblings as friends in later life. *American Behavioral Scientist, 33*(1), 81–93.

Crohan, S. E. & Antonucci, T. C. (1989). Friends as a source of social support in old age. In R. G. Adams & R. Blieszner (Eds.), *Older adult friendship: Structure and process* (pp. 129–145). Newbury Park, CA: Sage.

Ferraro, K. F., Mutran, E., & Barresi, C. M. (1984). Widowhood, health, and friendship support in later life. *Journal of Health and Social Behavior, 25,* 245–259.

Fitzpatrick, T. R. (1998). Bereavement events among elderly men: The effects of stress and health. *Journal of Applied Gerontology, 17*(2), 204–228.

Gass, K. A. (1987). Coping strategies of widows. *Journal of Gerontological Nursing, 13*(8), 19–33.

Giranda, M., Luk, J. E., & Atchison, K. A. (1999). Social networks of elders without children. *Journal of Gerontological Social Work, 31*(1, 2), 63–84.

Gold, D. T. (1987). Siblings in old age: Something special. *Canadian Journal on Aging, 6,* 199–215.

Gold, D. T. (1989). Sibling relationships in old age: A typology. *International Journal of Aging and Human Development, 28*(1), 37–51.

Gold, D. T. (1990). Late-life sibling relationships: Does race affect typological distribution? *The Gerontologist, 30*(6), 741–748.

Greenberg, J. R. (1991). Problems in the lives of adult children: Their impact on aging parents. *Journal of Gerontological Social Work, 16,* 149–161.

Hagestad, G. O. (1986, Winter). The aging society as a context for family life. *Daedaelus, 115*(1), 119–140.

Hodgson, L. G. (1992). Adult grandchildren and their grandparents: The enduring bond. *International Journal of Aging and Human Development, 34*(3), 209–225.

Hoffman, L. W., McManus, K. A., & Brackbill, Y. (1987). The value of children to young and elderly parents. *International Journal of Aging and Human Development, 25*(4), 309–322.

Johnson, C. L. & Catalano, D. J. (1981). Childless elderly and their family supports. *The Gerontologist, 21*(6), 610–618.

Johnson, C. L. & Troll, L. E. (1994). Constraints and facilitators to friendships in late late life. *The Gerontologist, 34*(1), 79–87.

Klingelhofer, E. L. (1989). *Coping with your grown children.* New York: The Humana Press.

Langer, N. (1990). Grandparents and adult grandchildren: What do they do for one another? *International Journal of Aging and Human Development, 31*(2), 101–110.

Lester, A. D. & Lester, J. L. (1980). *Understanding aging parents.* Philadelphia, PA: The Westminster Press.

Lund, D. A., Caserta, M. S., & Dimond, M. F. (1993). Spousal bereavement in later life. In M. S. Stroebe, W. Stroebe, & R. O. Hansson (Eds.), *Handbook of bereavement* (pp. 240–254). New York: Cambridge University Press.

Miller, B., & Cafasso, L. (1992). Gender differences in caregiving: Fact or artifact? *The Gerontologist, 32*(4), 498–507.

Nydegger, C. N. & Mitteness, L. S. (1991). Fathers and their adult sons and daughters. *Marriage and the Family Review, 16,* 245–256.

Osterweis, M. (1985). Bereavement and the elderly. *Aging, 348,* 9–13, 41.

Preston, D. & Grimes, J. (1987). A study of differences in social support. *Journal of Gerontological Nursing, 13*(2), 36–40.

Rubin, S. S. (1993). The death of a child is forever: The life course impact of child loss. In M. S. Stroebe, W. Stroebe, & R. O. Hansson (Eds.), *Handbook of bereavement* (pp. 285–299). New York: Cambridge University Press.

Seidler, V. J. (1992). Rejection, vulnerability, and friendship. In P. M. Nardi (Ed), *Men's Friendships.* Newbury Park, CA: Sage Publications.

Swain, S. O. (1992). Men's friendships with women: Intimacy, sexual boundaries, and the informant role. In P. M. Nardi (Ed), *Men's friendships* (pp. 153–172). Newbury Park, CA: Sage Publications.

Thomas, J. L. (1988). Predictors of satisfaction with children's help for younger and older elderly parents. *Journal of Gerontology: Social Sciences, 43,* 59–514.

Thomas, J. L. (1994). Older men as fathers and grandfathers. In E. H. Thompson Jr. (Ed.) *Older men's lives* (pp. 197–217). Thousand Oaks, CA: Sage Publications.

U.S. Bureau of the Census. (1999, March). *The older population in the United States: Population characteristics.* (Publication No. PPL-133). Washington, DC: U.S. Government Printing Office.

Vinick, B. H. (1978). Remarriage in old age. *The Family Coordinator, 27*(4), 359–63.

Wheeler, J. A., Gorey, K. M., & Greenblatt, B. (1998). The beneficial effects of volunteering for older volunteers and the people they serve: A meta-analysis. *International Journal of Aging and Human Development, 47*(1), 69–79.

Wright, P. H. (1982). Men's friendships, women's friendships and the alleged inferiority of the latter. *Sex Roles, 8*(1), 1–20.

12

Cohorts and the Future

In this book we have offered descriptions of widowers and their experiences, as well as our findings relating to patterns among them. Now we must consider whether this information is helpful in understanding widowers of the future. To do that, we must consider the effects of cohort experience.

The Cohort Effect

It is tempting to say that old men are basically patriotic, frugal, and value hard work. However, it is impossible to completely separate the effects of age from the circumstances of the cohort's life experiences. We found our respondents to be basically patriotic, frugal and valuing hard work. We must ask ourselves: are these characteristics of older men in all times, or are they characteristics of older people who experienced the Great Depression and World War II at a particular point in their young lives? Will researchers in 2020 find the octogenarians they interview to be patriotic, frugal, and believers in hard work? Or will youthful memories of a family living in suburbia (with a television), the civil unrest and social change brought by various social movements and an unpopular war, and a sexual revolution call forth a cluster of different predominant characteristics?

Hultsch and Plemons (1979) make a case for putting life events into a cultural-historical context as well as an individual one. Life events may be the kind that are experienced in the typical life course (such as getting married and having children) or they may be cultural events not part of the usual life course and experienced by many (such as wars and depressions). The individual responds to life events using his inner resources (such as physical health and intelligence) and external resources (such as money and social support). The individual's adaptation to an event "involves changes in affect (e.g., fear, anger), changes in orientation (e.g., beliefs), and change in activity (e.g., increasing, decreasing, adding, abandoning). These processes may lead to either functional or dysfunctional outcomes" (p. 10). Thus, the case is made for an analysis of life experiences that considers cultural life events as they affect the adaptation of individuals.

Persons in the same cohort do not experience all events in the same way, even if the events, such as a worldwide depression or a world war, impact large numbers of people. Not every American family "lost everything" in the Great Depression, nor did they all enter the Depression with similar assets. While the second World War disrupted family life for many, making life and love poignantly precious, and rallied many to a patriotic identification with cause and country, that was not the case for everyone. One of our respondents has medals for five battles in Europe; another missed those battles because he was incarcerated in the U.S. for being AWOL, another worked stateside as a chemist developing materials for use in battle. World War II affected all of our respondents, but we would be wise not to generalize too much about the effects on a cohort.

If there is any desirability to considering the effects of events on a group of people moving through the life span at the same time, the concept of cohort itself needs some refinement. Research by Elder (1999) calls into question even a time frame as short as 10 years. He analyzed two samples of people who were "young" when their families experienced the Great Depression. One group was born in 1920–21 (the Oakland Growth sample), the other in 1928–29 (the Berkeley Guidance sample). His findings illuminate the differential impact of the Depression on males and females in these two groups. His findings indicate that even a 7to 9 year difference in age brought significant differences in the ways that people's lives were affected by the economic downturn. He concludes:

> Central themes from this analysis emerge from the interaction of person and situation; of children characterized by a specific life stage, gender, and family environment during the early 1930s, and their developmental course in relation to Depression hardship. The Depression experience was not uniform. . . . In short, the impact of historical change in lives varies according to what people bring to the new situation; their resources, interpretations, and relationships pattern modes of adaptation and options (p. 156).

The cohorts studied by Elder are within the group of men we are including in our study. Eight of our respondents were born within 1920–21; three were born in 1928–29. Of course many more were born around those years, a total of 31 were born between 1915 and 1934 (five years earlier and five years later than the people in Elder's study). Not having access to the data used by Elder, and not having a common research design with those earlier studies, we are not able to compare our respondents with the Oakland and Berkeley samples. We refer to the work of Hultsch and Plemons (1979) and Elder (1999) for the philosophical perspectives that they offer to a consideration of cohort effect upon the lives of our respondents. Is the cohort effect of twentieth century events so dramatic that we cannot presume that widowers of the future will resemble the widowers of today?

Our respondents ranged in age from 58 to 104 years and thus were at a range of developmental stages during times of war and depression. In spite of these different timings, it seems useful to look at the juxtaposition of events and points in the lifespan in order to consider how much of what we have learned from the 51 men in our study might be applicable to widowers of the future. Hultsch and Plemons (1979) point out that major cultural events may affect generations not yet born at the time they occur because of the changes that these events bring within the culture. The 20th century was a period of life-shaping events; they had world-wide impact as well as particular influence on the lives of men in the United States. Those events include two world wars, the Great Depression, massive immigration into the United States, and the civil rights and women's movements. Whether or not one felt touched directly by these events, they influenced the societal context in which every individual lived, and have continued to influence societies and individuals. Thus, we see a Depression-originated social program called Social Security keeping many elderly out of poverty in the twenty-first century. We also find individuals who recall their life during the Great Depression and relate that directly to their current perspectives on spending money. We find younger people who say they grew up with certain values because of their parents' experiences in the Great Depression.

The Immigration Experience

Our Jewish respondents were much more likely to have immigrant experience in their backgrounds. Indeed, none of the non-Jewish respondents had parents who were born outside of the United States or

Canada, except for the one Asian-born respondent who had recently moved to the United States. Two of the Jewish men were born in Europe. Louis was born in the Ukraine in 1904 and was brought to the U.S. as an infant in the early 20th century wave of Jewish immigration. Jacob left his native Germany in 1937 when there were ominous signs that Jewish people there were in trouble. Most of the other Jewish men had parents who emigrated from their European homelands in the early twentieth century. Immigration trends in recent decades would suggest that future widowers with recent immigration experience in their backgrounds will be Hispanic or Asian, two groups who regrettably are not adequately included in this study.

The Depression Experience

The Great Depression was mentioned by many of our respondents. Al spoke of the struggle he and his wife had supporting their young family during that time. Frank was younger. He spoke of the Depression disrupting his education and, therefore, affecting the rest of his life:

> I came up through the Depression. At first to me that was just a way of life for everybody, until I was old enough to realize there is a problem. It stuck with me that you had to get out and work to keep things, once you could go out to work. There was a long time you couldn't do nothing. That's one reason I went to CCC camp, to help the family feed everybody. I took my mouth out of the house, which I know I made a mistake doing it. I should have gone to school and finished school. The schooling didn't hurt me financially, but socially it made a difference. . . . Quite a bit of difference there. A number of times I wished I would have gone to school, but I never had the desire of going back. For some reason or another I never gave a thought to ever going back to school.

Born in 1920, Frank is in the cohort that Elder (1999) described as (a) passing through the Depression as youngsters, (b) being a major source of manpower in the armed forces in World War II, and (c) providing the "Baby Boom" children who became the generation-gap protesting students of the 1960s. Thus develops an historical context for cultural events, such as described by Hultsch and Plemons (1979), that continues to influence lives and societies.

Frank's example speaks clearly to the impact of the Depression and World War II on his education. His story is not unique. There is a clear trend toward increasing levels of academic achievement during the twentieth century. However, achievement is lower for the men in their 70s now, and then is higher for succeeding cohorts. The G.I. Bill

(Servicemen's Readjustment Act of 1944) was designed to assist young men such as Frank, who had served in the armed forces, in returning to school. Its stated purpose was "to restore lost educational opportunities and vocational readjustment to service members who lost these opportunities as the result of their active military duty" (DeWan, 2001). Approximately 8 million veterans received educational benefits from the G.I. Bill: 2,300,000 for attending college, 3,500,000 for "school training," and 3,400,000 for on-the-job training (UCLA Graduate School of Education & Information Studies, 2001). Why, then, the undeniable dip in educational achievement among our respondents born in that cohort? Frank's statement of vanished motivation may be the answer. In his mind, the time had passed for going to school. He married soon after returning from the war. He needed to be earning an income.

World War II Experience

According to the U.S. Bureau of the Census (1975), 16,354,000 individuals served in the military during World War II; 10,022,000 of those were drafted. The Selective Training and Service Act of 1940 was the country's first peacetime draft (Parrish, 1978), although the world was hardly at peace at that time. Minimum and maximum ages for serving changed during the war years. After Pearl Harbor was bombed in December 1941, men up to age 44 were eligible to be drafted; within a year, 18- and 19-year-olds were made eligible. Whether they were drafted or joined voluntarily, wartime service represented a sizable disruption of the usual life plan for young men, their families, and the young women who were, would be, or would have been their partners.

While most who were of age had served, only three of our respondents spoke of battles in which they had taken part. Clyde, in showing the interviewer his medals, said that he had not, in 50 years, shown them to anyone. "Anybody who's been there knows what these stars are earned by. But people here don't care. They don't care the least. They don't care if you got your head shot off. They don't." He said if he heard someone talking about where he had been during the war, he would let them know if they were right or wrong, but would never just start "bragging."

Social Movements After World War II

This was not a topic deeply and uniformly explored during the interviews, but respondents spoke occasionally about civil rights and often about differences in the status of women. Civil rights of course hit right at home for the African American respondents. Claude had been born on a plantation in Louisiana at the beginning of the twentieth century. From his description, a listener could imagine his life taking place during the era of slavery; so little had changed. He was bone weary from a life of hard work, and in his tenth decade of life still felt a lack of ease between himself and his white neighbors. Arch said he and his wife tried to buy a house in a nice neighborhood in the 1960s, but the builder shut down the subdivision project rather than sell to them. When interviewed, he lived in a middle-class African-American neighborhood.

Most men commented in some way about changes that had taken place for women, usually regarding the opportunities to be educated or the expectation of staying home with children rather than working. Most of them had followed conventional mid-century gender patterns in their own families, but they did not speak disparagingly of choices made by modern couples. They may have felt constrained in making negative comments if they were so inclined since the interviewer was an educated, working woman. On the other hand, they spoke with pride of their wives' intelligence, whether or not the women were highly educated. They spoke with pride of the achievements of both granddaughters and grandsons, acknowledging that young people face a different world than they did. They noted these "signs of the changing times": (a) women are more independent, and men do more parenting, (b) more education is needed now, (c) social problems such as crime, drugs, poverty, and immoral behaviors have increased, (d) changes in the workplace have made it less personal, and (e) there is more emphasis now on money and personal gain.

Constants Behind the Cohort

In summary, factors affecting the cohort experience for our respondents include immigration into the United States, two world wars, the Great Depression, and the social movements in the second half of the twentieth century. Factors that are part of the usual life experience of a man took place within the context of these large cultural life events. What, then, might be held constant? The men spoke of gaining an identity as a man, which included going to work, finding a sweetheart, getting married and in most cases having children. Gaylin (1992) wrote of men's defining roles as protector, provider and procreator. Schoenberg (1993) wrote of "characteristics that men by tradition are encouraged to internalize into their own personal codes" (p. 92). He listed honesty, integrity, behavioral directness, belief in justice and fair play, and being "calm rather than emotional, empirical rather than rational. He can be both gentle and sensitive, especially to women and children, but aggression channeled into a keen competitive spirit tends to mask these softer characteristics in his interaction with other men" (p. 92). Bly (1990) wrote that there is an energetic, fierce (in passion for life), primitive male psyche waiting to be discovered inside each modern man. Bly commented that wielding a sword need not mean being warlike but can symbolize "joyful decisiveness" (p. 4). We did not ask our respondents if they could identify with Robert Bly and the mythopoetic men's movement, but we suspect they would have said no. The conventional masculine characteristics had become internalized at a time when they were not questioned. Only the youngest men, still in their late 50s, gave indication of having matured with some awareness of changing gender relations. For all of the men, pride in their integrity, their fortitude, and their dedication as family providers and members figured prominently in their stories. Perhaps these factors form the basic sense of manhood for these older men. Then each of them experienced at least one very great loss, the loss that made them eligible for this study. Many had faced other losses as well. Such losses may be influenced by external factors, such as we described in the Caregiving and Grief chapters, but finally they are felt in the heart of the individual who has suffered the loss. Several of the men touched their chests as they indicated their grief, memories, and loneliness. When we look to the future widower, we expect to find that identity as a man and as a family man will still be important considerations, and that the experience of loss will still be a painful and private event.

COHORTS OF THE FUTURE

Reports and Trends

When asked to give advice to widowed men of the future, our respondents assumed that widowed men will be much the same as they are today. None of us cannot foresee cultural life events that will develop into new cohort experiences, but we can look at trends that seem to be taking place that have predictive value for the next generation of older people. Many of the predictions look very positive.

Preston (1992) foresaw "enhanced well-being . . . as later and better-educated cohorts replace earlier cohorts" (p. 50) and suggested that the need for health services and welfare-type supports might be reduced. A federal report, Older Americans 2000: Key Indicators of Well-Being (Federal Interagency Forum on Aging Related Statistics,

2000), agrees that older Americans are better educated, and that can positively influence socioeconomic status and health. According to the report, people are living longer and feeling better at older ages. The majority of both men and women rated their own health as good or excellent. Men continue to describe themselves as more active than the women describe themselves. Activity contributes to better health and well-being in older age. In 1985, 34% of men reported that they were sedentary, in 1995 the percentage had dropped to 28%.

A report on trends in cigarette smoking (American Lung Association, 2001) shows a decline in the prevalence of smoking between 1965 and 1990, but says there has been no change in the decade of the '90s. More men smoke than women, but more male smokers have quit smoking. As we saw in comparing our respondents with their siblings, quitting smoking seems to contribute to longevity.

According to the report from the Federal Interagency Forum on Aging Related Statistics (2000), disability rates are declining, but many older citizens still find their health threatened by memory impairment, depression, chronic conditions, and disability, especially at very advanced ages. In 1995, nearly 60% of those age 70 or more report having arthritis. Other chronic conditions often reported include hypertension, heart disease, cancer, diabetes, and stroke. One-third or more of men and women 85+ have moderate or severe memory impairment; 23% have severe depressive symptoms.

On the other hand, life expectancy has risen almost 30 years over course of the twentieth century. Our centenarian respondents were in a group with a life expectancy of 48 years. Disability rates were projected to increase with the increased aging of the population, but they are lower than the increase that was projected. Only 21% of Medicare beneficiaries in 1994 had a chronic disability, which was down from 24% in 1982.

The older population is growing in both number and proportion. That trend is expected to continue at a very rapid rate. As the 85+ segment grows, according to the report from the Federal Interagency Forum on Aging Related Statistics (2000), there will be more health care and assistance needs, contrary to the suggestion of Preston (1992). Those 85 and older are most likely to live in nursing homes; in 1997 nearly 20% did. The trend is for those residing in nursing homes to be more functionally impaired (incontinent, need help eating, dependent on others for mobility). About three-fourths of nursing home residents are women, which is approximately equal to their proportion in the general population at that age. In the early 1990s health care expenditures both public and private increased above inflation. The oldest and those in nursing homes incurred the highest expenditures.

The report of the Federal Interagency Forum on Aging Related Statistics (2000) finds home health care is still mostly provided by family and other supports within the community, but since the 1980s, more use has been made of formal agencies for that service. More than a quarter of care situations in the community in 1994 were a combination of formal and informal care. The growing older population, according to the report, will be increasingly diverse in racial and ethnic identity. While the economic picture for most older Americans is improving, there are significant disparities in income and wealth between black and white households. Poverty has dropped drastically, but is still very high for some groups. Social Security benefits and pensions have taken on greater importance. Social Security payments account for about 80% of income for people in the poorest two-fifths in the older population. Poverty among the elderly has been reduced substantially in the past four decades, from 35% in 1959 to 11% in 1998. The poverty rate increases as age increases. It is higher for women than for men, and higher for minorities than for whites. As reported in the chapter on Living Alone, our respondents—all males and most of them white—did not have serious financial difficulties. To the extent that resources can get a person what he needs to be healthy and comfortable, these white men had those advantages available.

How the economy will function in the coming decades and how public policy affecting the elderly will be shaped cannot be foretold. Trends would indicate that Americans will live longer and will be healthier longer. They are still likely to need services at the end of their lives, and those services are likely to be costly.

SERVING WIDOWED OLDER MEN

Service providers for older persons are faced with many more older women than men. While some researchers (Kaye, 1997) have reported a lack of appeal to older men and their needs, we found in informal contacts with service providers that they are quite interested in being helpful to older men but do not know how to engage them. In this section, we present some ideas gleaned from current service provider—senior center directors, hospice workers, hospital and home health care social workers, nursing home staff, funeral home counselors—that may help others who are serving older men now and in the years to come. The ideas in this section do not come from a formal study of service providers; the ideas have emerged from the comments received after data and findings from our study have been presented to service providers at conferences and in one-on-one conversations.

Service providers agree that older men want to feel self-reliant. That leads to an unwillingness to seek help, to agree to offered help, or to express feelings that might indicate that they need help. Men are not attracted to groups or activities geared toward women, although they can sometimes be persuaded to join in activities when there is little else to do, such as in a nursing home setting. They tend to congregate on their own. One nursing home director said that male residents say hello to each other in the hallways and end up playing cards in one of the men's rooms. Many of the men have known each other in the community; they renew old friendships. It is also important, she said, to encourage links with organizations and clubs to which the men had belonged. Some of the men could still attend a meeting if someone would provide transportation. Also, visitors from the organization provide welcome camaraderie for the man who lives in a nursing home.

Computers are not readily available to all older men, and not all men are interested in them, but some older men enjoy playing with the technology. We have had follow-up contact with several respondents by e-mail; they also communicate with family members that way, they told us. Computer technology is a possible avenue for connecting older men with each other, too.

A community-based service provider cautioned that "just being together" should not be overlooked as significant support among older men. She said that widowed men might golf together, saying things like, "Yeah, I've been there too. It's rough." Then they go on to other topics. But such a sparsely worded exchange may be helpful to the man who feels alone with his feelings of loss, and the male companionship helps him move on with his life.

Service providers may be well advised to facilitate older men meeting in informal ways, rather than trying to get them into formal groups. One hospice worker said they had instituted a men's lunch bunch. The attendance was good; being there did not appear to be asking for or needing help. Out of the lunch group, three men decided on their own to join the formal bereavement support group. When a man is invited to the bereavement group, this worker said, he invariably asks if other men attend. So having three men in the formal group held promise for attracting others to the group. Harris (1993) recommended a male leader and a female nurse co-leader for caregiver groups appealing to men. If the person inviting an older man to attend a bereavement group is a male, the man might be more likely to give the group a try.

A home health care social worker said she tried to create informal ways to keep in touch with caregiving or widowed men. She would encourage them to call her for information or would drop by to check in with them. She found that the men often would have something to ask or talk about when she made such contacts.

Service providers describe bereaved older men as lonelier than widowed women. One hospice social worker said that she worries most about them because they are so isolated, staying alone with no distractions and no support system, unwilling to ask for or accept help. She sees men wanting to remarry as soon as the initial grieving passes, since they need a person to take care of them, and they need companionship. Women, she said, tend to grieve for seven or eight months and then begin to blossom with the freedom of living on their own schedule and according to their own interests.

Are men changing? The composite answer seems to be "yes," but not very rapidly. The young man of 30 years is likely to have a much broader range of interests than his grandfather of 80 years. He will have had some experience living on his own, cooking and doing his own laundry, because he did not marry so young. He will have had a broader range of occupational possibilities and more money to spend doing different things and meeting different people. However, his father who is now in his 50s is the man whom today's service providers may encounter as a widower in the next decade or two. He may be in a state of transition—a little more willing to share his feelings, more active in organizations away from home, more involved in his children's activities. We saw these tendencies in Jerry and Earl, the two men in our study who were in their mid-50s when widowed and in their late 50s when interviewed. However, programs serving men in their 40s and 50s find them still reluctant to seek services because it is still not the thing for a man to do. Self-reliance, even in the face of greatest need, is a cultural issue that will continue until boys and men are given the message by their families, their peers, and public opinion that seeking assistance is not unmanly. In the meantime, the ways in which men give each other support should be recognized as useful to them, and such contacts should be encouraged and facilitated.

SUGGESTIONS FOR FURTHER STUDY

Our findings should not be generalized to the entire population of older widowers in this country because our respondents may not be representative of that population. A similar qualitative study using a representative sample would be advised. Our study did not adequately represent the racial and ethnic diversity within this country. Interviewers fluent in the languages of immigrant groups should be used to be certain that the sample does not have an English-only bias, as ours did.

Whitbourne (2001) refers to further study of generativity as challenging but writes that it can illuminate changes in people in their later adult years. Further research might explore more deeply the relationship between parental and societal generativity, as well as the benefits of generative activity to the older men who undertake them. Additional research can seek to understand how practitioners could facilitate older men taking on a broader societal interest when their parental generativity was no longer so immediate. It would be helpful to explore the possible existence of a "window of opportunity" soon after the loss of a wife, during which time a man could become engaged in activity that might benefit himself as well as those who would receive the services he provided. Further study could seek to better understand the ways in which a Jewish upbringing contributes to the strong desire to serve others.

Our consideration of the Jewish men also suggests religion in men's widowhood as another area for further study. Much more remains to be discovered about religion's influence in men's ways of grieving, their successful adaptation to loss of wife, the ways in which their faith sustains them in everyday life, and the sources of their optimism.

More attention should be given to the role of the caregiver's health in adjustment to widowhood. Becoming widowed, whether that involves years of caregiving with the sense of impending loss or a sudden and shocking loss, is a very stressful adjustment for anyone. If one is already in declining health when called upon to make that adjustment, does health not play a major role in one's ability to absorb stress and be resilient? Health considerations limit the options a man might pursue, such as moving to another state to be close to children or marrying again. We would expect that a man in poorer health would have a harder time adjusting emotionally, would need more help from a support system, would be less hopeful about his future, and would suffer further declines in his health as the result of bereavement stresses. It would be particularly interesting to look at cases where that did not happen. Such cases could help determine what other factors helped those individuals manage to be resilient in spite of declining health. Such an assessment might lead back to a couple of factors that we found salient in our group of men: a lifelong optimistic outlook and an effective support system.

The questions about intangibles are intriguing and deserve further study: (a) How does one define oneself as old, when and with what meaning? (b) Do the optimistic survive? What are the limits of optimism in the face of physical decline and loss of loved ones and loss of one's belonging and participation in the wider world? (c) What faith questions do bereaved people ask, and how are questions answered for them by faith?

Men's studies should look more closely at the issues of older men in general, including their experience of widowhood. Male emotional expression in grief needs further study, including the possibility that lack of expression may not mean lack of grieving. Military experience has practical and emotional implications for adjustment to loss of wife in old age, and should be further explored. Sexuality issues for older widowers would be more freely discussed with a male interviewer. Bereavement support groups need ideas for appealing to widowed men, and once men are participating, the outcomes of their participation can be assessed.

Research could provide a basis for determining how to facilitate communication with emotional content between husband and wife about impending death and life thereafter for the surviving spouse. It would be interesting to explore whether processing the spouse's impending death with him or her is actually beneficial to the bereavement of the surviving spouse.

Remarriage is deserving of further study. Such study might include: (a) looking at the quality of remarriages, with consideration for the length of time between being widowed and remarrying, (b) a study of adult children and how they emotionally and intellectually process seeing a widowed parent remarry, (c) a study of the role of possessions in the remarriage of widowed people.

The baby-boom generation has been of interest to educators and marketers for a long time; now longitudinal studies must begin to note the cohort effect for those born in the 1940s, 1950s, and 1960s as they age. Events of the early twentieth century have had major impact upon the older people of today and upon the shaping of our society. Cultural events of mid-century and later likewise shape those who will be old in the early twenty-first century: the married, the single, and the widowed of the not-too-distant future.

Advice for Men from Widowers

Keeping in mind the purpose of our study—to illuminate the situations of older widowers in order to help men and their families in the future—we asked each respondent what advice he would give to other men now, in case they would someday face widowhood themselves. The advice ranged from very practical to very emotional and heartfelt. Here are the suggestions: Make sure finances are in order for paying bills, taking care of the mortgage, paying for illness-related expenses. Have wills made out and trusts arranged. Learn to do household chores. Learn to cook something. Do things you both want to do. Fulfill the wife's needs in illness. Help her disperse the possessions she values. Cherish the moments with her. Never give up.

Some of the men decided to answer in terms of giving advice to other men once they are widowed. Here are the suggestions: Stay busy and involved. Have interests. Develop new interests. Rely on religion to help with acceptance of the loss. Get professional help. Look for another companion.

REFERENCES

American Lung Association. (2001, January). *Prevalence based on revised national health interview survey* [on-line]. Available: http://www.lungusa.org/data/data_102000.html.

Bly, R. (1990). *Iron John: A book about men.* Reading, MA: Addison-Wesley.

De Wan, G. (2001, January). *The hunger for learning: Fed by the G.I. Bill of 1944, the Island's postwar demand for higher education explodes* [on-line]. Available: http://www.lihistory.com/8/hs805a.htm.

Elder, G. H., Jr. (1999). *Children of The Great Depression: Social change in life experience.* Boulder, CO: Westview Press.

Federal Interagency Forum on Aging Related Statistics (2000, August). *Older Americans 2000: Key indicators of well-being* [on-line]. Available: www.agingstats.gov/chartbook2000/pr0810000.html.

Ferraro, K. F., Mutran, E., & Barresi, C. M. (1984). Widowhood, health, and friendship support in later life. *Journal of Health and Social Behavior, 25,* 245–259.

Gaylin, W. (1992). *The male ego.* New York: Viking.

Hammel, J. & Walens, D. (1999, December). Testing a model for examining how older adults develop a self-care manager role following acute and long-term disability experiences. Paper presented at The International Meeting of the Rehabilitation Engineering Research Center on Aging, National Learning Center of the American Society on Aging and the Rehabilitation Engineering and Assistive Technology Society of America, Arlington, VA.

Harris, P. B. (1993). The misunderstood caregiver? A qualitative study of the male caregiver of Alzheimer's Disease victims. *The Gerontologist, 33*(4), 551–556.

Hultsch, D. F. & Plemons, J. K. (1979). Life events and life-span development. In P. B. Baltes & O. G. Brim, Jr. (Eds.), *Life-span development and behavior* (Vol. 2) (pp. 1–36). New York: Academic Press.

Janoff-Bulman, R. (1992). *Shattered assumptions: Towards a new psychology of trauma.* New York: Free Press.

Kaye, L. W. (1997). Informal caregiving by older men. In J. I. Kosberg & L. W. Kaye (Eds.), *Elderly men: Special problems and professional challenges* (pp. 231–249). New York: Springer Publishing.

McMillen, J. C. (1999). Better for it: How people benefit from adversity. *Social Work, 44*(5), 455–468.

Parrish, T. D. (1978). *The Simon & Schuster encyclopedia of World War II.* New York: Simon & Schuster.

Preston, S. H. (1992). Cohort succession and the future of the oldest old. In R. M. Suzman, D. P. Willis, & K. G. Manton (Eds.), *The oldest old* (pp. 50–57). New York: Oxford University Press.

Rubenstein, R. L. (1986). *Singular paths: Old men living alone.* Guildford, NY: Columbia University Press.

Scheier, M. F. & Carver, C. S. (1985). Optimism, coping, and health: Assessment and implications of generalized outcome expectancies. *Health Psychology, 4*(3), 219–247 .

Schoenberg, B. M. (1993). *Growing up male: The psychology of masculinity.* Westport, CT: Bergin & Garvey.

UCLA Graduate School of Education & Information Studies (2001, January). *1944: G.I. Bill of Rights* [on-line]. Available: www.gseis.ucla.edu/courses/ed191/assignment/ gibill.html.

U.S. Bureau of the Census (1975). *Historical statistics of the United States, colonial times to 1970 bicentennial edition, part 1* (Publication No. 003-024-00120-9), Washington, DC: U.S. Government Printing Office.

Whitbourne, S. K. (2001). Generativity. In G. L. Maddox (Ed.) *The encyclopedia of aging* (pp. 418–420). New York: Springer Publishing.

Wortman, C. B. & Silver, R. C. (1989). The myths of coping with loss. *Journal of Consulting and Clinical Psychology, 57*(3), 349–357.

Appendix A
Methodology

Purpose

The purpose of the study was to understand the experience of widowhood in an older man and more specifically to understand how an older man was able to re-establish a life with meaning and satisfaction after the loss of his spouse. We hoped to identify characteristics and patterns of behavior that might help other older widowers adjust satisfactorily to their circumstances.

Research Design

This study of 51 widowed older men was qualitative in nature, a research method that Gubrium (1992) identifies as a valuable "way of knowing [and] . . . documenting the aging experience" (p. 582). We were guided by the "grounded theory" approach of Glaser and Strauss (1967), an appropriate strategy when little is known about a population and the study seeks to understand the respondents in the context of their lives. Early findings contribute to new understandings and help to "ground" later interviews in the lives of the men. Thus topics of import to men in early interviews were included in subsequent interviews with other respondents. Likewise, we employed theoretical sampling, wherein intriguing questions emerging from early interviews led us to seek representatives of certain groups to help answer those questions. For example, two Jewish respondents with very different adjustments in widowhood stimulated us to find more Jewish widowers. Questions raised in early interviews with remarried widowers led us to search for other remarrieds to understand the role of remarriage in the adjustment to loss of a spouse in old age.

Seeking a Sample

Locating a sample of older widowers was challenging. They are a very small proportion of the general population, and their widowed status may be masked by remarriage. We sought respondents through our networks of professional and personal contacts. While we sought diversity in our sample, it cannot be taken as representative, nor can generalizations be made without great caution. Our original parameters limited attention to men who were 60 years of age or older and had been widowed between three and six years. We wanted to interview men who would have had time to get through the most acute grieving but who had not been widowed so long as to have forgotten important details of their married life and of their widowhood experience. However, on several occasions we were led to men who—we found out during the interview—were outside of those parameters; we also noted they were contributing in valuable ways to our understanding of widowhood. We found that some men were ready to move on in their lives much earlier than others, and we discovered that men have vivid memories for decades after the loss. As this was not a study of acute grieving, and grief researchers note the two year mark as the approximate boundary for acute grief (Lund, Caserta, & Dimond, 1993), we set two years from loss of wife as the lower parameter for subsequent interviews and eliminated the six-year-from-loss-of-wife parameter.

We had no upper limit on age, but set 60 as the lower parameter since we were determined to focus our study on older widowed men. By working definition, these men should have been living alone with their wives when the deaths occurred; children would have been grown and gone, the couple in or close to retirement. Again, opportunities arose just outside that age cut-off. We decided to conduct interviews with a few men who were widowed in their 50s. Again we found good advantage in those outside-the-parameter interviews. The issues and prospects for the future of these middle-aged widowers were different; the contrasts heightened our understanding of the situations of the older men.

Our contacts who located men for us to interview were mainly middle-class, and they tended to refer us to men who are currently living a middle-class lifestyle, although many had come from backgrounds of poverty and working hard to get by. We suspect our contacts also referred us to "nice" men who would be "interesting" to interview, in other words, men with fairly good social skills. We were also referred to men who were lonely and would enjoy some company. Additionally, there was an element of self-selection. Those who agreed almost invariably were men who said they would do it "if it would help someone else." So our sample is skewed in favor of such men. Still a variety of personalities was evident.

Respondents

Our 51 respondents ranged in age from 58 to 104 years old. These men currently live in 11 states scattered throughout the United States and in two Canadian provinces; their origins are even more diverse. Those whom we found in retirement areas had come from many different states. Two were born in Europe, one in Asia. All of them were widowed: four had lost more than one wife. Fourteen had remarried by the time they were interviewed; three remarried after the interviews. To date, seven respondents are deceased.

Procedure

Because of the problems with gaining access to an older population in their own homes (Wallace, Kohout, and Colsher, 1992), we enlisted the help of professional and personal contacts who knew of men who would qualify for the study. Thus, our respondents were first contacted by someone they knew. Those contacts ascertained the men's willingness to participate and informed them that they would soon receive a letter from the researchers. In the letter, we told the men we were interested in their lives in general, in the loss of their wives, and in their adjustment to life after that loss. Interviews were identified as confidential and voluntary. The man could refuse to answer any question he wished, and he could terminate the interview if he so desired. The letter was followed by our phone call to set up interview dates and answer any questions.

Some men declined to participate in the study. This occurred most frequently in the early months of seeking respondents. The message we received back in those rejections was that the man did not want to think about or talk about his wife's death. Length of time since the wife's death was a likely factor also. One man declined when he had been widowed just two years but then agreed to be interviewed quite willingly three years later. Another described a prolonged grieving period but was willing to be interviewed when he was in a new relationship. Two men agreed, but then declined by making themselves always "unavailable." One man declined saying he was now finally happy in a new relationship and did not want "to dredge up all of that pain." One man declined when he found there was no chance for a romance to develop with the interviewer.

Most of the men contacted did agree to participate. Many said it would not be their favorite thing to do, but they were willing if it would help someone else. Others seemed almost immediately happy to have someone interesting in listening to them. Whether eager or reluctant in the beginning, the respondents seemed to enjoy the conversational interviews and were willing to be contacted again. Still, we must note that our sample is of men who were willing to talk to a stranger about personal and painful events in their lives; that is not every man.

Because of our broad interest in the lives of these older widowers, an ethnographic interview seemed most appropriate (Spradley, 1979). Moreover, based on Moore's (1989) experiences with elderly women who would not participate in a research project if it involved tests and questionnaires, we suspected that an older population of men might too be reticent to participate in such a structured study. Rather than have the men respond to questions based on our naive assumptions of their widowed lives, we wanted to understand widowhood within the context of their lives and in their own words. Thus, we formulated general, open-ended questions to guide the interviews, which were highly conversational in nature, always keeping in mind that the "act of speaking-with itself gives texture to what is reported" (Gubrium, 1992, p. 581). Our interview schedule was by topic, not by specific wording of a question. The schedule ranged from life history questions to emphasis on life with the wife, her death, and his adjustment to life after loss. (See Appendix B for a list of topical questions.)

The interview format called for two sessions conducted a day or two apart so both interviewer and respondent could reflect on what had been discussed and what had not. The first interview was much more open to direction by the respondent, with topics generated by him. The second was more directed, with the interviewer asking questions on topics that had not come up in the first interview. In this way, the interviewer could make certain that particular topics were covered across all interviews, while allowing the respondent to indicate what was of particular significance to him. Also, in the second interview, with rapport established, we could ask questions that might have been too intrusive at the first interview; we could ask about finances and about the importance of the sexual relationship, for example. The two-part interview also reduced the problem of respondent fatigue noted by Wallace, Kohout, and Colsher (1992) in the study of the oldest old.

Almost all of the 51 interviews were conducted in the men's homes so their circumstances and surroundings could be observed. In the cases of the men who had remarried or had a live-in companion, we stated we would need to talk with the man alone for reasons of confidentiality. In all cases, we were able to meet the women in their lives either at the beginning or end of the interview and hold a three-way conversation that allowed us to see something of the relationship.

Our data collection format depended upon two important relationship qualities: friendliness and trust. In all but one case, by the end of the second interview we were able to open the door to future contact. In some cases, a phone call was made after the interview to clarify certain points or to ask additional questions. Follow-up interviews were conducted approximately 18 months after the initial interviews either by phone or in person to update records of the respondents' health, living arrangements, activities, and marital status. In most cases, we were able to secure additional information from our professional and personal contacts and relatives of the respondents. While most of the interviews were conducted by one researcher, we did conduct joint interviews with three respondents at first interview and six respondents at follow-up interviews. In some form or another, we both met or talked with 12 of the respondents.

Data Analysis

The interviews were tape-recorded for transcription. Field notes and an information cover sheet completed the data collection. Transcribed interviews were then entered into a computer software program entitled QSR NUD*IST 4 (Qualitative Solutions & Research Pty Ltd., 1997). NUD*IST stands for non-numerical unstructured data indexing, searching, and theorizing. The program facilitates the coding of transcripts, the development of an index of codes, and the search and print-out of specific topics and themes across transcripts. Initially, we and several assistants coded the same transcript for factual information. We organized the information by periods of life (i.e., premarriage, marriage, postmarriage) with factual information about jobs, health, relationships, residence, military experience, life skills, religion, finances, etc. a part of each period. The men who had more than one marriage had more periods, of course. Central to our study was the information about death of wife, grief, and recovery. As we worked with the initial transcripts, themes emerged such as husbands' regrets and dying wives' predictions. We utilized open coding (Corbin & Strauss, 1990) wherein each sentence of the transcribed interview is given a name or label which conceptualizes the phenomenon represented. When possible, these labels are words or phrases used by our respondents (e.g., "getting by") termed *in vivo codes* (Strauss, 1987). One researcher then coded all interviews to ensure coder reliability. Each transcript added to the development of the coding scheme. Earlier coded transcripts were re-examined for newly identified themes. Thus, the coding scheme was in constant evolution. We then conducted computer searches by topics (e.g., death of wife), key words (e.g., funeral, service), and themes (e.g., memorialization of wife, aftermath). In this way we were able to look across the 51 transcripts for commonalities and differences, to check for the salience of the themes for all respondents, to develop typologies of our respondents (e.g., caregivers), and to begin to understand adjustment to loss in our respondents. Theoretical insights which emerged served to further guide the exploration of concepts and categories which represent the phenomena of widowhood in older men. Of particular interest were the patterns represented in the men who seemed to have adjusted satisfactorily to life after the loss of a spouse, since the purpose of the study was to identify characteristics and patterns of behavior that might help other men make a more satisfactory adjustment to widowhood.

REFERENCES

Corbin, J. & Strauss, A. (1990). Grounded theory research: Procedures, canons, and evaluative criteria. *Qualitative Sociology, 13*(1), 3–21.

Glaser, B. G. & Strauss, A. L. (1967). *The discovery of grounded theory: Strategies for qualitative research.* New York: Aldine de Gruyter.

Gubrium, J. F. (1992). Qualitative research comes of age in gerontology. *The Gerontologist, 32(5),* 581–582.

Lund, D. A., Caserta, M. S., & Dimond, M. F. (1993). Spousal bereavement in later life. In M. S. Stroebe, W. Stroebe, & R. O. Hansson (Eds.), *Handbook of bereavement* (pp. 240–254). New York: Cambridge University Press.

Moore, A. J. M. (1989). *Life moves on: An exploration of motivation in elderly women.* Unpublished doctoral dissertation, University of Illinois, Urbana-Champaign.

Qualitative Solutions & Research Pty Ltd. (1997). QSR NUD*IST (version 4) [computer software]. Thousand Oaks, CA: Scolari.

Spradley, J. P. (1979). *The ethnographic interview.* New York: Holt, Rinehart & Winston.

Strauss, A. (1987). *Qualitative analysis for social scientists.* New York: Cambridge University Press.

Wallace, R. B., Kohout, F. J., & Colsher, P. L. (1992). Observations on interview surveys of the oldest old. In R. M. Suzman, D. P. Willis, & K. G. Manton (Eds.), *The oldest old* (pp. 123–134). New York: Oxford University Press.

Appendix B

Interview Topics

The following are the open-ended questions and statements utilized in this study of widowers. While the topics represented by the questions and statements were addressed with all of our respondents, the men often initiated these topics in the flow of conversation. If they did not, we used the following items in the approximate order shown to gain the topical information.

Describe your home and family in childhood.

What are the lessons you learned early in life from your parents?

What kind of education did you have?

Tell me about the work you did.

Tell me about your military service.

What major moves have you made in your life?

Describe your wife for me. What was her personality?

How did you meet your wife?

How did you and your wife divide chores in and around the house?

How did you and your wife settle disagreements?

Tell me about your wife's death.

Who helped you at that time? (Caregiving/illness questions as appropriate)

Did you have any changes in eating and sleeping habits at the time of your wife's death?

What role did religious beliefs play in your grieving process?

What is your belief about an afterlife?

What does it mean when a widowed person says he has "gotten over it"?

Describe loneliness for me.

How did you deal with your wife's possessions?

What is a typical day like for you now?

What kind of meals do you prepare?

What activities do you have outside of the home?

What health problems do you have?

What medications do you take?

Whom would you call if you were in bed with the flu and needed assistance?

What are your sources of income in retirement?

Why do so many widowed men remarry so quickly?

How important is sex to an older man?

What advice would you give to men whose wives are still alive but who might someday face the situation you faced?

Appendix C

Respondents and Characteristics

Respondents and Characteristics

Study Name	Year Born	Religious Affiliation	Highest Educational Achievement	Occupation	Marital Status at Interview or Follow-up	Number of Children Reared
Al	1905	Methodist	10th Grade	Factory Engineer	Single	2
Alvin	1920	Reform Judaism	Bachelor's	Business Owner	Married after interview	2
Arch	1929	Baptist	Doctor of Osteopathy	Medical Doctor	Single with companion	2
Arnold	1917	Reform Judaism	High School	Salesman	Single with companion	0
Art	1904	Reform Jewish background/ nonbeliever	9th grade	Business Clerk	Single	2
Bapuji	1915	Hindu	Bachelor's	Teacher	Single	4
Benjamin	1917	Conservative Judaism	Bachelor's	Corporate Accountant	Married	2
Bert	1915	Jewish background/ not active	High School	Wallpaper Hanger	Single	1
Bill	1920	Non-denominational Protestant	High school	Engineer	Married	2

Bruce	1914	Covenant Church	10th Grade	Salesman	Single	5
Carlo	1904	Catholic	2nd Grade	Factory Worker	Single	4
Charles	1906	Methodist	Master's	Salesman	Single with companion	2
Clarence	1907	Christian Church	Bachelor's	Teacher	Single	2
Claude	1904	Quaker	G.E.D.	Small Business Owner	Single	0
Clyde	1920	Baptist	7th Grade	Construction/ Factory Worker	Single with companion	5
Conner	1910	Catholic	Master's	Government Economist	Single	3
Cordell	1920	Catholic	J.D.	Lawyer/Politician	Live-in companion	11
Craig	1923	Baptist/Nazarene	High School	Military/Missile Specialist	Single	2
Curly	1908	Brethren	10th Grade	Business Manager	Single	1
Daniel	1912	Conservative Judaism	Master's	Chemical Engineer	Single	2
Don	1927	Reform Jewish background/no identification	G.E.D.	Salesman/Courier	Committed companion	1
Earl	1938	Baptist/Free Methodist	High School	Business Manager	Married	5
Eldon	1896	Presbyterian	8th Grade	Dairy Farm/Business Owner	Single	5

Respondents and Characteristics *(Continued)*

Study Name	Year Born	Religious Affiliation	Highest Educational Achievement	Occupation	Marital Status at Interview or Follow-up	Number of Children Reared
Frank	1920	Catholic/Lutheran	10th Grade	Factory Worker	Single with companion	2
Garrett	1926	Church of Christ	Bachelor's	Farmer/Teacher	Married	5
George	1921	Conservative Judaism	High School	Corporate Lab Manager	Single with companion	2
Harry	1899	Christian Church	8th Grade	Maintenance Worker	Single	6
Henrik	1921	Lutheran	High School	Butcher/Grocer	Married after interview	2
Jacob	1914	Orthodox Judaism	Ph.D.	Professor	Single	0
Jerry	1939	Catholic	High School	Office Worker	Single	2
Jim	1929	Presbyterian/ Methodist	Master's	Nonprofit Association Executive	Single	3
Joe	1917	Nonbeliever	High School	Mechanic/Salesman	Single with companion	1
John	1922	Brethren	High School	Shipping Clerk/ Salesman	Single	6
Karl	1909	Dutch Reform/ Presbyterian	High School	Restaurant Owner	Single	1

Kenneth	1916	Methodist	High School	Office Worker	Single	3
Leroy	1915	Methodist	7th Grade	Factory Worker	Single	1
Louis	1903	Conservative Judaism	High School	Business Owner	Single	2
Mack	1931	Catholic	High School	Labor Relations Negotiator	Single with companion	5
Malcolm	1925	Latter Day Saints	10th Grade	Factory Worker	Married	2
Michael	1915	Reform Judaism	Bachelor's	Business Owner	Single with companion	4
Ned	1899	Presbyterian	Bachelor's	Accountant	Single	5
Richard	1911	Christian Church	Bachelor's	Professor	Single	1
Robert	1920	Catholic	High School	Corporate Manager	Single	0
Russell	1929	Baptist	9th Grade	Construction Worker	Married	6
Sam	1926	Quaker	High School	Computer Technician	Married	2
Stuart	1934	Lutheran	Bachelor's	Civil Engineer	Married after interview	2
Sy	1916	Conservative Judaism	High School	Grocery Store Owner	Married	3
Terrence	1931	Methodist	High School	Military/Craft Maintenance Engineer	Married	5
Walter	1913	Disciples of Christ/Quaker	Bachelor's	Accountant	Married	2
Will	1918	United Church of Christ	Bachelor's	Newspaper Editor/Owner	Single	2
Yussef	1919	Baptist/Presbyterian	High School	Military/Ordinance	Single	2

Subject Index

Author Index